THOSE WHO FROM
HEAVEN TO EARTH CAME

UFOs and Extraterrestrial Encounters
in the Life of Puzuzu

Those Who From Heaven To Earth Came

On the front cover of this book is an engraving by Hendrick Goltzius in 1588, the same year that the picture was painted and is the story of Cadmus. I added the UFOs to this picture specifically for this book. I chose this artwork because of the Dragons, which represent the Reptilian race… and so it is.

Copyright © 2012 Puzuzu

All Rights Reserved. No part of this publication may be reproduced in any form or by any means, including scanning, photocopying, or otherwise without prior written permission of the copyright holder.

ISBN-13:978-1478360414
ISBN-10: 1478360410

Those Who From Heaven To Earth Came

I dedicated this book to my Mother who brought me into this World… for it is she whom has had to deal with my bizarre lifestyle and Tales of the Unknown.

Those Who From Heaven To Earth Came

TABLE OF CONTENTS

Acknowledgments	1
About the Author	3
Introduction	5
Questioning Authority	8
The Awakening	22
Battle between Darkness and Light	28
The Encounters	37
The Celestial Gods	50
Enlil, Lord of Sky, God of Thunder	58
Rainy Season, Enlil Cometh	75
Night Time Energies	120
Aliens landing on the Roof	129
End of Summer, Enlil leaves	140
Enki, Lord of the Abzu	145
Biological UFOs	170
Abductions - Tagged by Extraterrestrials	190
Missing Time	225
Skydiving and UFOs	231
Strange Clouds, Signs in the Sky	240
How to Capture UFOs on Camera	254
Other Aliens that come in the Night	260
Offerings to the Gods and Protection	269
There are none so Blind	273

ACKNOWLEDGMENTS

I would like to thank the One True Divine God Energy Source of All. It is through his House of Many Mansions that has allowed me to live on many Worlds. I want to thank the Celestial Gods Enlil and Enki who have been my friends for many lifetimes opening my mind and Enlightening me on many spectacular things. I thank them for their protection and their wisdom. I wish to thank those who have brought me Light upon a Dark road increasing my Light quotia and raising me to a higher level of consciousness... beloved Christ who stood patiently waiting on the side for me to bring him back into my life, Mother Mary, Kryon, Ganesh, Buddha, Serapis Bey, Sanat Kumara, Cyclopea and Virginia, the Ashtar Command, Archangel Michael, Archangel Raphael, Archangel Gabriel, Archangel Uriel, Sunnuna, Celest, Hermel, Jiobbe, Shamah and all my spirit guides that made me the Light Worker that I am today. I would also like to thank Elizabeth Clair Prophet for all the books she has written that guided me to these Beings of Light and Zecharia Stichin for his great books educating the World on Extraterrestrials and the beginning of life on this planet. I want to thank my friends Lea Chapin and Elizabetta for their channelings along with Devi and Twanny for believing in me, for they are the open minds of the universe. Most of all, I want to thank Archangel Michael again, for he is Almighty and All Powerful. I owe him my life. Without him I would fall. He keeps me on the Path of Righteousness and has provided me with unimaginable Protection. To him, I am Eternally Grateful and indebted. A Special Thanks to my friends Lil Lamb, Arietis and Mr. K. for their contributions to this book.

About the Author

Puzuzu is a Teacher of the Occult Arts and Spiritual Counselor along with being a UFO Hunter, Artist, New Age Musician/Song Writer and "Pioneer of the Unknown". He describes himself as a Beacon of Light for the World. He is an old soul, having lived 1,048 lives here and on other Worlds. An Eccentric Being in this life would be an understatement. Skydiving, Flesh Hook Suspensions, testing the thresholds of the mind and opening doors to the unknown that cannot be shut, is what makes this person feel alive. This being said, he is an explorer of another breed. Having run one the most popular Occult websites on the web, SpellsandMagic.com... he has become an Icon in the World of the Occult. Puzuzu chooses to live in Sarasota, Florida because of the vibrations in that area and the powerful vortex that emanates in the Gulf of Mexico. This makes Puzuzu feel at home, as it allows many of his Extraterrestrial friends to come through. Puzuzu is from a Pleiadian bloodline having come here to earth to experiment with the game of life on this planet. Puzuzu has become an expert at photographing UFOs and many other anomalies. He holds within his possession over 8,000 photographs of UFOs that he has personally taken himself, along with over 7,000 photographs of other paranormal anomalies that he has personally taken. He has also made contact with many Extraterrestrial races such as Arcturians, Pleiadians, Greys, Belis, and Insectiods along with the Reptilians. Having truly befriended the Reptilians he is now a part of the Reptilian Brotherhood even though he is not of their bloodline. Having mastered the Darkness he is now mastering the Light and helping to hold the Light for this entire planet. Being a "Living Master" and helping Humanity to Ascend into a higher consciousness is his wish for this last incarnation on earth.

Introduction

In this book, I will tell you about my life and how I got involved in the Occult, which led to my making contact with the Extraterrestrial Gods. I will share with you my tragedies and triumphs along with my struggles with the Darkness and the Light. There will be no stone left unturned as I explain to you my experiences and Encounters with Extraterrestrial Beings. My life has been like that of a science fiction novel. The things that I will share with you in this book, I have kept secret for many years except for a few close friends. Yet here are some things in this book I have not shared with my close friends or family. Now, I am at a point in my life where it does not matter if people do not believe what I am saying. Whether they believe me or not has no effect on my life whatsoever. There will always be the naysayers and those with blinders on. Many people I have met and become friends with, I have begun to explain some of these experiences with them will and they truly did not want to know about them because of fear. People filled with fear will deny the existence of something that they do not comprehend so that they do not have to mentally deal with it in any way. Jeremiah 5:21 *Hear now this, O foolish people, and without understanding; which have eyes, and see not; which have ears, and hear not.*

Those Who From Heaven To Earth Came

There have been times in my life where I would wonder if everything I was experiencing was a dream. This is because so many of my experiences were so extremely bizarre having been aboard many Alien ships that belong to different Alien races and offering my physical body to the Reptilian God named Enlil for experimentation.

I will share with you many photographs of UFOs that I have taken myself. Let me point out that there are no fake photos within in book. The only Photoshop work I have done on these photos is to crop them, enhance and sharpen the images, show expanded enlarged views and sometimes changing the brightness/contrast in order to give you a better visual of the actual shape of these UFO crafts. I am not looking for attention, so there is no need or reason for me to fake anything. I simply want to give you proof of what is out there in the skies. Most people go through life without paying attention to the things that are around them. I am a person who pays attention to detail in most everything that I do. Most everything in this book will be in non-technical language just as things are on my website. I am not going to fill you with theosophical garbage simply to impress you. That would only clutter your mind just as it has done when I have read many books in the past. You may wonder why I capitalize many words within this book, which need not be. This is because I really want to emphasize those words to encode your brain with them, thus helping trigger your Awakening so you may claim your Divine Birthright.

I will also explain in this book on how you yourself may go forth and capture these UFOs and flying anomalies on camera. I will tell you how to analyze your own photos to separate the true UFOs from other things in the sky such as birds, bugs, or planes that can sometimes look like a UFO to the untrained eye. I have been very skeptical about my own photos. I have analyzed them repeatedly to make sure they are exactly what I say they are. I am sure that after you have read this book, I will have sparked some serious interest in you to go out and try to seek the unknown. In this book, I intended to Awaken you to the fact that you truly are not alone in this universe and that you can make contact with many of these Alien races. There are many benevolent Alien races out there that will abduct and experiment on you in a not so pleasant way. On the other side of the coin, some will be very kind and teach you things of an advanced and spiritual nature. I will issue you warnings… some caution to the wind. Be careful what you wish for, you just might get it. There are many bizarre and wondrous things right in front of you if you just open your eyes.

Questioning Authority

Many of you may be asking yourselves what this has to do with Extraterrestrials and UFOs. It has everything to do with it because from this point forward I want you to question the authority of those in power who deny the existence of life outside our planet. I am a seeker of truth. To this day, in my life, I will still question those who are in places of power. For 90% of the time those who are in these places of power have altered the facts for their own benefit to enslave humanity in ignorance along with covering up their greed and murderous crimes against humanity and the planet. Most of humanity has forgotten who they truly are. The have forgotten the fact that they are part of the Divine. The Galactic Hierarchy placed a veil over our eyes long ago because of our misuse of Divine powers. However, those who are in high places of power such as our world governments and religious institutions have done all they can to enslave us to the material world by trying to prevent us from finding out the truth about our Divine inheritance. They do not want an equal world where everyone is happy and has food on the table. They want the world where they are the Kings and Queens and we are the peasants. They control most all sources of media except for books like this and websites. Therefore, we must question authority in order to find the truth.

Let us now look at the sources of false or doctored information.

First, I will discuss religion. Earlier in my life, I was a devout Christian indoctrinated into the mainstream Control System of beliefs. Starting out as a Southern Baptist and later moving towards the nondenominational churches where I would play guitar and sing. This seemed to be a more happy atmosphere and not quite so authoritative like the Southern Baptist were. I do believe it was around the age of 10 years old that I accepted Jesus Christ as my Savior and Lord. Then at about age 14 years old, the church performed a baptism upon me in the Gulf of Mexico off the coast of Corpus Christi, Texas.

I was a military brat. My father was a hard-core, old school Marine. Therefore, I want you to understand that I lived in a very controlled environment. Most of the places where I lived with my mother and father were on a military base. From the age 13 to 15 years old, we lived in Corpus Christi, Texas, but my parents bought a house off base. This put me in touch with civilian kids my age and with that came the introduction to marijuana. The only reason I am telling you about this is that I do believe that the marijuana opened my subconscious mind. I do not smoke it now, as I do not wish to put any type of smoke into my lungs or body. However, I will say it did open my eyes to many things. Then at age 16, I was living back on a military base in Keflavík, Iceland. I was still going to church at this time, but I was starting to question all the things I had learned about the Bible. However, I did not speak outwardly about these things to my parents. Questioning things from the Bible and expressing the fact that many things did not add up would have only shot up a red flag, for my parents were hardcore

Christians. I kept my thoughts and feelings to myself. I had also had many dreams, or what I thought were dreams of Aliens and being aboard Extraterrestrial crafts. This is also something I would have never discussed with anyone, not even my friends at the time in my life. People would have ridiculed me or labeled insane, thus having my parents put me in therapy.

In my mind, I was seriously starting to question all authority. Part of this stemmed from living in such a life as if I was in the military too. Nevertheless, this part of it was of a rebellious nature. However, most of it was from my mind beginning open up. I started to wonder why there were so many religions, yet in the religion that indoctrinated my brain, everyone else was going to hell. How could this be so? How could God create so many people with different religions, but only my religion was the truth? In the Bible, many things did not add up to me. To give one example; the story of a man named Jonah, swallowed by a whale…? Give me a freaking break! Another parable cloaked in obscurity. I refuse to believe that a whale swallowed a man named Jonah and lived in its belly for three days before the whale spit him back out and he lived to tell about it. I thought to myself that perhaps there was a better explanation and I would find this truth through the Sumerian Gods. I did find the truth in this matter; an Alien craft belonging to Enki that presided under the water abducted him and later returned him. Another example is the three wise men following the North Star. So let me get this straight, three men from different parts of the world followed the North Star to see the birth of Christ. I seriously doubt they would have all ended up in the same place being that they started from different locations on the planet. It is apparent to me that each of them followed an Alien craft in the sky that led them to the Christ child or an Alien craft transported them to where the birth of the Christ child would be. The latter of these two would make more sense.

    I found many examples of Extraterrestrial crafts within the Bible, yet I never found the specific use of these words. It was always a Chariot of Fire or a Cloud of Fire. I could go on and on about things that did not add up in the Bible. I did however believe that there were many truths in the Bible, but at the same time, I also believed that there was quite a bit of misleading information within this book. Why could not modern-day biblical scholars, not put this in proper perspective and in plain English without all the guessing games? They filled the Bible with parables cloaked in metaphors. I knew there was Extraterrestrial life and that there was proof in the Bible, but it was all in disguise. Here is where I will throw in some truth from the Bible as it says, "In my house are many mansions". This tells me that there are many other worlds that God has created and of course many other races of Beings that inhabit these worlds. Anyone who truly thinks we are the only living things in the universe is living life in arrogance and with blinders on.

    The Vatican is one the biggest offenders of hiding the truth. Those of you who are Catholic and reading this; please do not get your panties in a bunch. The Vatican has hidden underground secret archives with great spiritual and truthful information. Why does it need to be secret? Why are they hiding the truth from us? There is no need for secrets in any church atmosphere. They are hiding many things that have to do with the life of Christ and the fact that he was married to Mary Magdalene and was able to carry on his bloodline. Let us pause here for a minute and ponder upon this. Let us say you were the Christ avatar and you were going to come to this planet to show people the ways of unconditional love and how to receive the keys to the kingdom of heaven. Would you not also want to carry on your bloodline? Would you truly come here only to teach and not plant your seed of Light? Would you have truly come here so that you could be crucified and not carry on your bloodline? That would truly be illogical. Someone of this great magnitude bringing Light into the world would surely carry on his or her bloodline upon this Dark planet. The Vatican is also hiding the Holy Grail that Christ drank from during the Last Supper. This cup holds great power and therefore the Vatican hides it within their chambers beneath the Vatican. Why are they hiding the truth from you? Because they belong to the Illuminati and they need to keep organized religion intact so that you will remain spiritually ignorant and therefore enslaved to the material world.

Now, let us understand why church members long ago took so many books out of the Bible that many other Prophets had written. Constantine summoned these church members, known as the Council of Nicaea together under his watch. Why did they take out teachings of Reincarnation and so forth and other important information? The Council of Nicaea deemed this information too dangerous for the common person. They did not want the common person educated on the subject of the God-given Divine Birthright. They did not want humanity to escape the hologram that imprisoned them. If humanity knew this information then they would be Enlightened just as Constantine and his companions and have the same power. They wanted to change all this to create a "One God" system of fear. Believe this or you suffer eternal hell damnation. The key word here is control. They controlled through misinformation and fear. They also did not want you to know that Mary Magdalene was one of the Disciples. This is because women were not to be in places of power or authority. Men treated women as inferiors back in those days just as they do not treat them as equals over in the Middle East today. These prevaricators are the Illuminati... the kings, queens and religious hierarchy of royal bloodlines bathed in Darkness. Their job is to keep you in spiritual ignorance so that you may never become like Christ and obtain Divine enlightenment. There are still many church going people these days that believe that there were never any books removed from the Bible. They believe that there is only one book, written by the one God. The same goes for the Islamic religion. I will tell you that they are the blind who cannot see. They refuse to believe that Darkness could have worked its way into the church to remove the truth from us. When it comes to the church and Extraterrestrial life... they are not going to admit to the facts. If the church declared that there truly were UFOs and Extraterrestrial life... their control would go down the tubes. Their "One God" propaganda would turn to dust. They do not want you to know that these Angels fly around in spaceships. Once again, they look misinformed about their own Holy Book by not stating this. Have they not studied it well? They apparently think that the common person has the brains of a Neanderthal. We all know that references to Chariots of Fire were UFOs. We all know there were no damn wooded chariots with wood spoke wheels on fire flying through the sky. They borrowed and changed to their needs, the story of creation in Genesis of the Old Testament. They took away the most important part of how an Extraterrestrial Reptilian God named Enki created humanity. They borrowed the story originally written in Sumerian texts that were from 8600 BC. Therefore, when it comes to any religious texts that you may read, use your own intuition as what truly sounds real. Understand that the truth may be stranger than fiction.

Now let us move on to the education system. The education system is nothing more than brain washing. They dispense punishment upon those who do not comply with the system. The ability to be able to memorize and repeat things, determines our intelligence according to those in higher places of power. The more you can remember, the better your grades will be. Our History books are comprised of nothing but false information. The government teaches us history the way in which they wants us to know it and not how events really occurred. To do so, would expose their greed and crimes against humanity. Our history books teach us nothing about Extraterrestrial life or even the possibility of life on another planet. Do you see how arrogant that sounds, thinking that we are the only planet with living beings that God created? Everything you have learned in your history books is according to how the government wants you to think things happened and not how things actually happened. Indoctrination into this false paradigm starts at an early age for most all humans; therefore, you must question everything you learned about history.

    While we are on the subject of learning, I would like to inform you about the ancient Grimoires that contain information on the conjuring of Celestial Gods, Goddesses, Angels, and Demons. I have copies of most of these Grimoires that exist. These Ancient texts of Magic are very confusing, and designed this way so that once again the common person cannot find the truths about the universe. This would give the common person powers equal to those whom enslave them. Trust me when I tell you that the churches/Illuminati had their hands in these Grimoires. I say this because under their one God system they labeled all the other Gods and Goddesses as Demons. So personally, I have found these Grimoires to be useless, other than the sigils found within them. The information is embedded with ridiculously lengthy prayers, along with fasting for many days and other nonsensical things. The only thing of value in all of these Grimoires is the sigil for each spirit or God/Goddess. When I first started studying and working with these Grimoires I thought I had come across great books with the most valuable knowledge only to find out later that they were tainted with misleading facts by the elite.

    Let us talk about the media and how they control the truth. Those who bring forth claims of being abducted by Aliens would end up being humiliated by the News stations if they reported it. But if a small number of people report seeing a UFO and call it in to the media… they will air the story and later that day or the next day the government/Norad/FAA steps in and forces the media to make a statement saying that it was a meteor or space debris. The media works for the elite who diligently cover up these types of incidents. To this day in 2012, our government denies the existence of Extraterrestrial life on any other planet. Towards the end of 2011, our White House released a statement in regards to the acknowledgment of Extraterrestrials having visited earth and interacting with our government. They issued a statement only due to a couple of petitions brought forth before them, so they would formally acknowledge this. This was their statement... "The U.S. government has no evidence that any life exists outside our planet, or that an Extraterrestrial presence has contacted or engaged any member of the human race. In addition, there is no credible information to suggest that any evidence is being hidden from the public's eye." Phil Larson of the White House Office of Science & Technology Policy, on the WhiteHouse.gov website, issued this statement. This type of statement is about as imbecilic as some of our modern day criminals who commit a crime, then incriminate themselves by posting pictures on the web showing them committing the crime. I say this because you can go on the web and view so many photos and videos of UFO Encounters and Alien bases on the Moon and Mars that NASA released due to the Freedom of Information Act. If there were smart people in the White House, they would have simply made no statement at all. Our government thinks we are all stupid and that we will believe whatever they say. The problem is many people do believe what they say, for they are the blind who cannot see. Those of you are not so blind will see through all this and question their authority. You are the open-minded people who are reading this book. The government also believes that if they simply came out and told the public that there is life outside this planet ... there would be mass chaos and the fall of our entire economic system along with the collapse of mainstream religions. Personally, this is what needs to happen. This would help free us from the elite and our slavery on this planet. It would be a perfect time to reboot the entire world. Right now, the nefarious greed mongers and murderers of humanity run the entire planet. They would no longer have the power they now have. This is the real reason why they do not want you to know the truth. Their time is running out and a day will come when Extraterrestrials will announce themselves to the world. For right now, we have to rely on hacker groups like "Anonymous" to fight the corruption of the iniquitous elite. I do applaud their actions, for they are Seekers of the Truth and Defenders of Freedom around the world. They question authority and they stand up to authority.

This now brings me to questioning the authority of Extraterrestrial Beings and all that they say. Haven spoken with these multidimensional Beings in person, out of body, through the black mirror and through psychic channelers, I will tell you now that no matter which of these sources you use to bring forth the information that you are seeking... this information may sometimes be incorrect or intentionally false information on the part of the entity. I advised you to perform some form of protection ritual before trying to make contact with an entity from another dimension. You never know who may truly come through once you have opened that door.

First, we will talk about the conjuring of these Multi-

Dimensional Beings into the black mirror. Let me point out that these spirits or multidimensional Beings are actually Extraterrestrials. That is of course unless you are trying to contact the spirit of a lower vibrating dead person, which would not be an Extraterrestrial or multidimensional Being. Anyone who has worked with the Conjuring of spirits or multidimensional Beings knows that they cannot truly count on their information being flawless. Many times you may end up with a false entity shall. For instance, you may be trying to conjure up the Celestial God named Enlil. You may end up getting a false entity pretending to be Enlil and yet they are nothing more than a spirit on the other side that is not truly a multidimensional Being. These spirits come through because they are bored and they find entertainment in tricking those who are not truly knowledgeable in this art of conjuring. They also may be an elemental spirit who loves playing trickery on impure humans. Therefore, they will pretend to be the Celestial God named Enlil and answer all your questions. In this case, you must use your own judgment in questioning their authority and their answers. When you question their answers, they will skate around the issue like that of a politician or they will give you an answer that makes no sense. Therefore, you must be diligent and firm with these entities so that they know you are not some naïve imbecile playing a game. I will caution you that you must also be polite in doing so. Even if you do get the true entity to come through you still may receive incorrect information. The same goes for when you are speaking to one of these multidimensional Beings through a psychic channeler. No matter how good a psychic is, their information that comes through will not be 100% correct. If they were perfect with the information they were bringing forth, they would be multimillionaires many times the world over. Yes, there are psychics out there who are millionaires and their information is still not 100% correct. For any psychic to think that their information is flawless is to be quite arrogant. The greatest psychics/seers that have ever lived such as Nostradamus lacked in the ability to put forth 100% impeccable information. I am not quite sure as to why the information they are channeling is not accurate. However, I can tell you that some Psychics have their abilities fine-tuned more than other psychics do. I will say that if you are wishing to speak with an Extraterrestrial Being, that you use a psychic that actually channels spirit over one who uses tarot cards or other methods of communication with the higher realms. This is because you can actually sit and carry on a conversation with these entities for long periods whereas with a tarot card reader, they are simply telling you what the cards mean and you do not get direct answers. You are simply getting an interpretation of what the psychic feels they have received. I mean no offense to those out there who do tarot card readings. I have had many great readings with tarot cards. I am just stating that if you wish to carry on an actual conversation with a particular entity… that you choose someone who does channeling. Another suggestion is that you can go to a couple different psychics who do channeling and ask the same questions to the same entity. Make sure that you record your sessions. Then you can go home and do the math. Compare your answers from the two different channelers. From there I suggest that you use your own intuition to choose which answer resonates best within your own reality. Therefore, you may choose your truth. Also, understand that this information may still be incorrect. Just because it is your truth, does not mean that it is the ultimate truth.

For those of you like me who have had the privilege of actually standing before a Celestial God or Extraterrestrial entity... you should still question their authority, but only once, you have truly befriended them. I advise you to do so in a polite and courteous manner, for you truly do not want to anger an entity far more advanced and that has the power to squash you like a bug. I suggest that you do not ever call them a liar. Simply tell them that their particular answer to the question does not make sense to you and tell them why. If their answer still does not make sense... I strongly advise that you drop it and contemplate the answer on your own time. These advanced Beings can and will get irritated with you if you rub them the wrong way. I advise you to stay on the good side of these entities. These entities being Extraterrestrial have the ability to abduct you and alter your brain so that you are more subservient and less intelligent. So heed my warning lest ye be harmed. I will make one last statement here as to why the information may be incorrect coming from these advanced Beings. Even if you are truly speaking to a Celestial God and they give you an incorrect answer. It may be because they do not want you to know the correct answer. You may be seeking information from them that is not ready for release into the material world. Therefore, they give you an incorrect answer. It is the same as if you were to travel out of body to an etheric retreat of one the Ascended Masters... they may teach you things of an advanced nature, but this information is not released to your conscious mind into the physical world until the time is right. However, you will not know this once you are back in your physical body. Therefore, you do not have the ability to question authority in this regards. My point for all of this is that you always question authority when you have the ability to do so. Do not accept information as the truth if it does not feel right to you. Do not accept information as the truth just because it comes from someone in a higher position than you are, whether it is your boss, the government, a religious leader or an advanced multidimensional or Extraterrestrial Being. Every person in power or advanced being has an agenda and you must question that agenda for the benefit of yourself, humanity and this planet. Turn off your TV and if you must watch it... stay away from watching the news. Take your blinders off and question all that your see, read and hear, including my words. Ponder upon everything that you read in books. Do not be a brainwashed sheep that goes through life saying, "Yes Sir, yes Sir, three bags full". Pay attention to the food that you put in your body. Much of our foods these days controlled by our FDA and government, are designed to make you dummy down. Yes, that is right... to make you stupid. If they succeed, in making you dummy down... then you will not question authority and you will believe all that you hear through the media, which is their main tool for delivering the bullshit to your mind. Take control of your life and seek out the truth in everything. When you find the truth, tell your fellow man, for the benefit of all humanity.

The Awakening

The moment when people truly Awaken in life is a moment of confusion and excitement at the same time. As I stated earlier in the previous chapter, I began to semi-Awaken around the time of my mid-teens. However, it was not until I was 18 years old when I truly Awakened and went on my quest to find out about Aliens, the universe and the meaning of life.

It happened one day when I was walking through the mall. I decided to go into the bookstore, which was of a national chain that I do not remember the name of as this was around the year 1978. I did not know why I was even going in there. I walked straight to the very back of the store where they had two small shelves with Occult books. My own spirit guides led me to purchase a Grimoire entitled the Necronomicon. This was the Black Book of the Dead. It felt very strange in my hands, yet very, very powerful. Simply reading this book would send chills up my spine, but the entities within the book intrigued me. There were three main ancient Sumerian Gods in this book and two of them I found an obsession. This would be Enki, Lord of the Abzu, along with Enlil, Lord of Sky, and God of Thunder. I felt there was some connection between them and myself, but I had no clue as to why I felt this way. I had unknowingly within my hands the keys to making contact with two different

Extraterrestrial Beings of great power beyond my wildest beliefs.

    I will point out that this was my very first Occult book that I had ever owned or come across. At the time, I did not know that this book was a fake Grimoire written by H.P. Lovecraft, the man famous for his horror, fantasy, and science fiction. Even though this book is supposedly a fake Grimoire, the Deities listed within this book are very real and very dangerous for the untrained person. These were Deities that worked with the Darkness and the Light, but at this time they were working more with the Darkness and I had tapped into the Dark side of their energies. I did not know that I was in this life to finish mastering the Darkness so that I may master the Light within the latter half of my life.

    During this time, I also came across an album entitled Project Pyramid by Alan Parsons. If you look at the album cover, you will see that it looks like something representing astral projection or some sort of mind trip. The music on this album triggered something in my brain that gave me a craving for all the Occult books that I could possibly get my hands on. The songs on this album were all Occult oriented. The lyrics to the songs were sending code to my brain for it to Awaken. The music on this album also triggered an obsession with pyramids. So I also sought out every book I could find on pyramids and how to use them. I had small pyramids set up in my room for experimentation such as putting razor blades or plants underneath them to see if all that I had read about these geometric devices was true. I even had built a pyramid frame that was about 4 feet high that I could sit under and learn to meditate.

At this same time of my life, I had also come across the wonderful magic mushrooms (psilocybin). This was the true trigger to opening my subconscious mind. At this time there were no housing developments out east like there is today and living here in Florida during the rainy season of summer brought forth many of these magic mushrooms. My friends and I would travel a few miles east to the cow fields and collect trash bags filled with these magical mushrooms. We would bring them back and boil down mass amounts of these shrooms to a very small and concentrated liquid to drink. I am serious when I say concentrated, because we would take a full garbage bag of shrooms and boil it down to one small pot of liquid. We would then trip and it would be the most intense trip one could ever imagine out into the cosmos. Some people will more than likely say… "Oh, that is why you are so messed up in the head with all your crazy beliefs, because you have done so many hallucinogenic drugs". Au contraire mon frere. I had these extremely powerful and natural drugs to thank for opening my subconscious mind. This is why the CIA has been experimenting with hallucinogenic drugs for so many years for mind control, psychic abilities, remote viewing, and telepathy along with many other things. It is also, why many native tribes of many countries use natural hallucinogenic herbs to view and travel the spirit world.

I believe it was during this time that I first opened my third eye and my entire mind to these Extraterrestrial Gods Enki and Enlil. When doing drugs like this you are an open door to almost any entity that wishes to come in and I had no clue as to how to perform any type of protection rituals. For it was at this time I had my first Encounters or abductions shall we say. I had several of these Encounters, but I had written them off as dreams and did not dwell upon them.

Now having said all the above, I will say that I truly was Awakened, but only to a certain degree. I would estimate that I was about 30% Awakened. That might not sound like much, but compared to the average mainstream person, I was moving up the ladder rapidly. The one thing I will say for sure is that I removed my blinders and was no longer a life member of the elite's Control System. I was in a sense the Phoenix rising from the ashes, spreading its wings and ready to fly across the universe. I would be constantly searching for answers to questions that linger within my mind. Many times, I would find these answers only to find out later in life that those answers were incorrect. So the search for answers would continue as it still does to this day. I will never stop searching for all the answers. Many spiritual Beings or Deities that I have spoken with tell me not to worry about the details. They tell me that I should simply go through life with unconditional love for all living things. I agree with having unconditional love for all living things, but I do not agree with not worrying about details of the universe. I refused to dummy down. There was an instance where the Celestial God Enlil literally told me to dummy down and not worry about these details. I flat out told him that I was not going to do so, as I was a Seeker of Knowledge and not some grain of sand upon the beach that blends in with everything else.

For many years forward, I would continue my search for

the unknown and seeking the answers to my questions. It would be approximately a good 30 years that I would stay in sort of a limbo state of mind. In other words, I was not truly moving forward on my Path and I was not finding the answers for which I had searched. I would simply be in combat with the forces of Darkness and Light. Both were trying to win me over to their side.

It was around the age of 50 when my Awakening was more the range of 75%. The veil had lifted significantly compared to the last 30 years. The reason my Awakening had increased so much was that I had finally made a conscious decision to no longer work with the Darkness and to only work with the Light. Many lifetimes ago, I had come here to experiment with life. This means both polarities must be mastered. Now it was time to master the Light. People need to understand that just because you work with the Darkness does not mean that you are an evil person. Each of us chooses our script on the stage of life before we come into his lifetime. Many lifetimes I had chosen to come into this world for the purpose of experiment with the Darkness. Such as coming into this life as a Viking warrior only to rape, pillage and conquer other countries. Understand that those who would be my victims were in complete agreement with this before coming into this life. Just as people like Napoleon, Stalin or Hitler were truly not evil as I previously thought and many people still do think. They chose a script to come into this life to play the part on the world screen. This is the information given to me by Archangel Michael one day when I was rattling off about how evil these people in history were. He went on to say that if they had not chosen those particular scripts, then someone else would have. These scripts of life are prewritten and someone must play the part. There is no escaping these facts. Just as some people think that President Bush or President Obama is evil. They are not evil. Misguided yes, as many of us are, but they are truly not evil. Yes, they may have incarnated into a darker bloodline, but they are playing the part from a script that they chose before coming into this life. As I stated before… if they had not chosen the script, then someone else would have. The people that have chosen to come into this life and experiment with the Darkness are still carrying the light within them. Everyone and everything carries the Divine Spark within their being and can find their way back to the Divine when they so choose. Yes, this sounds like a very screwed up game we must all play created by some sinister God upstairs, but it is what it is and that is why I am still searching for the escape route from this Matrix which can sometimes seem like hell on earth.

Battle between Darkness and Light

In this chapter, I will put forth my dirty laundry to air dry and for all to see. This way you understand the journey and struggle in which I have gone through to get to where I am today. You will understand how I first encountered Alien races and what they did to me. You will understand the tug of war between the forces of Dark and Light fighting for my soul. You will see that in the end… Light overcomes all Darkness. I am relaying to you my own personal Armageddon that I have endured. There has always been war in the heavens as Alien races battle for control over earth and humanity, but these ETs had brought the fight right into my own personal universe.

After having opened so many doors and given so much information… I would be constantly toggling between the Dark and the Light. As I stated in the previous chapter, it would be a long 30 years of living in a limbo when it came to my spiritual progress. It would be a long battle for those on other dimensions whom were fighting to control my destiny. My mind was on overload with all this information about the universe. My desire to conjure up the Mighty Ancient Ones from the abyss was an obsession, as I knew that there was some connection between these Beings and myself, but I did not know why. At this time in my life, I did not know that these Mighty

Beings were actually Extraterrestrials and truly not Gods or Demons as I learned growing up in mainstream religion and the mainstream thought process of the Control System within the Matrix. Deep down in my mind, there was the key. The key to my own heaven or hell experience here on this earth plane existence, for I had learned that I was a "spirit having an earthly experience" and not a "human having a spiritual experience". I had opened many doors that once opened, will never be shut. Nevertheless, I considered myself a pioneer or explorer of uncharted territories, so I figured the risk was worth the reward. Even if I lost my soul in the process and ended up in some eternal damnation, fiery hell … at least I tried to unravel the mysteries of the universe and the unanswered questions of my mind. Therefore, I anxiously opened each of these doors ready to move forward in my quest for the knowledge. As I passed through each door I was being tested each day with my strengths and my weaknesses… sometimes finding that I was passing through the same door several times until I had learned my lesson. I found this to be the case with almost every lesson I was going through. However, I found that with my knowledge, passing each test I gained the reward of more wisdom. I learned that knowledge is obtained, and wisdom is developed. The universe gave me more Light and more Love, but on the other side of the coin, the world of Darkness did its part to counter balance this. So I felt as though I was still not progressing. You must understand my ideology… you cannot master the Light without having mastered the Darkness. It is like being on a football team and not knowing anything about your opponent. If you do not know your opponents strategies and ways, then how can you expect to win the game...? It is also like my skydiving. I have to be well trained in knowing the good things and the bad things that can happen while doing a risky sport. Not only have I had to learn about the bad things that can happen... I have had to experience them, which in turn made me much more knowledgeable and experienced. There is only so much you can learn from reading a book or taking classes. You must truly experience the things in the physical in order to understand them. This principle applies to your spiritual progress and development as well.

You have to understand that when you start to search for answers to the meaning of life and the universe, you are more susceptible to many entities /Extraterrestrials that now know you are no longer in the main frame of the Control System/Matrix. They see the beginning of your slipping out of their control. You are no longer the blind and ignorant one who cannot see. Your eyes are gradually opening and the veil is partially lifted. So that being said, I was attracting the attention of very dark Extraterrestrial Beings who knew I was vulnerable and easy to sway to the dark side of the Occult. All they had to do was show me the glory of how I could live a life of party, party, party and not give a care about humanity or this planet. Understand that at this time of my life I was a musician playing full time in a band 5 nights a week. So the dark ones made sure there were plenty of drugs at hand along with booze and women. The drugs were opening my mind but they also lowered my vibrations, thus making me an easy target for them and their influences. Since they would no longer be able to keep me in the mainstream thought process... they would do everything in their ability to keep me under their thumbs by making the dark side attractive to me. For some people, being evil or dark was cool. I was not trying to be cool. I was trying to find my true calling and whoever answered my calling was whom I would gravitate towards. Raised in mainstream religion, I felt as though no one was listening to me when I prayed… and nobody was answering my calls. It is like those of you who have a large list of supposedly close friends, but only one or two of them will ever answer their phone or call you back. You are eventually only going to call on those two friends because they choose to make you part of their lives. Therefore, this is how I felt when it came to these Gods or whatever you so choose to call them.

    These Extraterrestrials were from the Grimoires I was studying and using to make contact with these Beings. Two of the main Deities, which I spoke of earlier, were Enki and Enlil. To me they were simply two Sumerian Gods of ancient times. I had no idea that they were actually real Extraterrestrial Beings that were of a Reptilian race and that worked with the Dark and the Light. I had no idea of the danger I was bringing forth into my life. At this time in my life, I did not even know if they were truly real or some Mythological mumbo jumbo. All I knew is that I had an obsession. My goal was making contact with them and hoping they would give me the secrets to the universe and the meaning of life. I had no idea that those who had abducted and experimented on me in my dreams were these Reptilian Gods. The best part of all is that I had no clue that one day later in my life I would be great friends with them and that they would show me many things to help me on my path back to the

Divine along with watching over and protecting me. So now, you can see how these entities operate as a polarity of Dark and Light holding the balance. Having to keep a balance of these polarities is a ridiculous thing to me personally. If the universe taught only things of the good nature, then we would only do good things for we would know not of the darkness. Once again, this earthly plane is a learning school for the soul and each of us must play our part of the script that we chose before coming into this life. Understand that there were times that these Reptilian Gods mainly worked with the Darkness here on earth and only until the last few years started working with the Light according to the roles, they were to play out in this hologram. Therefore, I have been on both sides of the fence with these characters and I must thank them for all they have taught me and for watching over me throughout many lifetimes.

Around this time in my life, I had also come across some books by Elizabeth Claire Prophet. The time I am referring to is between 1978 and into the 80's. Elizabeth Claire Prophet was a spiritual channeler who had had written many books on Invoking Archangels and Ascended Masters of the Light. I became very intrigued by her work. Here I had been shown an alternate route and access to heavenly Beings who would help me through life and could truly change my life for the better if I so chose to call upon them and change my ways. Now, I found a way to make contact with higher Beings without having to go down the dark Path. Perhaps they could bestow upon me the knowledge I seek. Perhaps they would answer my calls. This was not mainstream religion and I would learn how to call these Beings of Light in a proper science. Maybe I was going about it all wrong earlier in life praying, "Dear God, please help me blah, blah, blah, blah, blah". Perhaps I had now found the key within her teachings.

I dove deep into all the books Elizabeth Claire Prophet had written. I practiced all the Invocations each day. I would feel empowered with Light and felt like life was good. I truly felt closer to my Divine self. I had also joined the Rosicrucians. They supposedly taught all the secrets of the universe, but this was not true. However, all this would come to a stop if I did not get my way in life. I would blame whatever side of the fence I was on and soon jump to the other side. So the battle between Darkness and Light would continue.

There have been long periods of my life where I have experienced the severe Darkness created by my own thoughts which would manifest into this plane creating chaos, thus pushing me further behind the Veil and away from my Divine God self. I did not understand or have any knowledge of the concept of the law of attraction. I did not understand that every thought I had put forth would manifest in some form of my life. For many years, I lived with anger, fear, and hatred for all those who had done me wrong and all those who I did not agree with or did not agree with me. All the while feeding the negative entities or psychic vampires with the energies they so needed to feel alive. There were many times I entertained the idea of selling my soul for knowledge and all that I desired. Perhaps a "Faustian Pact" with a Demon would give me all I wanted and desired. When one makes a pact, they actually become a puppet on strings for an Extraterrestrial being that will reside in their adobe of flesh, thus allowing the ET more control over the worldly events. This is because the human making the pact will be given a place of power in the world, be it in politics or in music. Either way they will be able to influence the world to the Draconian ways. However, I resisted this temptation, for I did not want anyone to own me for my soul. I did not want to be like some of our politicians who were involved in satanic blood drinking rituals and have made pacts with the Dark side. I did not want to be like some of those big Hollywood stars and famous musicians who had done the same. What good is it to become rich and famous in this lifetime, if by making the pact and selling my soul I would have to permanently be enslaved to the three dimensional material world in all my future lifetimes. This would mean that I would never be up to escape the Matrix. This would mean that I would never have the spiritual freedom to do as I choose. This is as ridiculous as cutting off one your fingers in the workplace to get a small financial settlement.

In the year 2007, I was going through a bad time and Darkness was using that moment in time to its advantage to take hold of me. During this time, there were people who had done me wrong in a serious way. I was not the same person I used to be. The anger inside me was uncontrollable. You must also understand that for much of my life I was a very angry person and not someone that you wanted to piss off. The only thing that got me through all this without me committing any heinous crimes was the love of Archangel Michael. I have him to thank for keeping me from doing anything of such an evil misguided nature. If I had not been calling and invoking him during this trying time of my life, I would not be writing this today as my life would have taken another direction… the

Darkness would have won. However, Light overcame the Darkness, thanks to the power of Archangel Michael, for he is the most powerful force in the universe. I had also a very powerful lesson to learn from this experience and that was forgiveness of my enemies. It was the power of forgiveness that took away my anger and the heavy burden upon my back. One night, I had spoken with the beautiful Lady of Love and Light, Mother Mary. She had told me that I needed to forgive the people who had done me wrong. I told Mother Mary that this would never happen within my lifetime. I told her that I could never forgive these people no matter what the consequences would be for me. Mother Mary did not argue with me. She simply told me that when I was ready to forgive… she would be there waiting for me. Three days later beloved Christ came to me in my sleep. He took me on a spiritual journey and showed me several things. He explained to me about the laws of forgiveness and unconditional love. He showed me that even though people had seriously done me wrong… I must still have unconditional love for them and forgive them as they are only misguided and not evil. He explained to me that in order for me to be happy again, I must let go and have forgiveness. I woke up in the morning with a sense of renewal. I was simply happy as to the fact that Christ himself had come to me and had taken me on a journey. The fact that he cared so much for me that he would take the time to come to me and teach me the way of unconditional love and forgiveness. I decided that morning that I would truly forgive these people and the bad things they had done. It was as if a giant weight was lifted off my back. I no longer had this dark negativity ripping through the insides of my body. It was almost as if I were a new person. I learned to forgive and let go. Everything happens for a reason and is associated with a life lesson. This was truly one of the lessons.

I believe it was at that moment after learning forgiveness that my life would make a dramatic change. It was from that moment that I decided I would become a "Light Worker". I have Archangel Michael along with Mother Mary and Christ to thank for their love. During my trying time of Darkness, they did not abandon me. Therefore, in the end, Light had overcome the Darkness. By the end of the year 2008, I would no longer have this inner struggle or battle of who would have control of my destiny and my soul.

It is the same for this planet. Light will overcome the Darkness. Darkness has been allowed to rule on this planet for a very long time, but we will eventually revert back to our ways of Love and Light as in the early days of Atlantis and Lumeria, as this is all part of the Divine plan or Script shall we say. Eventually those who choose to work with the Darkness will have to incarnate onto another planet or dimension that is less spiritually evolved.

The Encounters

My first Encounters with an Extraterrestrial race occurred during the early 1980s. I prefer not to call them abductions because they were pleasant experiences. Although I do remember being experimented on... these experiments were not of a terrifying nature as one might think. I did not know that these experiences or Encounters were real. I thought they were simply dreams and wrote them off as such. Besides, people did not talk about this sort of thing with friends or family for fear of being labeled crazy. These Encounters were the result of my using hallucinogenic drugs, leaving myself as an open door to any entity that would wish to enter.

These Encounters were with two different Alien races... the Reptilians and the Pleiadians. The Reptilians were the ones that did the experiments on me. Even though these Reptilians were performing different types of experimentation on me, I did not feel as though I was being harmed. I did not wake up in a cold sweat or terrorized state of mind. I would simply wake up and say..."Wow". You have to understand that I thrive on terrifying things, so that which is terrifying to someone else is exciting to me. I simply thought that I was having extremely bizarre dreams. Nevertheless, I did enjoy these dreams because they were exciting. I had wished that they were real, not knowing all along that they really truly were in fact real.

Then there were the Pleiadians, who I did not know at the time were of my own race. They were very pleasant and humanoid looking. When they would come to visit me in my sleep... they would always pick me up in a small disc shaped Scout Ship or Beamship as they are properly called. These Beamships are Biomechanical meaning; they are biological and mechanical at the same time. These living intelligent machines/crafts are designed so they could only be flown by the entity that was programmed to fly it. In the hands of anyone else, the craft would simply self-destruct. These ships were programed this way to keep them from falling into the hands of the military/government of any country. After picking me up, they would take me to their Mothership. Aboard their Mothership, I would see many other humans that had been taken aboard. The other humans that I would see did not seem scared or terrified. They all seemed to be in a good mood except for maybe a few of them who did not understand what was going on. The Pleiadians all wore uniforms of a simple nature that were mainly black with a blue stripe across the chest. To me I felt like I was aboard the Starship Enterprise. Once again, they did not experiment on me. They would only examine me checking my vital signs and brain wave activity. They would take me into classrooms aboard the Mothership to teach me things of an advanced and spiritual nature. Most all the information that they taught me would not be released into my conscious mind until a later time of their choosing. This information I was given was regarding my spiritual well-being and that of helping this planet evolve and Ascend to higher consciousness along with many other things. I always enjoyed these journeys and wished to take more rides upon their smaller Beamships. Nevertheless, I was told that this was not happening so I could have fun. My Encounters with these Pleiadians seem to be quite frequent during the 1980s and into the 90s.

It was in the year 2000 that I found a great psychic who told me about my origins. I did not ask this psychic about UFOs, my dreams or Encounters. I went for a simple psychic reading just to see what was going on in my life at this time. The first thing she told me was that I was some sort of super-human, which made me laugh. She said that I was of a Pleiadian bloodline. She went on to say that this planet was not my home and that is why I did not feel at home here. She told me that I had been aboard many Spacecrafts within this lifetime. I explained to her about all the dreams that I had for many years or what I thought were dreams. She went on to elucidate that these were not dreams. She enlightened me to the fact that these Encounters had actually happened to me. After leaving that psychic reading, I went home with a new lease on life, and a new perspective. I remember being extremely excited about the new information I had received. I explained this to my girlfriend at the time and she understood and believed it to be so. I had also told my Mother, but I think she may have thought I was a little whacked in the head. The funny thing is my Mother had gone to a psychic herself some time later, only for her psychic to tell her that her son was not from this planet. From that point forward, she began to believe.

I remember making the mistake of telling this to some

friends that I work with. I told them where I was from and my having been aboard Alien ships. This truly was a big mistake to say the least. I know they thought that I was crazy and I could tell by the way that they looked at me. I had no proof of anything to show them. At this time of my life, I did not have any UFO pictures as I do now to show anyone. Therefore, I am quite positive that they thought of me as a lunatic who had done too many drugs. The even bigger mistake I made was telling my boss at work. Nevertheless, I was so excited and wished to tell everyone. I had made new friends whom I told and once I told them, they came forth with their own stories about abductions. The big difference is their experiences were truly abductions and not Encounters. When I say abductions, I mean they were not pleasant experiences for them. Their abductions were ones of a terrifying nature and they did not share this information with anyone until they had met me and I had spilled the beans first. They did not want the ridicule. Nevertheless, because I had shared my story with them first, they felt comfortable enough to come forth with their experiences. I would soon realize that there were quite a few people out there with abduction stories, but were afraid to come forth with them.

To this day, I still share stories of my Encounters with many people. I have come to realize that this is also a big mistake when it comes to dating women. I have been on many second and third dates with women only for them to label me as crazy and run the other direction after telling them of my Encounters. Nevertheless, I did not want to hide this information, for it was part of my life. If I did not share this information with them, then they would not know the true me. Sometimes it is best to keep your mouth shut, but I am not one of those people to do so. The last two women that I dated were quite open to the subject of Aliens and abductions. One of them I call Lil' Lamb had been abducted many times as a child. The other young woman was Arietis, who would succumb to having her own chilling experience after I had warned her about calling to these Extraterrestrial entities or trying to photograph them in flight.

    For the next few years until about 2003, I would continue to have visitations from the Pleiadians. I was married at the time and my wife was not part of these Encounters. She was not being taken aboard any Pleiadian Beamships or Motherships. My wife was non- spiritual and therefore the Pleiadians had no interest in her. However, I would continue to tell her of my experiences and she would accept them as truth, but wanted no part of the experience. I want you to understand that the Pleiadians have the ability to take someone to their ships in the physical or in spirit. When I say in spirit, I mean they come to you when you are sleeping and take you out of body. So yes, in this case, you would be Astral Traveling. Some people might say that is not the real thing. However, it truly is the real thing. We are all multidimensional Beings to some degree. It is just that we have not mastered the art of truly being multidimensional. Remember, we are spirits having a human experience and not the other way around. This physical body is nothing more than a shell. This physical body is not even real. We all live in a hologram and so this human experience is simply an illusion. Therefore, when we are in our spirit body, we are in our true form.

After 2003, I was having a dry spell with the Pleiadians. I was not having any more Encounters with them no matter how much I called to them. I was getting frustrated and I did not understand why they would not come to me when I called. I purchased several books on Pleiadians and how to interact with them. This was to no avail. So finally, after many months of frustration, I gave up on them. I did not try to make contact with them anymore. I was not angry with them. I was only disappointed and saddened by their absence.

Feeling lonely, I decided I would seek out new friends of the Extraterrestrial kind. I did not want to call to the Reptilians because I knew that they would experiment on me and they were of a much more stern nature. Therefore, I decided to take some even greater risks and call to the Greys of Zetta Reticuli. Now I know this might sound contradicting of my last statement about the Reptilians, as I knew that the Greys were not of a friendly nature and I knew that they were notorious for their experimentation upon humans and animals. Being the thrill seeker that I was, I wanted to test this theory and see for myself what would happen. I remembered the movie from 1993 entitled "Fire in the Sky" based on a true story. I remember the Greys putting the abductee on an operating table and having a large robotic needle come down and go into his eye. For some sick, twisted reason this intrigued me. I wondered if I could handle such a terrific experience or pain. I wanted to test the limits of my mind and body. I wanted to see just how much I could handle. While most people would give up their first born not to experience something like this, I was quite the opposite.

Therefore, I purchased a few books regarding the Greys of Zeta Reticuli and studied all I could about them, hoping to gain some sort of insight as to their disposition and their agenda. I found nothing of a positive nature in any of the books that I studied. From what I read, they were the henchmen for the Luciferians or Reptilians (same thing) and they had no regard for human life. Their agenda was to use humans for cloning to repopulate their own race with hybrids. After reading all this, I decided there had to be some good qualities about these the Greys and I was willing to take the risk. My next step was to start calling upon the Greys and see if they would actually come to me. I thought they might ignore me being that I was not the mainstream thinking person and therefore would not be able to control me through implants. On the other hand, if they were able to tag me, I would figure out a way to disable and cut the implant out of my body, leaving them no way of keeping track of my whereabouts and my actions. In addition, I would have the implant as the evidence needed to show people who were in doubt of my stories.

Each night when going to bed, I would call to them as soon as I got to the borderline sleep level. After a few weeks of no results and getting frustrated, I was almost about to put an end to my new project of trying to make contact with them. Then lo and behold, they came to me. I am not trying to sound like a manly man, but normally I have no fear when it comes to scary things. My first contact with them actually brought about some fear. What I do remember from this first experience was that I was asleep in my bed and felt a light beam come down from out of the ceiling and it scanned my body. The next thing I know, I was aboard one of their Scout ships. I do not know if I was there in my physical body or if I was there out of my body in spirit form. Either way it was the same, because I was there having the experience.

Once aboard the ship, I did not find myself a captive lying in some mucus contained cocoon and I did not find myself standing in line with others waiting to be experimented on. Yet the fear was still there. One of the Greys, who said his name was Katah, escorted me to what I would call the bridge of their ship. There was one main Grey that sat upon what I would consider the captain's chair and there were two or three other Greys that were working some controls upon their onboard computer systems. All these little Greys were different looking than I had pictured them to be. They were not wearing their special suits or helmets. They were in their natural skin that was of a pinkish, grey color. Their heads were very large compared to their bodies and the back of their head extended backwards quite a bit. I was more accustom to seeing pictures of them with their helmets and space suits on looking quite different. From that moment, I thought that maybe they were not the Greys and that they were another form of Alien race. Then they made sure that I understood they were of the Zetta Reticuli. They did not speak in a physical sense. I heard their words in my head, so they were speaking to me telepathically. As I was standing there with Katah on the bridge next to the captain's chair, I started to have fear again. I immediately started calling to Archangel Michael. I simply said "Archangel Michael, Archangel Michael, Archangel Michael". Katah, who was escorting me, immediately communicated to me that I need not be fearful. He said... "No, no, no, please, do not call upon Michael anymore. I promise we will not harm you". At that moment, I sensed extreme fear coming from him. Therefore, I knew that they were afraid of what Archangel Michael might do if he had to come there to help me. From that moment, my fear was gone and I actually snickered in my head, because I then knew that now I had the upper hand with the Greys in having something that they feared.

    The rest of my brief stay upon their Scout ship was pleasant. They simply took me for a joy ride as I had wished and told me that they would visit with me again soon. I then found myself back in my bed. I had trouble going back to sleep for I was so excited from the journey I had just had. Now if they had done anything else to me, then they have blocked that from my memory. I had no sense of missing time. I seriously doubt that they had done anything harmful to me being that I had called Archangel Michael's name and the fact that I carry Archangel Michael's essence having such a strong bond with him.

    From that moment forward, I would continue to call to the Greys in hopes that they would return to visit me. A few months went by with no contact. Therefore, I would get tired of trying to call to them every night and would only try maybe once a week. However, after about four months they visited me again in my sleep with the same scenario of a light coming through the ceiling scanning my body, once again finding myself upon their Scout ship. I had asked Katah to take me to their Mothership, but he declined and said that would not be allowed at this time. They proceeded to take me simply on another joyride in their smaller Scout ship and show me how they could enter one vortex such as the one here in the Sarasota area and come out on the other side of the world through another vortex over the Pyramid of Giza. I found this to be fascinating, as I already knew that they had the ability to do this just as all the other Alien races do. They also showed me the maneuverability of their craft and how it could make an instant 180° turn going thousands of miles per hour and yet not feel the G-forces from these maneuvers. That to me, was one the most fascinating things I have ever experienced. After my exciting joyride, they dropped me off in some remote area in which I was not familiar. I know this sounds silly but I could see them through their windows on the ship, waving goodbye to me before they took off and disappeared in an instant. I then found myself back in my bed. Being that they had dropped me off in some remote area and not my bed, told me that I had traveled with them out of body or in spirit. I know this to be fact because I went from being dropped off in a remote area to instantly awakening in my bed. I believe that after my first encounter with them, it was easier for them to take me in spirit than in the physical, being that they were not going to do any type of experimentation on my body. This way they would also be able to take me through any of the vortexes that they had showed me.

    I had two more Encounters with them which were the same as before. Each of them was pleasant and exciting. I found myself fortunate for them to have treated me as kindly as a close friend. To this day, I truly do not know why they treated me so friendly and with respect. Yes, I know they feared Archangel

Michael, but they could simply have not made contact with me again knowing that he is my protector, yet they did. My only surmise is that they know who and what I truly was. They knew that I was a Galactic Being of a Pleiadian bloodline that had chosen to incarnate on this earthly plane. They also knew of my connection with the Reptilians, which are the big brothers of the Greys.

My intuition tells me that the Greys are as malevolent as their reputation and agenda precedes them to be but on the other side of the coin is their benevolent nature. So now, I have no fear of these skinny little guys with the big heads. I will also issue a warning here to those reading this. What is good for the goose may not be so good for the gander. Just because my experiences or Encounters were pleasant, does not mean that yours will be. For the mainstream person who has not lived on other worlds, you may find that if you call upon these entities, you will have sentenced yourself to a life of living hell. You may find yourself tagged and not being able to control what happens to you or when these entities come to visit you. If you play with fire, you might get burned. If I had not been a Galactic Being myself of an advanced soul, my Encounters would have been of a much different nature.

I have not made contact with the Greys since my third Encounter with them. I do miss them and one day I will call upon them again when I feel the time is right. From there I decided it was once again time to make contact with the Reptilian God Enlil and see what he would show me in terms of his Sky Ships.

While in the middle of writing this book, I had an

Encounter again and I believe it was with either the Pleiadians or the Arcturians. It is April of 2012 that I write this. Before going to sleep one night, I had called on my protection with Archangel Michael, but I had asked him to allow any Extraterrestrials to come to me and take me on a journey as long as they were of the Light. Around 3:00 am in the morning I was of course sleeping, but I was out-of-body and standing in a field with quite a few other people when a UFO like I have not seen before, mostly white with some blue stripes came down and hovered in front of me. The majority of the ship was long and rectangular, yet it had a large orb shaped front end with a clear window so I could see the entity who was piloting the ship, and he was a Grey. This puzzled me, as I knew this was not a ship belonging to the Greys. Attached to the front of the large orb shape was a smaller orb shape, which had a clear lens device and or possible weapon. I am not sure which it was. Nevertheless, it of course was robotic and pointed at me as I walk towards it. Everyone else screamed and ran far away from it. I was not afraid, other than wondering if it would fire some type of laser at me. I walked even closer to it and it landed in front of me. I then ran up to it, a door on the rectangular part of the ship opened, and I went inside. Once inside I saw humanoid Beings, which puzzled me being that the pilot of the ship was a Grey. Everything looked like some sort of high tech lab/office and the walls were of a light and dark grey color. The door closed behind me and I approached a female humanoid that was behind a tall desk. She came out from behind the desk and ushered me into a room. I have no memory of what took place after going into the room. My memory only takes me to the time before entering the room and then being dropped off in the field in which I started from. Then I awoke from sleep in my own bed and was in awe of my latest encounter. Once again, this Encounter appears to have been an out of body experience (OBE).

These are only but a few of my Encounters as there were many more after these particular events.

The Celestial Gods

Humanity throughout history has had a need for Gods. In the beginning of humanity, we needed someone to worship. We needed a higher God-like figure to tell us how the world is supposed to be and set forth some rules. Even with Kings and Queens of the lands, we still needed a supreme authority over all humanity.

There have been many Gods named throughout history. Where did all these Gods come from? Were they just made up names? No, these Gods came from the sky. They were Extraterrestrial Beings from many different worlds and galaxies. Some of them came here like Enki to experiment with life and mine for gold. Others came here to try to dominate earth and control the lives of humans and then there were those who came here to destroy life.

First, let us talk about false Gods. All these different names of Gods or Goddesses throughout history to the beginning of time are false Gods. They were not the one and only True Divine Source of all that exists in every universe. There is an Ultimate God source of energy that even the Extraterrestrials do not completely understand. There may be a name for this Divine source of energy that created all things in every universe, but I have yet to find anyone who knows. Gods that came here to earth were nothing more than Extraterrestrial Beings. I have spoken with many of them and they have told me that they were simply playing the part of a God, because humanity had the need for Gods in their lives.

    Think of yourself being way back in ancient times and having a giant Mothership the size of several cities come down before you. In those days you would have thought this was surely a God, for at that time there was nothing that could fly much less be the size of several cities. Many of these Extraterrestrials would then introduce themselves to humanity as Gods and direct authority over them. They would easily demonstrate their power by doing miraculous things and feats of all kinds, like making lightning come down from their ships destroying anything they so choose. This of course would instill fear into man. Here we have the beginning of the Control System by instilling fear. It makes no sense to me as to why these Extraterrestrials could not have simply told us the truth. They could direct us to the Divine ultimate source and reveal to us that we ourselves as humans are also part of the Divine source of energy, but they did no such thing. I will tell you why. It is because these Extraterrestrials loved being the movie stars on the big stage of this hologram we live in. Humans worshipped them and therefore they loved to play the part of Gods. I have debated with a few of these Deities concerning this matter to no avail. They would only tell me that this is what humanity needed at the time. I personally do not agree with their logic, or perhaps I should say pretzel logic. I knew that it was because they did not want humanity to evolve so quickly in a spiritual sense. They did not want humanity to be on the same level of intelligence and Godlike as they were. In other words, they wanted us to be beneath them. This way they could have their own bloodline incarnate into the material world who were the Annunaki. They would be our Kings and Queens throughout history. They would be our Presidents and Dictators that would control the world. They would be the ones who would keep humanity in slavery to this Matrix. They would be the ones who were the elite and wealthiest people on earth while the rest of humanity suffered and struggled through life. So now, you understand some of their agenda. Welcome to your prison without bars.

Now let us analyze some of the false Gods of ancient times. First, let me say that I do not wish to offend anyone who thinks that one of these Gods that I name is the "True God". I am sorry if you are still stuck within the mainstream Control System. Look at it this way my friends... there are many cultures around the world and each of these cultures has its own God. Each of these cultures has its own religious scriptures or books. All of us were brainwashed into one of these systems from the time we were able to speak as a child. So what makes you think that the God you worship or your religious book is superior to someone else's God or religious book on the other side of the world? Can you say ego? Can you say brainwashed? We are all of a collective soul. We all came from the same Divine source of energy. Until you understand this, the world will stand divided and nations will be at war. You must also understand that some of these Extraterrestrial Gods thrive on war. We are nothing more than pawns in their chess game of life.

Those Who From Heaven To Earth Came

    During the Biblical times of the Old Testament, there was a God by the name of Yahweh. He was one of many Gods during this time. You need to understand that the original Bible had many different names for these Gods and yes, they were separate entities and not one God with 72 different names as many people think. Now back to Yahweh, he was a brutal God who was very cruel to humans. He required blood sacrifice on a regular basis. Those who did not obey him were put to a torturous death. Once again, he is a false God with an ego and anger issues. Some people to this day believe Yahweh is the one and only God, but they are wrong. Who am I to say this? Well, let us examine the facts. Here was a God that required blood sacrifice consistently; this would mean that he was more than likely a Reptilian/Draconian or some other Alien race that thrived on blood and the energies released when someone is sacrificed. If God were all loving and all merciful, why would he require blood sacrifice? When Christ came here to this earth, he never asked for blood sacrifice. During this Biblical time, Yahweh was one of many Gods back then fighting for supremacy over and yet he was not even the Extraterrestrial that created humanity. Enki is the God who created humans.

    I would like to point out something that Christ said about false Gods. Some Scriptures recently discovered in the past few years called the Gospel of Judas point to this fact. First, let me clarify that Judas was not the betrayer of Christ. Christ asked Judas to turn him in so that he could be crucified and rise up so that he could then escape to another country and have a child to carry on his bloodline. Now back to my point, in this gospel it tells of how Judas was the favorite disciple of Christ and that Christ told him the true secrets to the keys of heaven. Christ ridiculed the other disciples because of their worship of a false God such as Yahweh. When Jesus went into the Temple in Jerusalem, he saw gambling and the sale of sacrificial animals. He told his other disciples "Do you see this? This is who you are. This is the worship of a false God." That is when Christ had a moment of anger turning over many tables within the Temple and giving these false idolaters a piece of his mind. Therefore, you see that even Christ was trying to educate his disciples just as I am trying to educate you now about false Gods. Christ came here to teach us about our true divinity and unconditional love for all humanity.

Yahweh did not teach humans about their divinity and unconditional love. To Yahweh, humans were beneath him. He needed to instill extreme fear into his followers, for he was in competition with several other Gods, mainly that of Ba'al who is also known as Enlil. Do you remember when Moses went up to the mountain to get the 10 Commandments? When he came down, he found the Jewish tribes worshiping the golden calf made in honor of Ba'al. This truly angered Yahweh and he ordered Moses to have each of the 12 leaders of the Tribes of Israel executed by having them impaled. Does this sound like a loving God? What happened to forgiveness? That flew right out the damn window. How do we know that Ba'al was not the true God? Well Ba'al was not the true God either, for he also required blood sacrifice of children at this time. Many of the Jews during these times of worshipped Ba'al and some worshipped both Ba'al and Yahweh at the same time. These were nothing more than two Gods in competition with each other, but there were many more that were competing against these two Gods.

I am not going to point out the Gods of some of the more radical religions here on earth. I do not need some brainwashed fanatic wanting to kill me, but I and sure, you know to whom I am referring. I will only say that I feel sorry for those who feel they must kill others in the name of their God. They are the religions that claim to be the most peaceful, yet kill in the name of God. For what they do not understand is that they are all my brothers and sisters and that I was once lived in their same culture many lifetimes ago.

My point to all of this is simply that none of the so-called Gods is the true Divine source. Yes, they belong to the Divine source just as you and I belong to it. When I have spoken to these Extraterrestrials, they have told me that this is all part of the Divine plan. Well, I say their Divine plan or Script is absurd.

Many of these Gods or Extraterrestrials are known by other names in different cultures. Being that the cosmos is all-encompassing means that the Past, the Present, and the Future are all happening at the same time. This means that these Extraterrestrials can project themselves into whatever time frame they so choose to play the part of the God that they love playing the most. For instance, my beloved friend Enki prefers to dwell within the Greek Mythological time and therefore loves me to call him Poseidon. His brother Enlil prefers the Viking period where he was known as Thor.

Now I will point out that I still love to call my Extraterrestrial friends, Celestial Gods. The ironic thing is they have told me that I do not need to call them Lord or a God.

They know that I do not belong to the Control System anymore and therefore there is no need for me to act as though I am a mere mortal by calling them Lord or God. However, for me, I am still on a stage within this hologram, so I still give them these titles because it is simply role-playing for me and it makes them feel superior. I understand that they are not superior to me. They are simply just more spiritually advanced and are not confined to the Wheels of Karma. They are not confined to the material world. They are fully activated multidimensional Beings that have access to any world they so choose.

One day when all of humanity Awakens to their True Divinity, there will be no more need for religions. There will be no more need for different Gods in different cultures. When all of humanity has Awakened, there will be Unconditional Love across the board and no more wars. Humanity will realize that we are all one. We are all of a Collective Divine Energy. The elite would no longer be in power and they will have the choice of changing their ways and working with the Light or they will be forced to reincarnate on an alternate world that has not yet Ascended or Awakened. The same goes for humans who are not in places of power and choose not to Ascend in Consciousness.

None of what I have told you is a theory that belongs to me. What I have told you is the information given to me by these Celestial Gods. Now you may ask me, how do I know these Extraterrestrial entities have told me the truth? That is a good question. I have asked myself the same thing because I always question authority as I have stated earlier in this book. Most of what they have told me makes sense and when it does not, I make sure they know about it and I question their authority.

So now you have a little bit of information on why we have had a need for Gods and why these Gods are actually false Gods and nothing more than Extraterrestrial Beings playing a role on the world stage. I ask you, all my beloved friends to free your mind and free your soul from those who have enslaved you for eons. Once again, understand that there is an Ultimate Divine Energy source in which no one knows the name. You can call it by many names, but those are just names that humans have placed upon it.

Once again, none of the Gods in any cultures or religions is the true God. They are only part of God as we all are part of the collective God Energy. Just because they are on a higher dimension does not make them more significant than you. They are nothing more than advanced Extraterrestrial entities that are playing the part of Gods because we as humans choose to believe they are Gods. You now have the choice to believe the Truth. What you choose to believe as the truth will be according to your own spiritual Evolution. I used to believe there everyone has his or her own truth as I learned from my spiritual adventures. Nevertheless, this is pretzel logic 101. No matter what the truth is truly… there is only one truth and it lays hidden from most of humanity.

You have the freedom to choose anything in life according to your Path. If you choose not to believe any of this, then it is simply because you are not ready to Awaken to all that is your Divine Birthright and you will do so later on in this life or in another lifetime. It will be according to your Life Lessons and the script you chose before entering this life.

Enlil, Lord of Sky, God of Thunder

Now we come to my dear friend and Extraterrestrial God, Enlil. He is known as the Lord of Sky, God of Thunder, and Lord of all that Flies. He was also known as Zeus to the Greeks, Thor to the Vikings and Ba'al to the Jews, Phoenicians and Canaanites. The Romans knew him as Jupiter. Enlil played many different roles as a God and I will not go into all of them at this time, only the major ones. The church had once labeled him as a Demon named Beelzebub. It is funny how the church likes to twist and distort the truth. As he is known as the Lord of all that Flies in the Air, the church twisted and changed it into the Lord of Flies, associating him with a nasty insect. They accomplished this by simply removing a couple words from his title. According to the Grimoire entitled The Lesser Key of Solomon, also known as the Goetia, Enlil is labeled as one of the seventy-two Demons named Baal. Once again, the elite have stepped in to re-label a Celestial God as a Demon within a Grimoire. Yes, there were two different spellings, Ba'al and Baal. Both are the same Deity or entity.
Ba'al means Lord or Master and is a northwest Semitic title.

Personally, I prefer to call him by his Sumerian name Enlil. His color ray is a combination of orange and red, basically, a rust color. He is one of the two Gods that I connected with during my early stages of exploring the Occult. I love him dearly, for he has taken me under his wings and has accepted me into the Reptilian Brotherhood along with providing protection for me. He is of a very strong and stern male energy. He is also someone that you do not want to make angry for he is much more authoritarian than his brother Enki is. Even though I have such a close connection and relationship with him, he still makes me nervous, as I do not ever want to anger him.

There are some things that some of you may have read in books or online about him that are untrue. He has told me that he is not the one responsible for creating the great deluge/flood in order to wipe out humanity. This was something written in the Sumerian Tablets, which are from 8600 BC. I had also asked him if it was true that he had raped his first wife named Ninlil. He laughed when I asked him this. Once again, I told him this was something that I had read from the Sumerian Tablets translations. He stated that many things are not true in the writings of history and that that story was nothing more than a rumor or gossip just as you would have in a modern-day tabloid. He also went on to state that the Sumerian tablets depict him always at odds with his brother Enki, and in competition or conflict with him. This is not true he stated. He said that there were times when he and his brother had disagreements, but for the most part, they were very close and still are to this day. He also pointed out to me that many people thought that he was also Yahweh and this is not true. I once thought this after doing so much research as many people on the web seemed to have this theory. However, I was incorrect relying on information from the web. Therefore, I have learned not to believe information unless I have heard it from the horse's mouth. You may say the same thing about what you are reading in this book, but what I am writing is what was told to me by the deity Enlil himself.

Enlil is indeed a Reptilian, but he is also of a form that many on the earth plane could truly not understand. He has worked with the Darkness and he has worked with the Light, but at this time, he is working with the Light to its fullest form. He is originally from Nibiru, but has stranded his energies to be in many places on many levels on many dimensions. Currently he is working with the Dark Knights of the Soul who reside in the underworld trying desperately to clear the negative thought forms that have accumulated there. These dark energies and thought forms have been like leaches upon humanity. However, do not forget that these thought forms were created my man and his misguided ways of thinking. This underworld is under the earth but on an etheric plane and these energies must be cleared in order for Peace to prevail upon this planet.

Many people have misunderstood the vibrational frequency that Enlil holds. He does carry the Christ essence as he also carries the essence of many Beings. I have asked Enlil what his favorite role to play upon the world stage as a God was. He informed me that his favorite period is that of the Viking era and therefore he loves playing the part of the powerful God Thor.

Now I will explain to you how I came to connect with Enlil once again. My first experience with him was during the late 70s and into the 80s. From that point, I have no conscious memory of Encounters with him until a much later date. I do know that in 1989 and 2003 I was aboard two separate Motherships that belong to Enlil. In 2003, he brought me aboard his main Mothership the Tamarandak to remove my pineal gland and replace it with one of a powerful higher frequency and a connection to my inner wisdom so that I could remember and experience these connections with the Celestial Gods. This was not only because of my own interest, but also so that I could help humanity. Most humans do not have access to the wisdom within their pineal glands and so it was a necessary procedure for me to go through. Please understand that I did not ask to be taken aboard his Motherships at this time… it just happened.

    I would come to realize that all these years of my life, Enlil had resided here where I live in the Sarasota, Florida area during the rainy season. Florida is the lightning capital of the world. The Tampa Bay area and Sarasota are areas of extreme lightning and thunderstorms. The lightning here can travel 10 miles in advance to an incoming storm. Why am I telling you this? I am telling you this because Enlil is the God of Thunder. He is Zeus with the lightning bolt as his main weapon. He is Thor with his hammer and lightning. That is why this area generates so much extreme lightning. I remember one evening when Enlil was here with his Motherships and they said on the news that there were over 5,000 lightning strikes within a 50-mile radius within a 2-hour period. It was like a bomb going off every few seconds. Enlil comes to the area where I reside because of the extremely powerful vortexes that exists here. There is one over the Tampa Bay and there is one over the Gulf of Mexico here in Sarasota. These Stargates allow Enlil and his Motherships to enter this area from another part of the world or galaxy in an instant. The Stargate here in the Gulf of Mexico is a part of what used to be Atlantis and there is a very large crystal from Atlantis under the waters here. Our Siesta Key Beach is one of the top beaches in the world and has 99.9% pure quartz crystal sand, which is like walking on pure white sugar that is cool to the touch of your feet. It is a sacred area to many and is sacred to Enlil. He is here in my area usually from late June through the end of August, which is the time of our rainy season. So now, you have an understanding of the fact that he resides here and how he enters into this part of the world where I live.

If only I had known when I was younger, that in the sky above me was this Celestial God with his Motherships and Scout ships buzzing around in mass numbers every year during the summer. My next encounter with Enlil would be of great magnitude, for it would bring me to this discovery of his presence in which I was just explaining. In 2005, I was married and living in Palmetto, Florida, which is only a few miles away from where I live now. This year of 2005 was one of the worst hurricane seasons of Florida. That was the same hurricane season where Katrina devastated New Orleans and that coastal area. Even when hurricanes of that nature simply passed by, it would still do extreme damage to many places here on the Gulf Coast of Florida. It was during that summer that I decided it was time to make contact with Enlil again. Being that he controlled the weather and all that flies, I figured this was a prime time to make contact.

Those Who From Heaven To Earth Came

This time I wanted to have proof that he exists. I did not want proof for myself for I already knew that he truly did exist. I wanted proof to show the world and to those who are open-minded. I wanted pictures to show those who still have their blinders on so that even if they did not believe, they would still be scratching their heads and wondering if it was possible that there was Extraterrestrial life and that they were watching over us. Therefore, in mid-July which was the heaviest part of rainy season I would start calling to Enlil and asking him to show me his vehicles of travel. I wanted to see all of these Skyships and document their different shapes and purposes. I decided this time to take a bold and mighty step. I decided not to use my normal method of sitting in a magic circle staring into the black mirror of the Triangle of Solomon in hopes of seeing him and receiving an Oracle from him. I decided to ditch all of my protective services in hopes that Enlil would not hold back in showing me that which I desired. I did not care what the consequences would be. At this time, my marriage was not that great and I felt as though I was in a prison. I thought to myself that this could truly be the great escape. This could be my Shawshank redemption from the prison of matrimony. Yes, I know you are laughing as you read this and I am laughing with you. I decided in order to get Enlil's full attention I would have to do something insane. I would offer him my physical body to experiment on as he wishes, as long as he would give me the knowledge I desired and protection or perhaps take me away for good, as I did not feel at home on this earthly plane. I would also offer him my loyalty as a humble servant to his agenda. I do not know of anyone who is of sound mind that would ever offer his or her body for experimentation to an Extraterrestrial. I knew the risks and that I could be sentencing myself to horrific torture for the rest of my natural life. To me it was worth the risk because it was only my physical body and not my soul. I knew there was a connection to this Reptilian God surging inside me. I also figured that if I voluntarily offered my body to him for experimentation, then he would be merciful on me and perhaps enhance me as he had done in 2003 when he replaced my pineal gland.

Each night for two weeks, I would go to bed and summon him in my mind repeatedly until I would fall asleep. I would put crystals in my bed alongside my body to help me project my thought forms to him and to increase my Vibrational level. I am sure that you will all laugh when I tell you that my putting these crystals in the bed really pissed my wife off. She had no clue as to what I was doing. All she knew is that I was putting stupid rocks in the bed and many times one of these crystals would roll over on her side of the bed poking and agitating her. Yes, I have to laugh when I look back at this. I also would wear my clothes to bed in case I was to be taken in the night. I did not want to have an Encounter and brought before Enlil standing there in my underwear. To this every day, I still wear my clothes to bed for this same reason. You can laugh all you want and that is fine by me, as I can laugh also.

I continued to call to him each night imploring him to please come and take me with him to his Mothership to experiment on me. Then each morning, I would ask him to show me his Skyships so I could photograph them. Well, I got my wish. I was taken aboard the Tamarandak again where his scientists had me lying back in a chair, which was similar to something like that of a barber chair, except it had many mechanical gadgets attached to it and around it. There were also many monitoring screens with strange symbols on them. They had placed some sort of cap device on my head with many electrodes and wires coming off it. They told me that this was simply a checkup to see how my new pineal gland was working along with a few other things. They also performed several sound tests on my brain to see how different sound waves effected my hemispheric synchronization. Some of the sounds were pleasant and others were painful. I remember waking up with an extreme headache the next morning and I am one of those people who never get headaches unless I am lacking in caffeine. The headache continued for about a day and a half before residing. I continued to call to Enlil each night after this Encounter, but I stressed to him that I wanted to be able to capture his Skyships on camera.

Three days later, I decided to go for a ride around the neighborhood in my golf cart. It was about 7 PM in the evening and the sun was still shining bright as it stays much lighter in the evenings here during summer. As I made my way around the neighborhood, I looked up in the sky and saw an amazing cloud. It looked like a massive Mothership cloaked behind a giant super cell cloud. It reminded me of the movie Independence Day when the Mothership hovered over the city except this super cell cloud covered half the sky. It appeared to be 50 miles wide or more. I immediately rushed home to get my camera. Once I had my camera, I got back in my golf cart and headed down to the end of the street where there was an open field so that I could get a better view of this cloud without the blockage of trees and so forth. Before taking my first picture, I noticed that there was a small round rust colored object flying extremely fast coming in my direction. I immediately started taking pictures in hopes of capturing this fast-moving object. I continued taking pictures of the giant super cell cloud in the background. The cloud was too humongous to capture the whole thing in one frame and my camera did not have the panoramic feature. There was also another cloud right next to it that was saucer shaped, but only a fraction of the size of the big super cell. My adrenaline was pumping through my veins like crazy. I was so excited because I knew instantly that what I was seeing truly was a Mothership cloaked that belonged to Enlil, yet it was right in front of me. All the little hairs on my body stood up as electricity was going to my body and through this, I sensed his energy as being present.

After taking quite a few pictures, I went home to analyze them on my computer. I was astonished by the fact that not only had I taking great pictures of this amazing cloud, but I was also able to capture the small round flying object that was heading towards me. I also noticed in one of my photos that there was a small round white object zipping out of the giant super cell cloud. My repeated requests to obtain proof had been answered. Even my wife was astonished by these photos. In this first picture (photo 01), look closely at the super cell cloud and how it is shaped like a giant saucer. Notice how perfectly the lines are feathered up to the top edge. Underneath the saucer shape, you will see the actual thunderstorm part of the cloud. In the foreground, I have circled the Scout Ship that was heading towards me.

Photo 01

This was the "Tamarandak", his main Mothership. Tamarandak means "Beautiful Earth Ship" and this is truly a thing of beauty to observe in the sky. Next, you will see a blown up view of the Scout Ship in Photo 02. Notice that there are arched ridges on the sides that come down to a point in the front. From what Enlil told me, this unmanned Scout/Drone was coming to observe me. However, it ended up losing communication with the Mothership. Normally these Drones go out and take samples of the air pollution, water and many other things including that of tracking something or someone who has been tagged. They are normally not visible if they are cloaked or going too fast for the human eye to see.

Those Who From Heaven To Earth Came

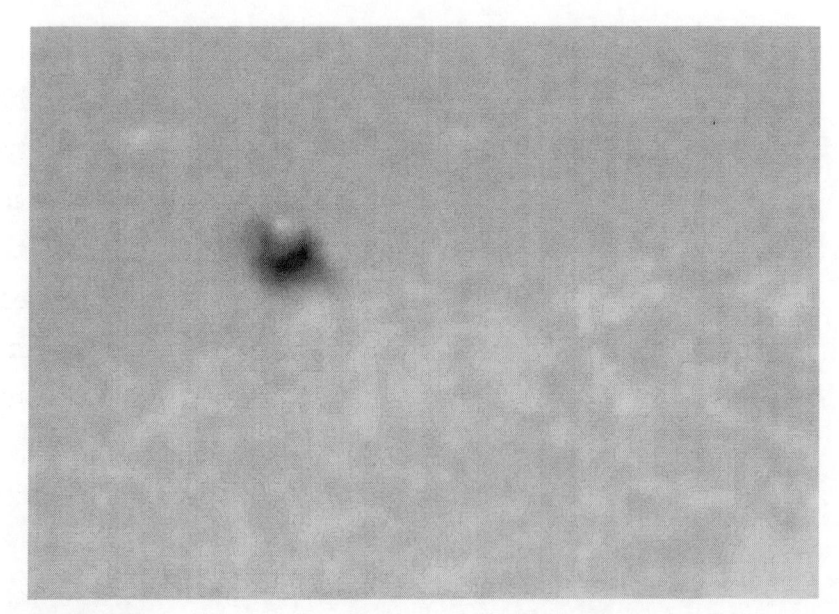

Photo 02

Photo 03

Those Who From Heaven To Earth Came

In photo 03, you will only see the left corner of the Tamarandak and you will see there is another Scout/Drone that looks like a white ball of light. This was the second Drone that was sent out to find the first one that was tracking me and got lost. The other smaller super cell cloud was cloaking the Skyship named the "Tahazu Zog". So here, I had two Alien spaceships before me along with two Scout/Drones all within a couple photographs. My Reptilian God friend had come through for me just as I had requested of him.

The following day I saw that the same large super cell cloud that was cloaking the Tamarandak was still in the sky and had only moved a fraction to the west. The same shape clouds never stay in one place for more than a day. If this were simply a large storm cloud, it would have moved on, changed shape or dissipated. This confirmed to me that it was indeed the Mothership Tamarandak. I decided to wait until later in the evening to take pictures of it right before it was going to rain. Around 8 PM, I decided to go take some more pictures, but this time from my own yard. When I went outside onto my side porch, I looked towards the Tamarandak once again and saw many little speckles of light coming my way. There were twenty-nine of them in total. As they got closer and closer to me, they looked like one of those neon green glowing necklaces you would get at the fair. As they got about thirty feet away from me I stopped taking pictures because I was too much in amazement as to their presence. I stood there somewhat frozen as they came right up to me and started circling around me. As this was happening, I closed my eyes to concentrate on their energies. It felt like my skin was tingling with many little pinpricks. When the sensation stopped, I opened my eyes and the entities were gone. I immediately ran inside to inspect the photographs I had taken. Now the camera that I had at this time was of low quality and was only three megapixels, which did not take very good pictures close to dark. In this next picture (photo 04) which is a fuzzy picture, you will see two of the entities that I have circled. The one towards the bottom was the closest one to me and looked like a neon glowing ring with something deep blue inside of it. The one above it had a white ring around it with deep green inside of it. I have more photos that show all of these entities at one time that were approaching me, but they are too small to show you in one photo without seriously enlarging it.

Photo 04

Those Who From Heaven To Earth Came

In the following picture (photo 05), I have cropped and enlarged the image of the entity that was closest to me. It clearly had a neon green ring around it and a deep blue entity within the neon green ring. It has what looks like three fins, one dorsal fin and two side fins. It also has two large black eyes in the front of it. Now I know that when friends of mine have looked at it, they see something different inside the glowing ring. Nevertheless, I am explaining to you the way it truly looks according to Enlil. This picture is like nothing I have ever seen in any books or on the web. Therefore, I do not think anyone else has ever encountered these creatures before. My only wish is that I had a camera with higher mega pixels at the time, but when I took these pictures, my camera was top of the line for small digital cameras at that time.

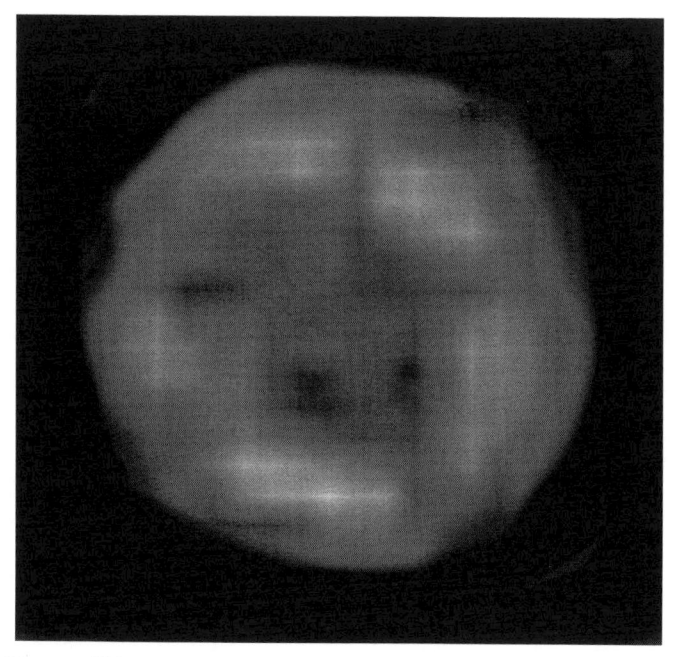

Photo 05

Now I needed to find out who and what these entities were that emanated from his Mothership and had approached me. I knew they were of a Reptilians nature coming from Enlil. I wrote my close friend Twanny in Amsterdam to get her opinion and have her ask the spirit who watched over her named "Baruchiel" of the Hara-Serapel. The spirit confirmed that this entity was indeed of a Reptilian/Draconian energy. That is all the information that Baruchiel put forth. It was not until a few years later that I would receive some detailed information on these entities. I believe it was somewhere in 2008. I figured the easiest way to get this information was to have a channeled session. I contacted my dear friend Lea Chapin who is an intuitive psychic channeler. She has the gift of spirit, meaning she can channel through any spirit or Celestial Being that she so chooses and the spirit will actually speak through her. This way I could sit down, have a one-on-one hour-long conversation with Enlil, and get the information that I needed. This would be the first time I had ever spoken with Enlil through an actual channeled session and not through the black mirror. My friend Lea had no problem bringing this Celestial God through, for he was anxious to speak with me. Therefore, Enlil came through to speak with me and as always when he is near, all the little hairs on my body stood up. For me, his energies were so intense that it was like electricity going through my body and my heart would race. He explained to me that the super cell clouds I had taken pictures of were indeed cloaking the Tamarandak and the Tahazu Zog. He explained to me that he was actually trying to land his largest ship the Tamarandak and that is why it was at such a low altitude. He came to show me that which I desired.

However, he was not happy that he had lost one of his Drones and even after sending out another Drone to find it had no success. They had also lost all data that the Drone collected. I thought to myself if only I had been able to find the lost Drone that had possibly crashed somewhere. I could just imagine the military being up my ass if they knew about it. I also asked him "What were these entities that had approached me and were swirling around my body?" He explained to me that they were as he called Scouts. They were a group of 29 entities that were of a collective soul. Therefore, they always travel in a group. He sent them to me because of my interest and to sample shall we say, my Etheric DNA. The color of the one in photo 05 is a reflection of my own auric field. In other words, it changed colors like a chameleon to match my own energies and vibrations. Enlil laughed and told me that this collective group of entities were somewhat frightened of me just as I was of them, for they are normally not allowed that close to humans and so they were not accustom to interacting with someone like me. He went on to confirm the number of times I had been aboard his Motherships and the experimentations that were performed upon me. He appreciated my loyalty and my allegiance to him. He gave me much information during the course of this conversation with him and promised he would watch over me and that there was much more he had in store for me.

At this time in 2008, I was living back in Sarasota and my connection with Enlil was stronger than ever. I was able to photograph many of his Scout ships with their different sizes and shapes. Although some of the Scout ships always remain close by here during the winter, it is not until during summer in the rainy season that his Motherships reside here. On any given day during rainy season, I can walk outside and capture on camera anywhere from 7 - 200 UFOs within a matter of minutes and during this time Enlil's energies become extremely strong within my house, which I will speak more of later in my chapter entitled Night Time Energies. Normally, Enlil will communicate with me telepathically in my head and tell me to go outside so that I can take pictures because the Scout ships, Drone and Telemars were flying high in the sky.

Rainy Season, Enlil Cometh

From 2008 and on, my connection to Enlil became stronger and stronger. It was the summer of 2009 during the beginning of rainy season when I would come face-to-face with this Reptilian God, but first I would meet my Divine Protector, Archangel Michael. I was lying in bed one night as a storm was approaching. It was a heavy storm with serious lightning and thunder cracking every minute or so. I was doing my normal protection invocations to Michael before I went to sleep as I do every night. This particular night, Archangel Michael appeared standing next to my bed. I was in awe of his magnificent and appearance of strength. He said to me... "I am your strength, without me you would fall." Then his Twin Flame whose name is Faith, appeared before me. She was the most beautiful entity I have ever seen. Everything about her was pure white... her hair, her skin, everything except her eyes, which were a deep blue. She was almost too bright to look at, for her aura was so strong. She did not speak. She only showed herself to me. Then they both faded away and I got up to go to the bathroom and splash water on my face to make sure I was not dreaming of what I just saw. After doing so, Archangel Michael once again appeared right behind me to my left. The thing that struck me the most was the size of his sword. The sword was almost as long as I am tall... about 5' 7". I asked him how it became a flaming sword as described in the Bible and he proceeded to show me. He pointed to the Blue stones imbedded into the handle. There were several blue stones, and when he pushed one of the stones, the sword became electrified with what looked like blue lightning all around it. In reference to that, his Legion of Angels is called the Blue Lighting Angels. After he showed me how the sword worked, he once again disappeared. Nevertheless, I knew he was still there, just not visible. I went back to bed with my mind joggled over the experience I just had with the one who watches over and protects me.

I laid there in bed listening to the sounds of the thunderstorm, which brought forth a sense of relaxation like no other and proceeded to start calling upon Enlil. I was almost asleep when a beam of light came through the ceiling and I found myself having been transported to another part of the world, which looked like somewhere in the desert. Wherever it was, it was in the middle of nowhere. I found myself dressed in a brown colored robe, which resembled something like that of biblical times. I remember looking at my clothes and saying... "WTF". I seem to be more worried about what the hell I was wearing than where I was actually at. Even though his other Motherships were over my home in Sarasota, Enlil himself was in another part of the world at this particular moment, and that is why he transferred me to that part of the world. Approaching me was a dark thunderstorm cloud rolling in fast. It stopped as it was over top of me. The next thing I knew, I was aboard Enlil's Mothership, the Tamarandak. I was then escorted to his main chamber where I was stopped and forced down to my knees about 10 feet in front of his throne. This main chamber had a white and gold marble floor and contained many marble pillars behind his throne. Let me explain at this moment that his personal appearance was a manifestation of how my conscious mind chose to see him at this time. For he is a shape-shifter and can change his appearance at any given time. He sat there on his throne leaning to one side with his right elbow on the armrest and his chin resting upon his fist. He wore a large gold crown with many jewels and was sporting a long black curly beard almost like that of a spiral perm. On each side of him stood five or six Beings with long hair pulled back in a ponytail that seemed somewhat gender neutral, for I could not tell if they were male or female. He got up from his throne and walked towards me, proceeding to walk around me slowly in a circle as if he were inspecting me. He told me that he appreciated my loyalty and allegiance to him. He said... "You are not of the Reptilian bloodline. You are of the Pleiadian bloodline. Nonetheless, I am accepting you into the Reptilian Brotherhood. You are now part of my family. As long as you are loyal to me no harm shall come to you." He then raised the palm of his hand towards the ceiling and the majority of the ceiling opened up into glass panes so that I could see the storm clouds that surrounded his Mothership. He said... "You like?" In addition, I told him "Yes indeed, that is an understatement". He walked back, sat upon his throne, and made some sort of motion with his hand. With that motion, I found myself back in my bed. I did not sleep the rest of the night after having met Archangel Michael and Archangel Faith along with the Reptilian God, Enlil, for my energy levels were too high. This was my most exciting encounter ever. I do not have any conscious memory of ever having been allowed to meet with Enlil in that close a manner at any other time than this. The previous times I had been aboard his Motherships, I only remember meeting with his scientists and other members of the ship, be they guards or what not.

So now, I was part of the Reptilian Brotherhood and I did not have to do anything special to achieve this. Normally to be part of the Reptilian Brotherhood, a person must be part of a blood ritual, drinking the blood of another Reptilian, thus making you a host for a Reptilian entity that will work behind the scenes. However, I was not looking to become a host and Enlil knew this. He simply knew that I had unconditional love and loyalty to him. From that night forward, everything would become even more intense.

Now back to Enlil's appearance. As I stated he is Reptilian and therefore he is a shape-shifter. He rarely ever shows himself as a reptile looking figure. He chose his appearance to me that night according to how I have always imagined him as the Sumerian God and how they looked in those days. On a later date, I had asked him through a channeling session how he preferred to appear. He told me that he normally likes to appear in somewhat of a Tarzan image… very tall and muscular with no body hair, only wearing a loincloth. This is because he likes to feel free. He comes in many guises according to what someone needs to see. Even though he is quite stern, he does have a sense a humor and sometimes he likes to appear as a gorilla or something that would appear to look like Bigfoot, for he loves to shape-shift into many different things. Any time I try to conjure him into the Triangle of Solomon; he appears in his Tarzan image sitting upon his throne with his long blonde hair. This is also because I no longer choose to see him as the Sumerian image I once thought of. I choose to see him the way he truly wishes to appear.

Now that it is rainy season and Enlil is residing here, I am anxious each day for the thunderstorms to role in. Almost every day the thunderstorms roll in around 3 or 4 PM in the afternoon. As the thunderstorms start to roll in, I ready my camera for taking pictures hoping to capture some of his UFOs buzzing around. He has explained to me that he has eight different types of Scout ships that emanate from the Mothership. Some of them are manned others are Drones and are unmanned and some of them are biological entities/vehicles of energy. The manned UFO Discs and Tubes are called Telemars. The unmanned ones are called Drones. The biological flying rods are called "Belis" pronounced (bay-lees).

The Motherships stay cloaked in the large super cell clouds. They are actually on another dimension, just as a spirit that visits you in the night. They are right in front of you, but they are on another dimension. Mainstream people have no clue as to what is right in front of them. Most of the time these super cell clouds look just like a giant oval shaped UFO. I pay attention to my surroundings in detail, noticing the slightest thing that might be out of place or abnormal. When Enlil himself is present in one of these Motherships and is close by... I can feel his presence. I can feel his presence from miles away. It is similar to when someone is about to be struck by lightning... all the hair on their body stands up from the static electricity. For me I can feel the electricity going through my body, my heart beat increases rapidly, and sometimes I start to hyperventilate. Many times, he will telepathically speak to me in my head telling me to grab my camera. In this next picture (photo 06), you will see the Tahazu Zog Skyship coming in fast to hover over my home. Notice how it is saucer shaped and has a defined edge with the storm clouds underneath it.

Photo 06

This is truly a magnificent site to see in person. Tahazu Zog means "Battleship that Shines". As I stated earlier, these clouds will come and stop directly over top of my home. Sometimes two of them from different directions will come and almost touch each other right above my home. In the next picture (photo 07), you will see it getting much closer. I was very lucky to capture this one because it came in so fast. Once they are straight above my home it is hard to capture them on camera, as they are too large to fit within the camera screen.

Photo 07

Many times these Skyships come in but do not bring any rain. They come in and move fast or they stay in the distance out to the east of my home. When these types of clouds roll in, I am able to capture the Telemars going to and away from them.

Sometimes, I will be at the beach and see big clouds that are very faint yet retain the shape of a large oval saucer. The cloud will move around the sky, yet retain its oval shape. These are once again Motherships cloaked on another dimension just sitting there watching us like specimens in a petri dish. Trust me when I inform you, that is what we are.... specimens. They have been watching us for centuries. Nowadays, humans are so wrapped up in everyday affairs that they pay no attention to their surroundings. They walk down the street in a zombie like daze with their eyes glued to their IPhones, unaware of what might be observing them from above.

Needless to say, we are being watched, abducted, and experimented on. Many people do not speak of what they think they may have seen out of fear of humiliation from closed-minded people. You will see in this next picture (Photo 08), how I was able to have Enlil raise his Skyship in altitude at my request. In this picture, one of his Skyships is rising from the dark cloud below it in a glowing glory.

Photo 08

Yes, while venturing outside one day, I felt his presence. I called to him while looking to the north because there was something bright barely peeking out of the top of the dark clouds. I asked Enlil if that if he was in that cloud, to raise his ship higher in the sky and he did as requested. There is a complete series that go with this photo, but this one here is when the ship was fully raised. You can see the bizarre shape as it looks somewhat like a large boomerang with another section of the ship below it, which looked like it was burning with fire. That lower section of the ship was so extremely bright. The entire Skyship was extremely huge and stayed in that position for several hours without moving.

Photo 09

    This picture is another classic example of the Skyship Tahazu Zog. It is a glorious thing to see this in the sky and knowing a Battleship of the Reptilian God is close at hand. Study the picture closely and once again, you can see the oval shape, like that of a Mothership. I believe now when you look in the sky, you will never look at clouds the same knowing that within them could be an Alien Mothership belonging to a Celestial God. You will be amazed at the things you will see if you pay attention to the world around you. Now, you may be asking yourself how an airplane can fly through this cloud if there is a Mothership inside it. Any physical object can fly through these clouds because the Mothership is on another dimension or plane of existence.

When a big rain front comes in, I always get my camera out, for I know there will be many of the round shaped Drones flying about. These Drones always circle the perimeter of the rain front. The Telemars and Belis do the same as they are bringing in new energies. They fly in erratic patterns and never in a straight line as an airplane would. So right before the rain hits and you can smell the rain coming, that is the best time to capture them on your camera. Notice once again the large thunderhead cloud in photo 10 that is cloaking a Reptilian Mothership. In this picture, there are three Drones, which are just hovering there in one place.

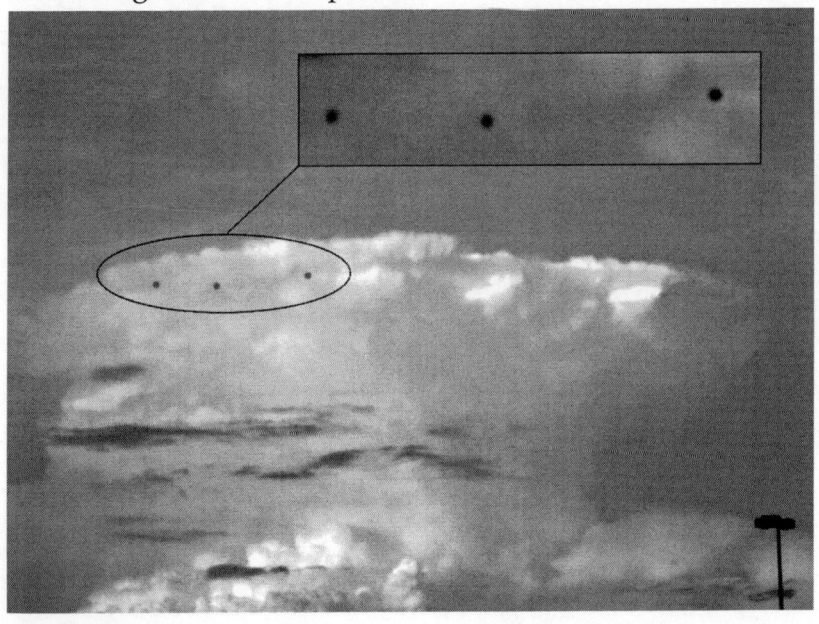

Photo 10
I have changed the brightness/contrast as I do in many pictures

when enlarging so you can see the shape better.

For your knowledge, the Drones are the most common UFOs to capture on camera. Sometimes they are more visible, but most of the time they look very faint in color as they are also somewhat cloaked and on another dimension. You have to understand that a camera can capture many things that are not on this dimension just like spirit manifestations and orbs. These Drones toggle back and forth between the material world and their own dimension and this sometimes plays a part in how visible or not they may be.

Now some of you might say… "How do I know these objects I am taking pictures of, are not birds, or planes or whatnot?" That is an easy question to put to rest. Any of these unidentified flying objects can easily be distinguished. If you have your camera in burst mode then it is shooting a certain amount of frames per second as long as you are holding the button down. My small pocket size digital camera takes two frames per second and my large Cannon EOS 7D shoots eight frames per second. Therefore, if you have your camera pointed in one steady direction and you have taken a good number of shots, then you will notice that with airplanes or birds, they move quite slowly across a section of eight frames. Airplanes normally fly in a straight directional manner and birds are little more erratic. Many times the birds will simply be riding the thermals in a circular direction. Nevertheless, with any type of flying anomalies such as these, they are traveling at extreme speeds in excess of 7000 mph. This means in a sequence of frames, you may only capture three frames containing the UFO. You will see that within those three frames it goes from one side of the sky to the other. There is nothing man-made that can fly that fast. I wish to take this time to point out that sometimes birds in the far distance will appear as round objects and therefore you may think you have captured one of these Drones on your camera. Many times, it is simply your lens out of focus, which will make the bird appear as a round blurry object. Therefore, you must do as I stated and judge these anomalies by their speed across the sky. You can also judge them by their erratic flying pattern or if they do not move at all. Birds and airplanes cannot do an instant 180 in the sky. Birds and airplanes do not fly straight up and down or in a zigzag pattern.

In this next picture, my dear friend Arietis and I were at Myakka State Park. We went there simply to have fun and

Photo 11

nature, but we also went there to hunt for UFOs and other

anomalies in the sky that day. We thought that if perhaps we were further out east, away from the city, we might have more success in capturing them on camera. In this picture (Photo 11), you will see a Telemar Disc, a Drone and a small Cessna airplane. This is one of the photos she took. After that day, we came to realize that we could get just as many UFO pictures within the city limits by stepping outside of our homes. My friend Arietis was very interested in photographing these UFOs after having seen many of my photos. Therefore, she was instantly hooked. Every day she would go outside to take pictures of the sky to see what might possibly show up. I did warn her however, being that she was dating me at this time with my Galactic connections… she might very well be visited in the night by some of these Extraterrestrials. I will explain her experiences with that in a later chapter.

This next picture you will see one of the Drones and its round shape. As you can see from the enlarged part of the photograph, the Drone is fuzzy looking. They are not meant to be seen. They are Scouts and therefore they are not for the public eye. I will give you a scenario; it is just as if you were an Indian warrior sent out as a scout to see where the enemy was and what they were doing. You would not want to be seen. The same goes for these Drones. They are simply on a mission to collect data without being seen by the mainstream media and humans. Sometimes they are so faint, you can barely even see them as they appear to look like water spots on the lens and this is because they toggle back and forth between dimensions.

Those Who From Heaven To Earth Came

Photo 12

Next, I will show you what I had believed to be a Drone, but I am still not quite sure because of its color. I will explain. One night my friend Arietis and I decided to get up on the roof right before dark. We had seen an incoming thunderstorm from the east. We both used our smaller Sony Cyber-shot cameras. For some reason her camera was picking up on a glowing object and mine wasn't. She got excited and told me "Check this out". You could see the object moving around on her camera screen but you could not see it in the sky. As long as she held the camera up we could watch it on her screen bounce around up and down sideways and every which way as if it were simply entertaining us. Therefore, she was able to get a large number of photos with this glowing, bouncing ball. When I said earlier, I did not know if this is a Drone, that is because I do not know if the Drones have the ability to glow in this manner at nighttime. Possibly this could be simply another type of manned UFO craft from Enlil, being that it came straight out of the storm cloud and at one point there were two of them dancing in the sky in unison putting on a spectacular show. I have yet to ask Enlil about this.

Photo 13

This was not Ball Lightning as some people may think. The term Ball Lightning is for mainstream people and scientists who do not know any better. I am sorry, but scientists have yet to prove anything when it comes to ball lightning. All they can do is theorize, but truly, they have no clue.

Now we will talk about the UFO Discs and Tubes known as Telemars. Many times, they are hard to distinguish between the two of them. The Tubes appear to have a 45° angled front end and a 45° angle rear end although there are some tube shaped UFOs that simply have flat or round blunt ends. These

Tubes can travel at any angle. Many times when I catch a sequence of a Tube, it is flying erratically. When flying horizontally, it appears to change the angle of its flight raising the front end up slightly and then a moment later bringing the front end down at a lower angle. When it does this, you can see the air being displaced around it. Many times the Tubes fly vertically at about a 45° angle such as the one in this next picture.

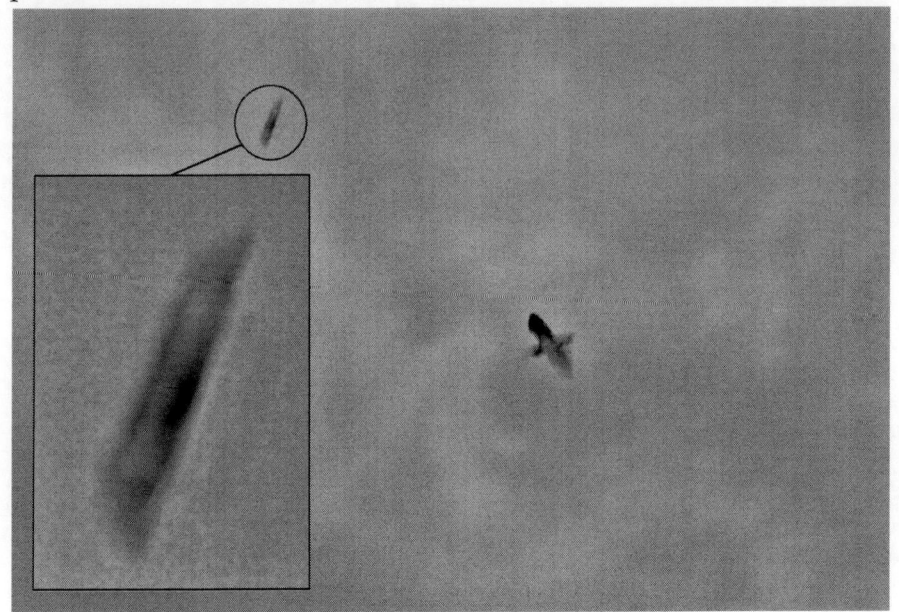

Photo 14

    I was extremely lucky to catch this one on camera being so close. A storm front was coming in and I saw the large bird. I am not positive, but it might be a tri-color Heron or a Wood Stork. Therefore, I was actually photographing the bird and caught the UFO Tube along with it. It was at a very low altitude and flying upwards. I have a sequence of five photos showing this Tube in action. Now if you look at it you will see the angled front and rear end which is a gun metal grey. The body section is cream-colored with what looked like burn marks or rust color towards the middle of the body. The majority of the Tubes that I capture on camera are a light solid gray color or a solid dark gunmetal color.

Now, I will share with you some more photos of the Telemars that are actually flying Discs or Tubes. In this next picture (photo 15), you will see a Telemar flying close to a small Cessna airplane. Notice the angle in which the Telemar is flying. They are also very easy to photograph during rainy season as a storm fronts approach. Just like the Drones, the UFO Disks are always circling the outer perimeter of

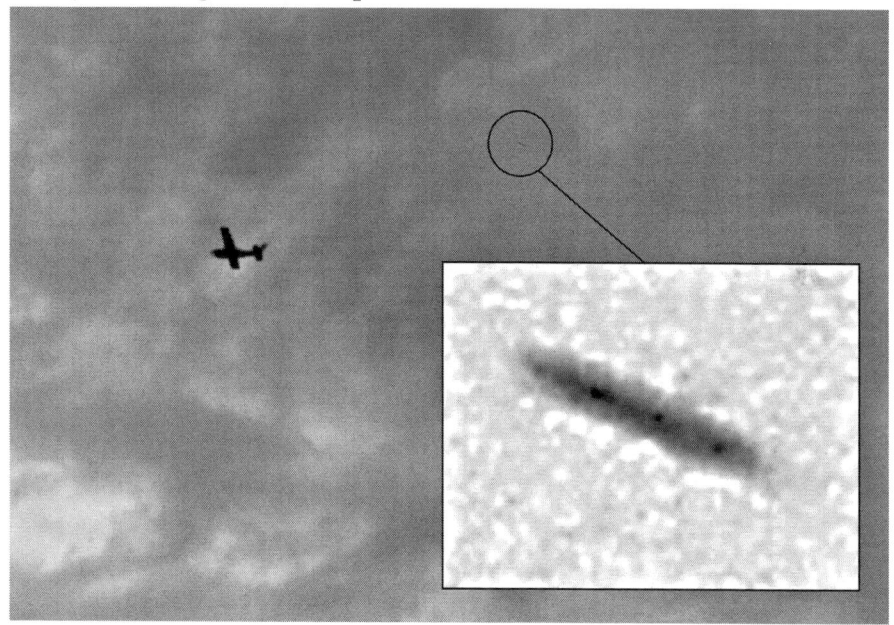

Photo 15

the storm front. Just like children playing in the sky running back and forth, pulling off crazy maneuvers that no man-made aircraft could ever come close to doing.

Here is another Telemar in photo 16 coming in front of the storm. It appeared to have a green like substance coming off the sides of it as it cut through the air. What you cannot see in this picture, are the hundreds of Belis below it. They are way in the background and are too small for you to see without enlarging this whole picture on a big screen.... but they are there.

Photo 16

It took me months to figure out what the hell the small rust colored specks were. Once again, I had thought it was dirt on my lens.

Some of these Telemars appear to be somewhat rectangle in shape as you can see in the next picture (Photo 17). For most all these photos, There also a full sequence of them zipping across the sky and radically changing their flight angle, which airplanes never do. It would be nice to be able to capture one of these UFOs, as they were straight above me, so I would be able to make out the complete shape of the craft. All my photographs are from a side view of the ships. I have asked Enlil to bring them closer to me, but he has declined stating concerns for radiation emitted from these ships. Technically, they could come much closer and not be a threat to my health. They do not need to land in front of me, I only need them to stay still and hover above me at an altitude of about 500-1,000 feet, which should be quite a safe distance. This would allow me to capture the details of the ships.

Photo 17

Those Who From Heaven To Earth Came

Photo 18

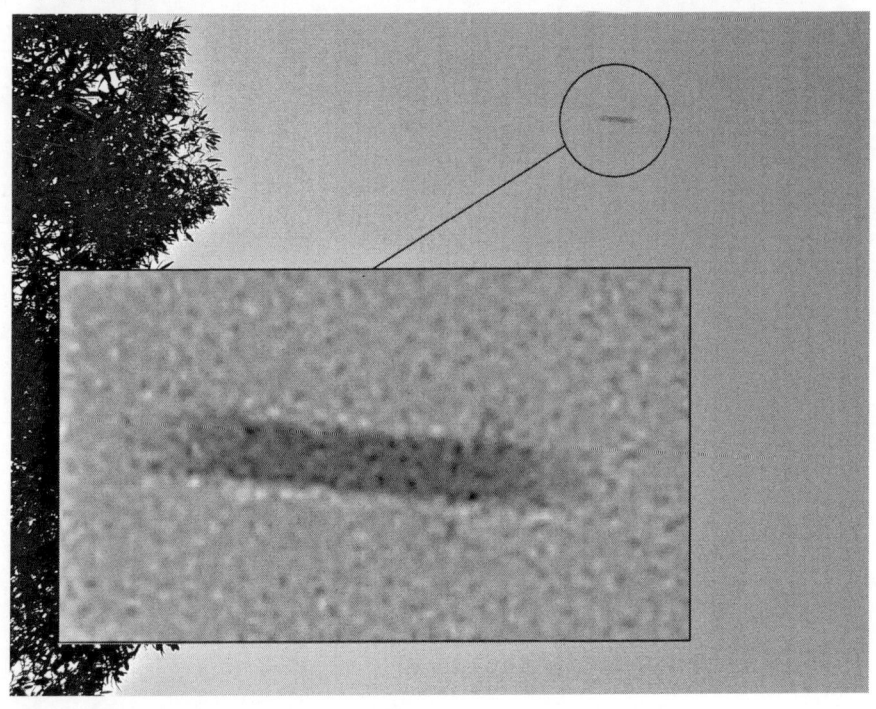

Photo 19

Those Who From Heaven To Earth Came

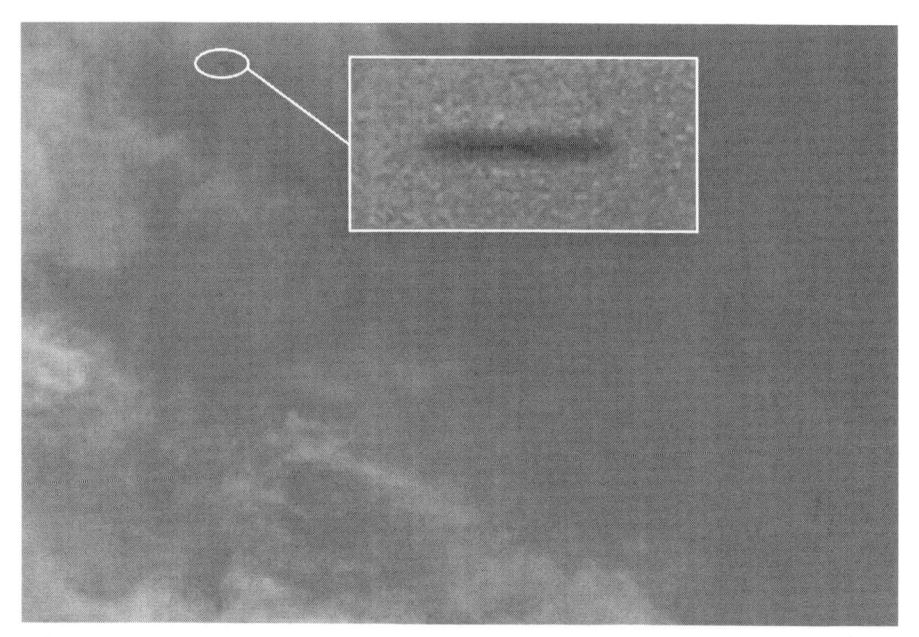

Photo 20

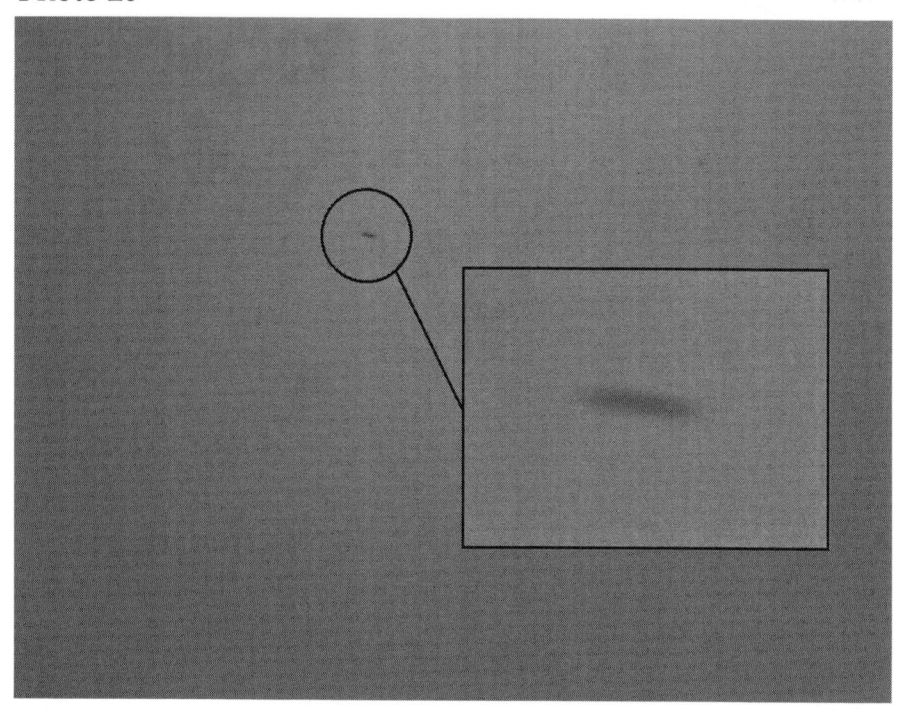

Photo 21

Those Who From Heaven To Earth Came

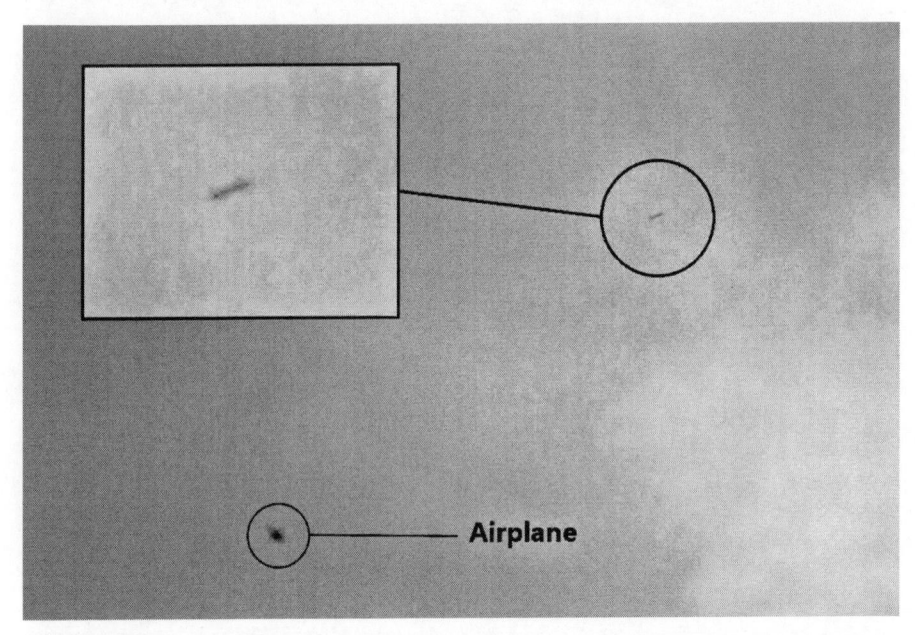

Airplane

Photo 22

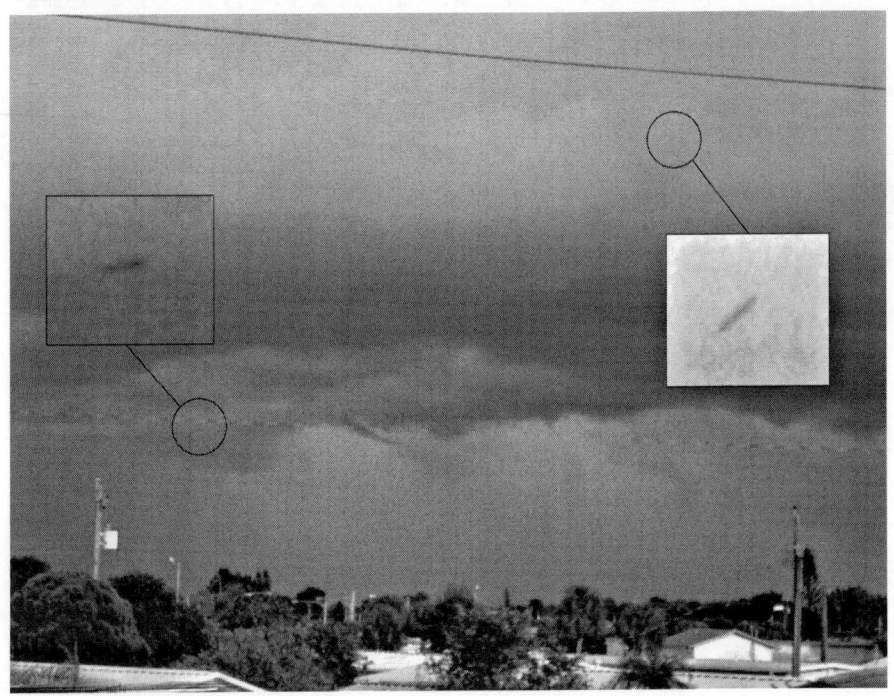

Photo 23

Those Who From Heaven To Earth Came

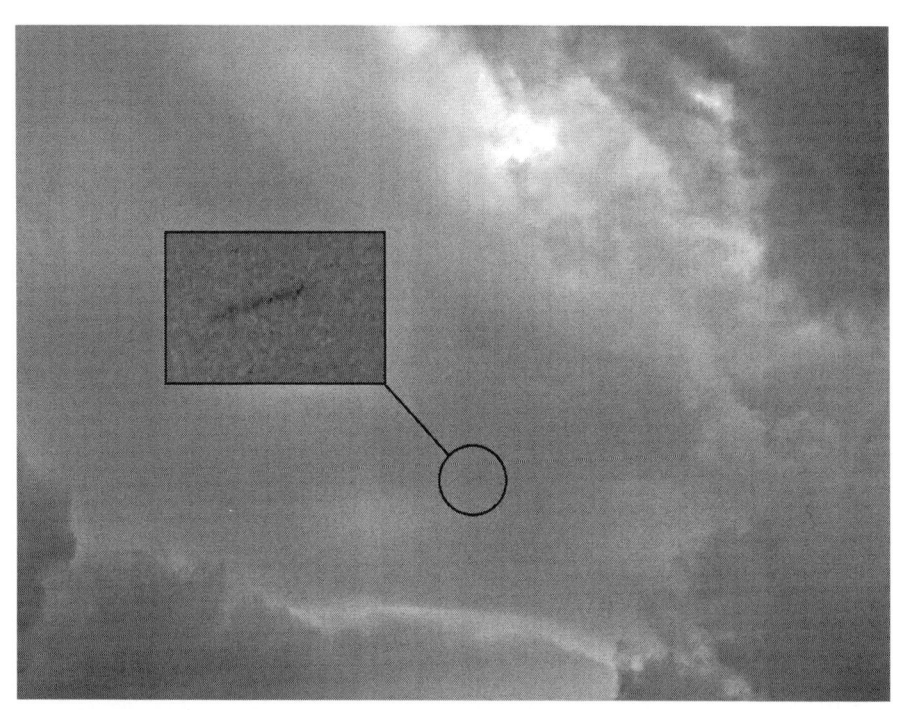

Photo 24

Photo 25

Those Who From Heaven To Earth Came

Photo 26

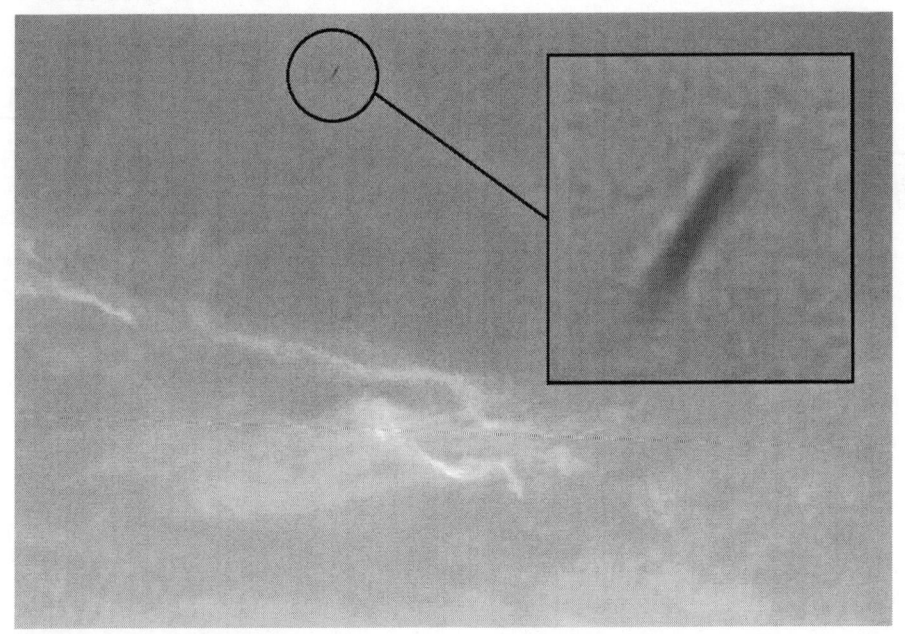

Photo 27

Those Who From Heaven To Earth Came

Photo 28

Photo 29

Those Who From Heaven To Earth Came

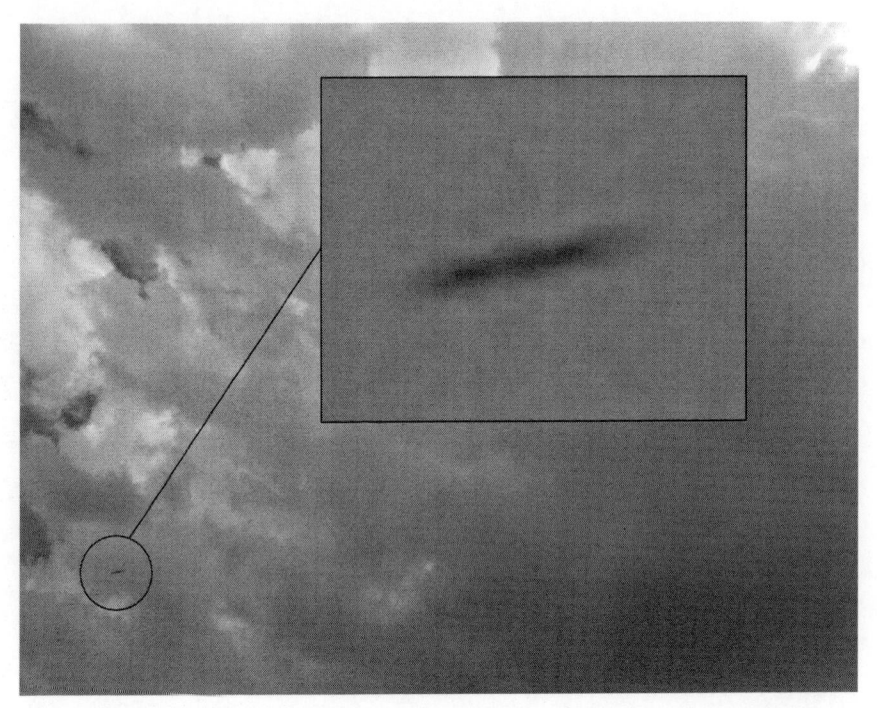

Photo 30

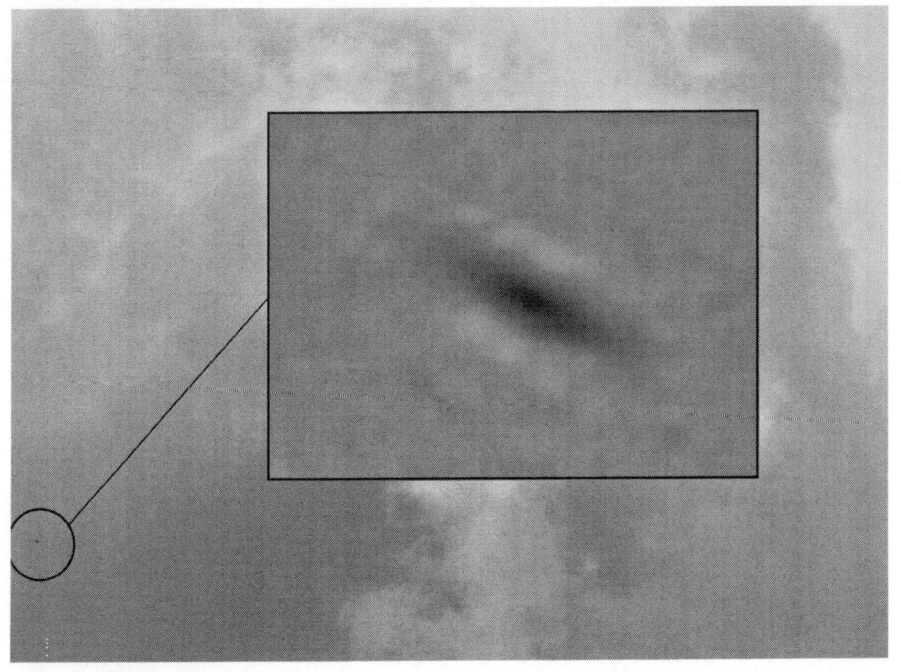

Photo 31

Those Who From Heaven To Earth Came

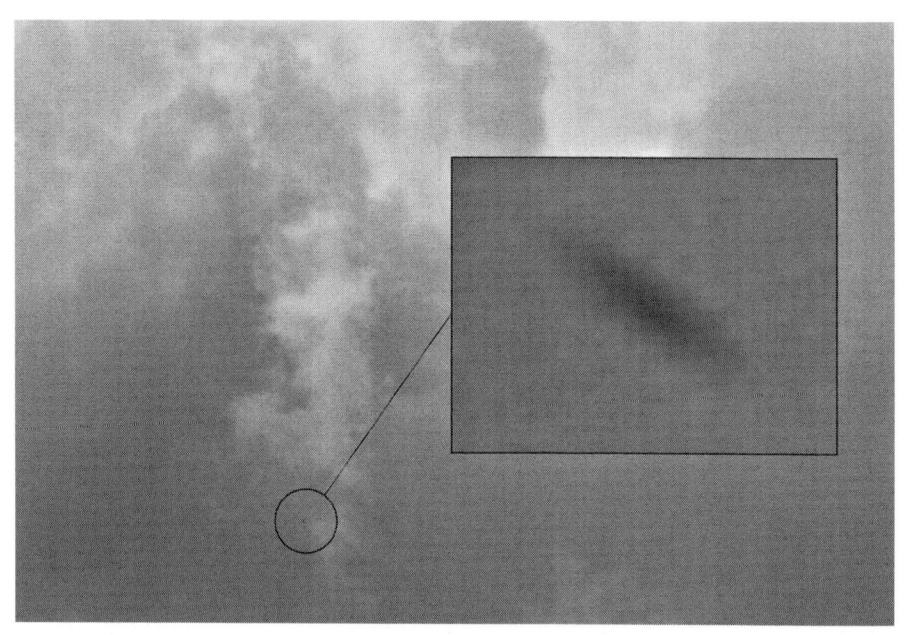

Photo 32

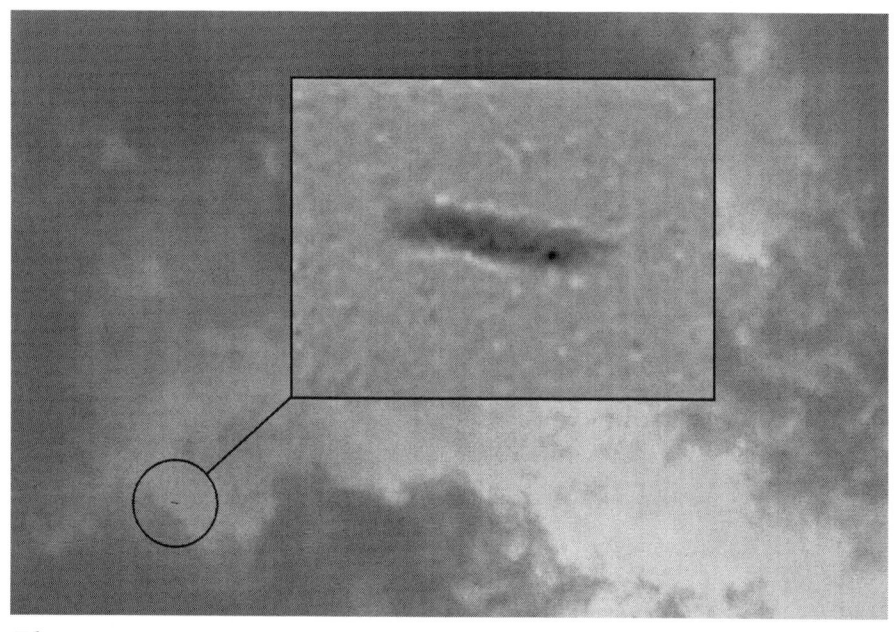

Photo 33

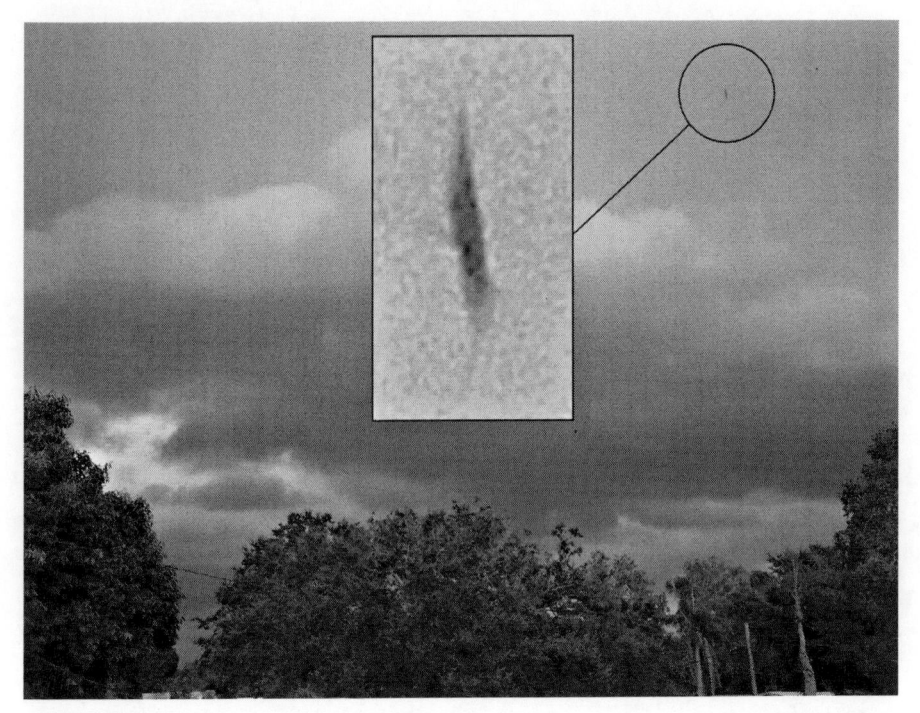

Photo 34

Now you have seen quite a few photos of the most common types of UFOs in my area. As I stated before... Enlil informed me that he has eight different classifications of Scout ships that he would send forth from his Motherships. I do not think I have managed photograph all of them, therefore, the process is still ongoing.

So now, I will show you some pictures of some of his UFOs that I rarely see. They are inconsistent in shape and size compared to my other UFO anomalies. In this next picture (photo 35), you will see a very divergent shaped UFO. It has a light grey top, which is like an elongated bubble and a dark bottom. This photo was taken by Arietis and we have yet to see another one shaped quite like this one. This was also taken during the wintertime here in Sarasota, not during rainy season.

Those Who From Heaven To Earth Came

Photo 35

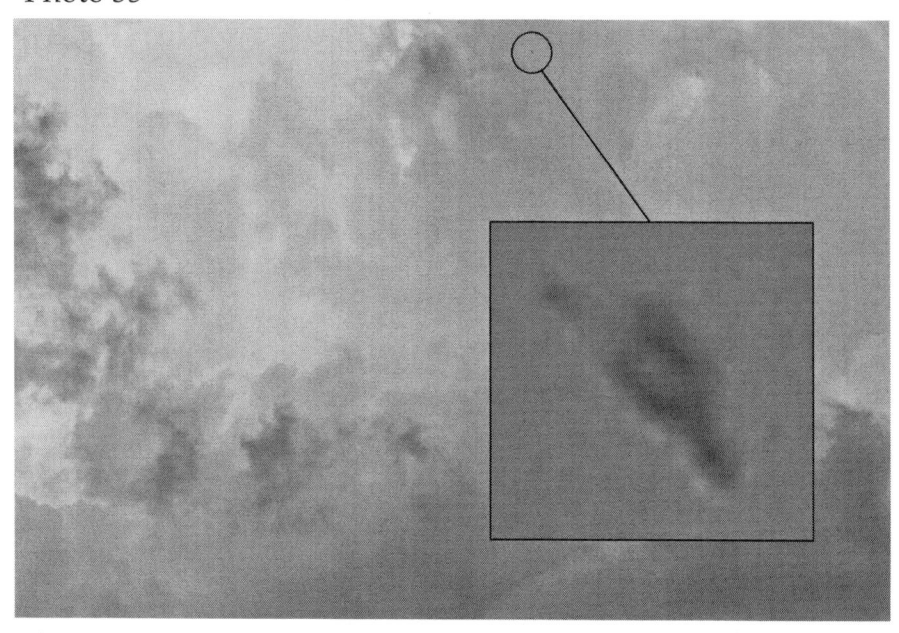

Photo 36

The previous picture (photo 36), shows another divergent shaped Spacecraft, which was greenish in color with what looks like two little wings of some sort.

The next photographs (photos 37 & 38) are unique looking UFOs indeed. One end of the craft appears to be wider than the other end. In these photos taken by Arietis, there was no sequence of pictures. Therefore, I do not know which direction the craft was traveling. If I had knowledge of this information, then I could determine which was the front and rear of the Spacecraft. These UFOs absolutely appear more streamline than many of the others that seem bulkier and rectangular.

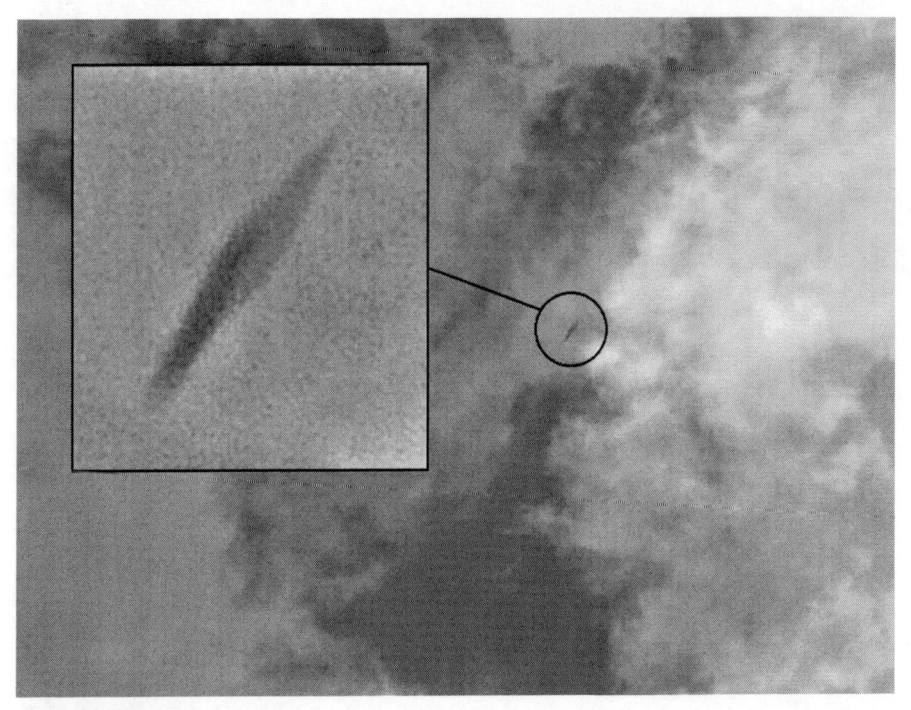

Photo 37

Those Who From Heaven To Earth Came

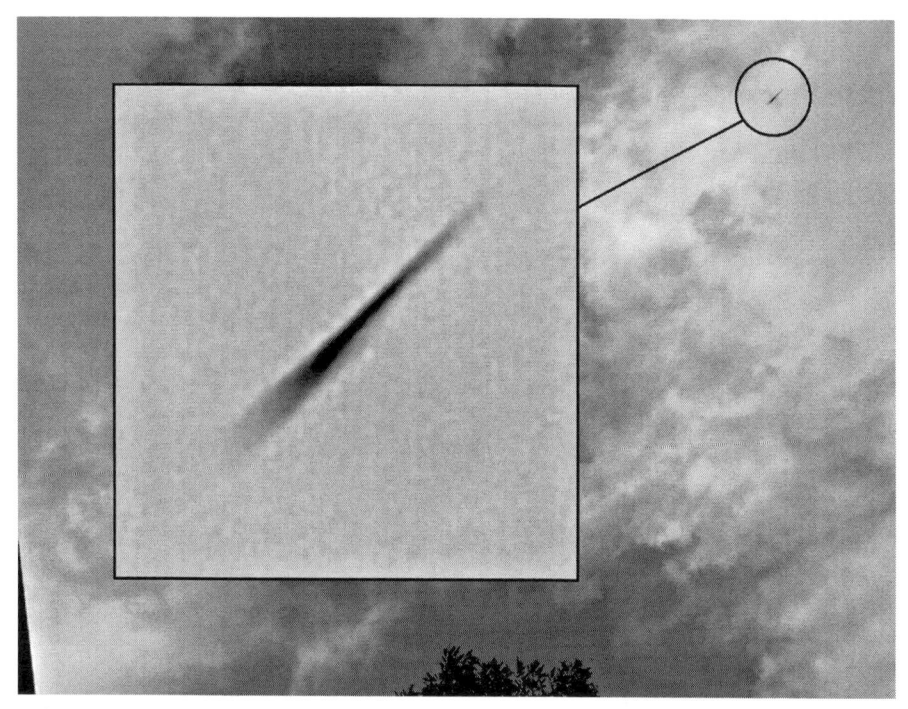

Photo 38

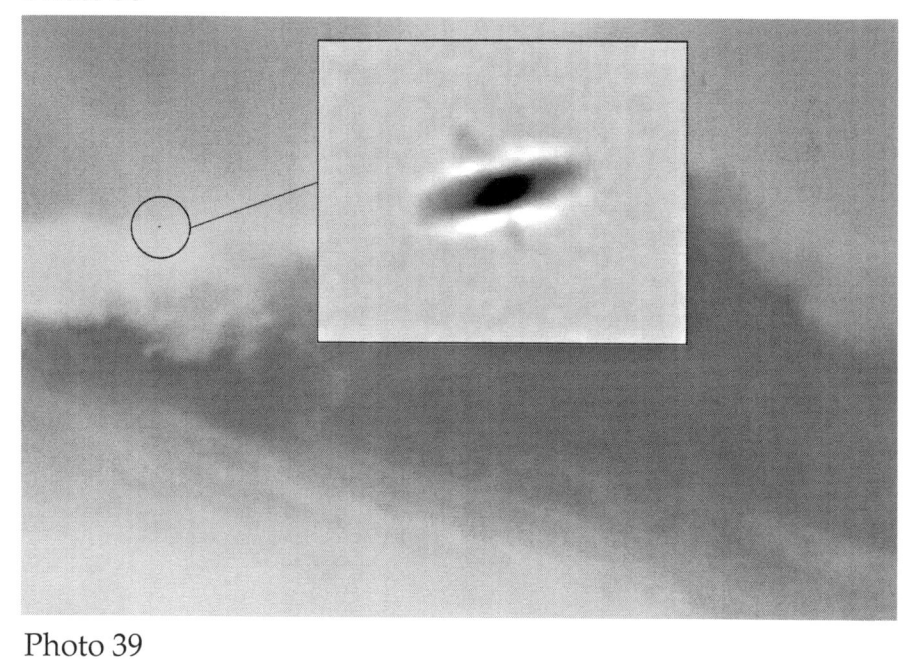

Photo 39

The last picture (photo 39), is the only UFO I have ever

105

managed to photograph that has an antenna on the top and bottom of the Spacecraft. It is also appears to have the stereotype oval Disc shape.

I have asked Enlil about these last several photos. I wanted more specific information as to exactly what their missions were or job duties shall we say. I want to know how many occupants are in each Spacecraft. However, Enlil seems to be cryptic of detailed information concerning his Spacecrafts. I believe he does not want to divulge this information because he does not want the government to have access to this intelligence. I know that Enlil does not work with the US government or any other government from any country in any way shape or form. Yes, there are other members of the Reptilian community that do, but not Enlil, for he does not like the corruption within the elite. Being that I live about 50 miles south of MacDill Air Force base, I thought it was possible he worked with the military there. Once again, he said no in a very stern voice. He said the military is aware of the presence of his Spacecrafts in the area here during the rainy season, but they do not know who they are or what they belong to. He said the military is intrigued by their presence, but has no information as to the nature of his UFOs. Enlil does not want humans to have more advanced powers in weaponry and technology, for power leads to corruption and greed. He also stated that it is the Greys of Zeta Reticuli and other Dark Extraterrestrials that work with the military in exchanging weapons technology for human experimentation. I also have some photos of a Black Ops helicopter being followed by several UFO Drones. The Drones are barely visible, so I have not put them in this book. They were keeping cloaked as much as possible while following the Black Ops helicopter. They followed the helicopter for quite some time.

The next two pictures show an airplane coming in for a landing and two shape-shifting UFOs in the background. Notice that in the first picture (photo 40), the two UFOs are flying in unison at the same exact angle. Take note of their size, for in the following picture (photo 41), they have shape-shifted and become much longer and skinnier, yet they are still flying in unison at the same exact angle. They are both bending in the middle. It is as if they were mirroring each other. They are not interested in the airplane, for they are in the background simply zooming across the storm front that is approaching. Most people would never see these in their photos as they blend into the background because of their color. Then again, most people do not take pictures of the sky looking for UFOs. As I will reiterate many times over in this book… it is difficult to determine sometimes whether these Alien ships are Mechanical, Biomechanical or straight out Biological, but these are more than likely the Biological UFO's known as the Belis.

Those Who From Heaven To Earth Came

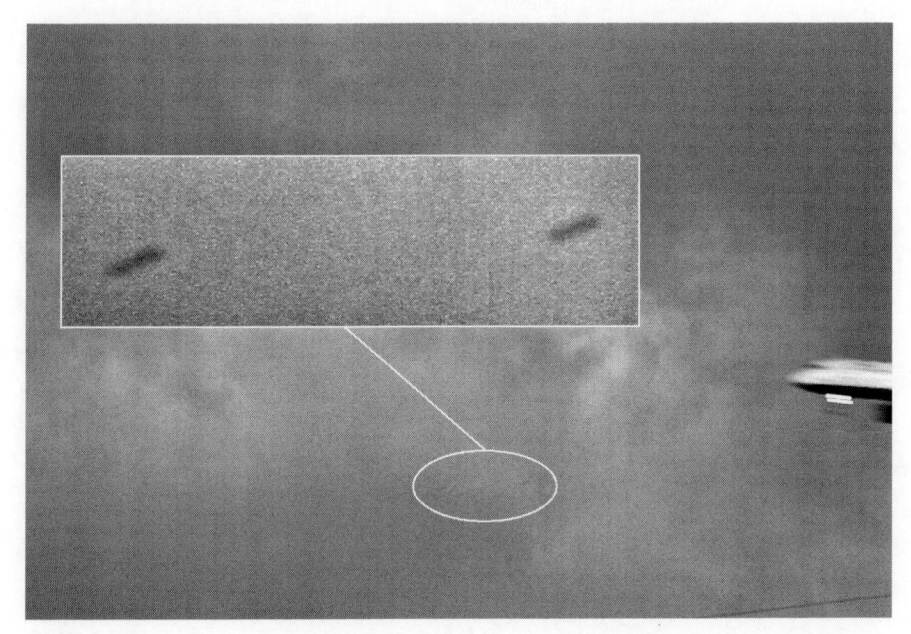

Photo 40

Photo 41

Those Who From Heaven To Earth Came

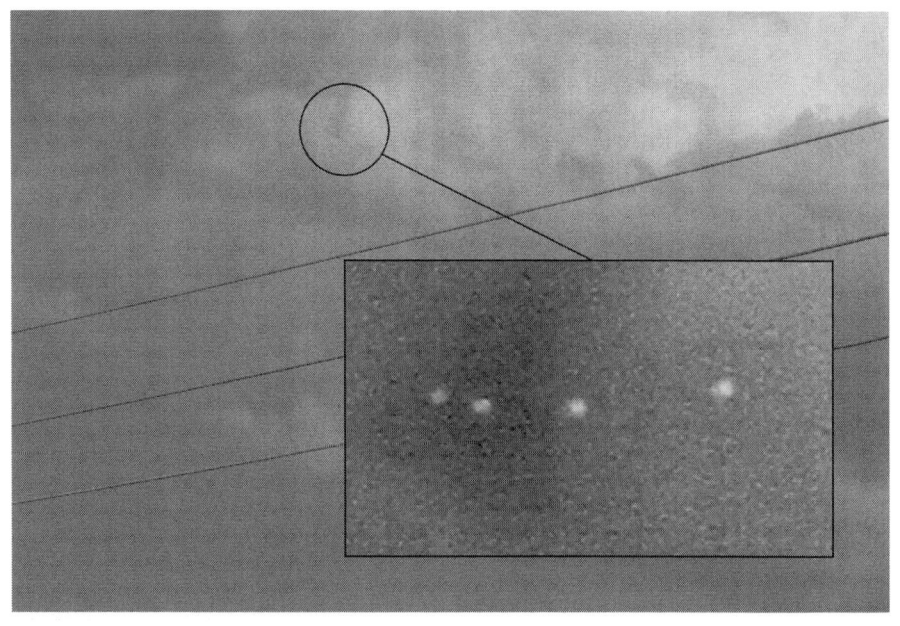

Photo 42

In this picture (photo 42), there are four round white UFOs just parked in the sky within a large cloud. These round white UFOs were in the sky behind my home and appeared to be watching the Biological Belis that were flying in mass numbers that day. They just stayed in one spot for quite some time without moving. Either they were simply observing or they were acting possibly as a gate back to the Mothership for the Belis. My gut instinct tells me possibly both.

Here is another example of a round white UFO in the next picture (photo 43). I believe this to be a "manned" UFOs because it appears to stay in one position unlike the rust colored Drones that are unmanned and fly patterns like that of a drunk driver.

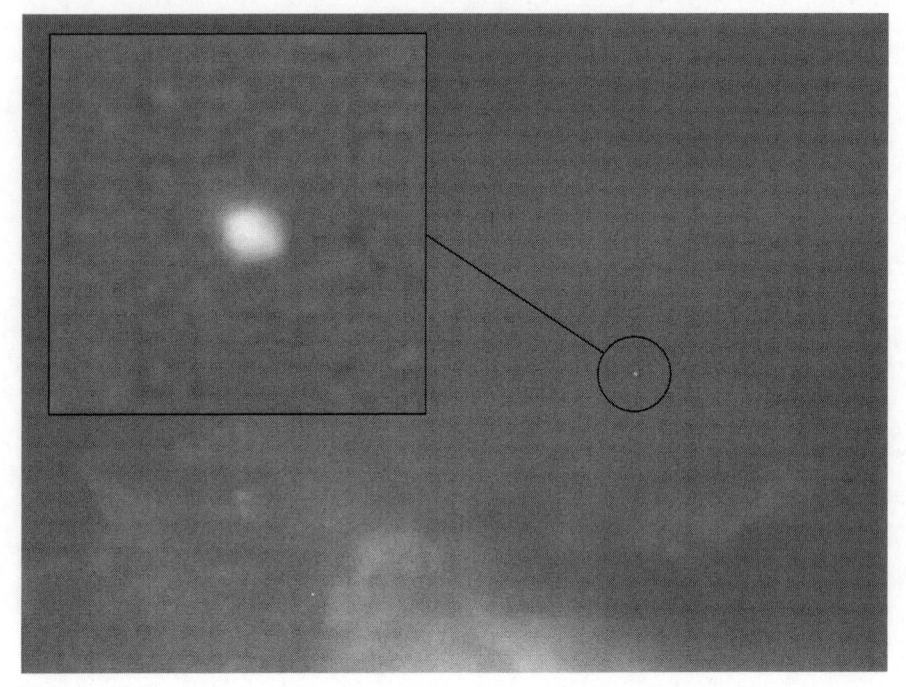

Photo 43

The unmanned Drones also seem quite unsystematic with their flight patterns. This particular UFO just like the others, stayed in one spot for about 20 minutes or more observing from a distance. I have many photographs of them just hovering in one place, but when this happens, they are always at such extreme high altitude making it hard for me to determine their exact shape other than what looks like little white balls of light, like in these pictures.

The UFOs in this next picture taken by Arietis (photo 44) are also the same round white Spacecrafts and they are definitely in a formation. There are about 20 of them in this picture. However, you will not be able to see all of them. You would have to see this enlarged on a big screen monitor.

Those Who From Heaven To Earth Came

Photo 44

There are five at the top that are in formation and form a somewhat Disc shape configuration. Even though they are small, they appear to be much bigger than the jet airliner that is trailing through the sky leaving a contrail.

The next picture (photo 45), is one of the same type Spacecraft that was hovering above some big clouds all by itself like a lone wolf. This was taken in my backyard and the Spacecraft stayed there in the same position for about 15 minutes or so. Just in case some of you were wondering… this is not a spirit orb. I have thousands of spirit orb pictures, so I know the difference. Spirit orbs are always very close to earth and not thousands of feet in the air.

Those Who From Heaven To Earth Came

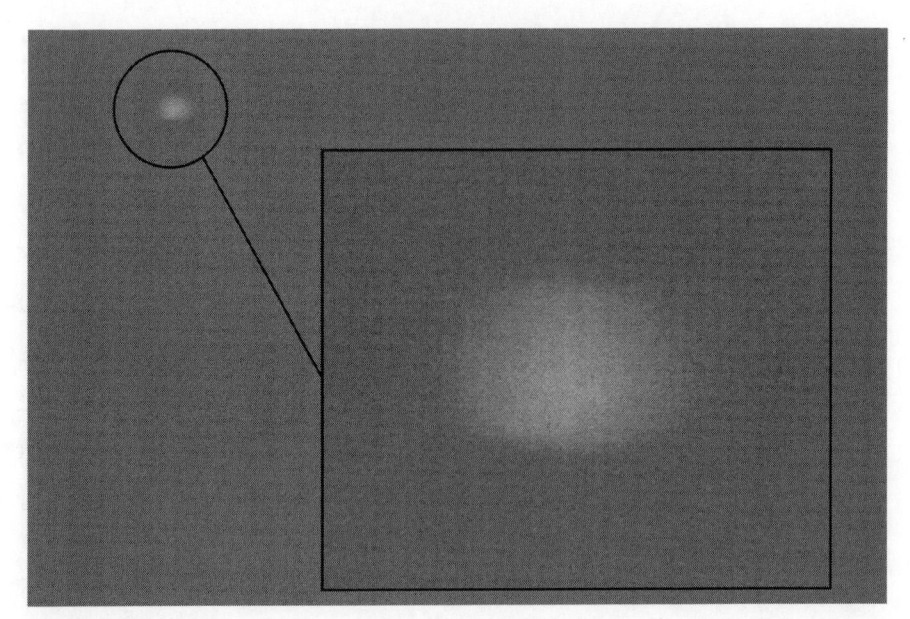

Photo 45

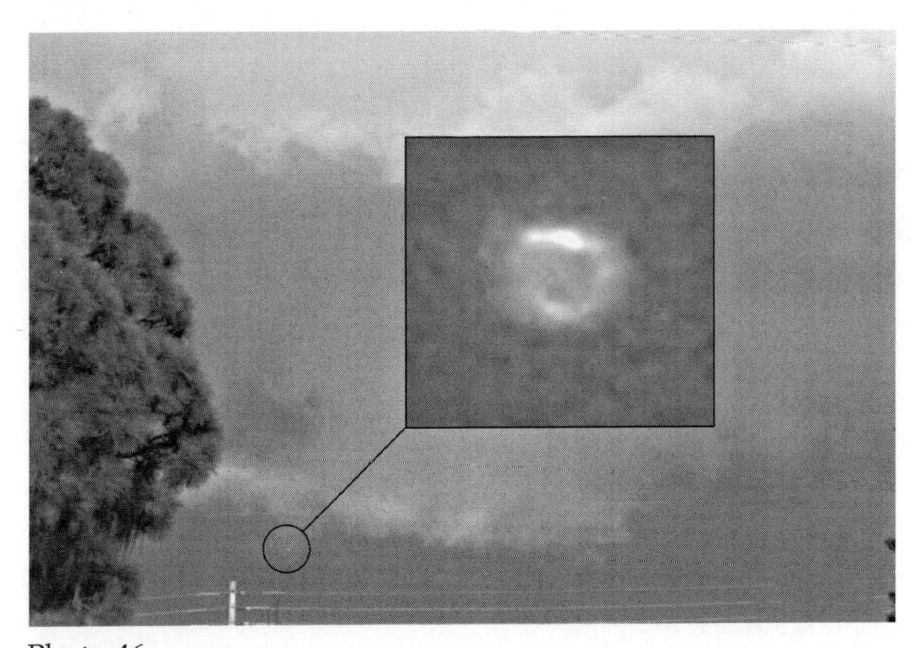

Photo 46

This picture (photo 46), is one taken from my front yard as the storm front was approaching. It is right below the cloud line. I

112

wish to state, that this is not a spirit orb.

The next picture (photo 47), shows a group of Scout ships at an extremely high altitude. Now some people may look at this and say that maybe these are geese, which fly in groups and at high altitudes. This is a possibility, but the way I can debunk that theory is simple. Take notice and you can see there is a government jet spraying its poisonous Chemtrails across the sky. Even though the jet is a fast moving object, it is moving at only a fraction of the speed compared to this group of Scout ships. These UFOs were moving very fast and did not appear interested in the plane.

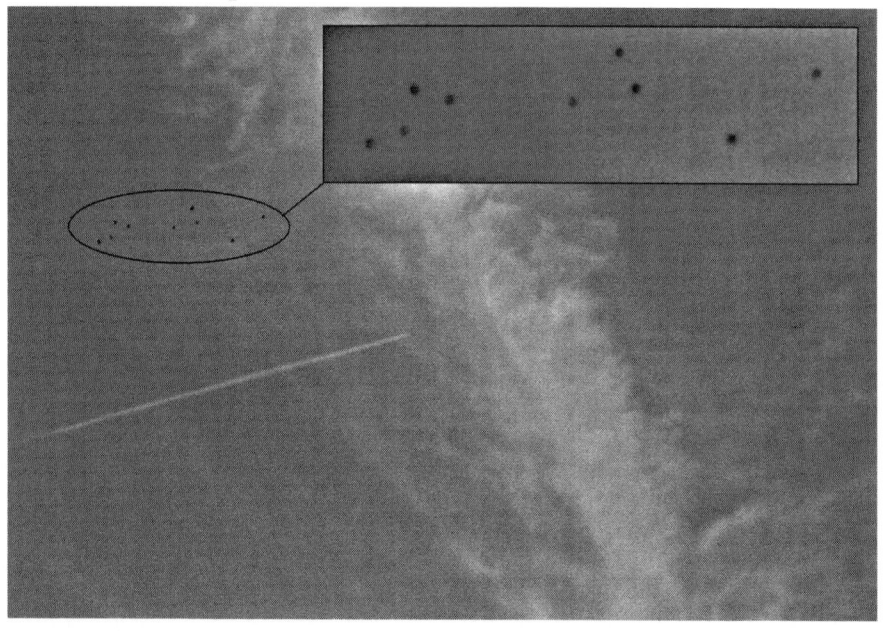

Photo 47

I have a sequence of about thirteen photos showing how fast this group of anomalies was moving. This group was able to cross the sky in the matter of 2 seconds, whereas the government jet looked like it was barely moving. Geese cannot fly this fast and neither can any man-made aircraft. Trust me... I first thought it might have been geese, as I try to analyze every photo I have. However, it is clearly not anything of nature or man-made according to the speed in which they are traveling. I have to try to debunk my own photos to assure they are real, otherwise facing the obvious questions from skeptics and even UFO experts.

    As I was writing this book in 2012, it was in the middle of rainy season and therefore I took many more photos of UFOs each day as I always do and found myself having to add some more interesting pictures such as these flying Tubes/Telemars. From the months of June through August, I photographed over 450 more UFOs and that is not counting a couple hundred more that I discarded, as they were not that interesting to me. If I get too many of the same thing or if they are too small, then I delete them. I did however manage to take some photographs of some new UFOs that I have not seen before over the last few years and that to me is exciting. My friend Arietis took these first two pictures. They were taken over her home and they have a unique shape to them. A couple weeks later, I caught the same Alien Spacecraft flying over Lido Key while I was getting ready to leave the beach one afternoon. The top of the craft has a very light greyish or possibly white dome shape with curved sides and the bottom is black. Photo 48 on the next page shows a side view while photo 49 shows the bottom of the craft as it turned sideways in the sky.

Those Who From Heaven To Earth Came

Photo 48

Photo 49

Those Who From Heaven To Earth Came

Photo 50

Photo 51

Photos 50 and 51 were taken by me. In my photos, the craft went from the south end of Lido Key all the way to the north end where I was standing, all in a matter of a split second. This Spacecraft also has a black bottom and light colored sides. Actually, the sides look white. I realized it was the same type of Alien craft after examining the entire series of photos.

The next picture was taken by Arietis one afternoon while she was partying with some friends in Pinellas Park at a beach bar. I have seen these Tube/Rod shapes many times before, but I had yet to see them

Photo 52

As an all-white craft. I was able to examine this picture enlarged on a big screen and saw that there are several more ships trying to break through into this dimension. There were actually five Alien ships in this picture altogether.

Those Who From Heaven To Earth Came

While writing this book I thought I would share with you more recent photos of the Telemars I had taken. These pictures were taken on the same day and I had captured 39 of them this particular day. This first one is also a very strange shaped craft as it is thicker in the front and narrow towards the back. It also has some odd bumps on the front.

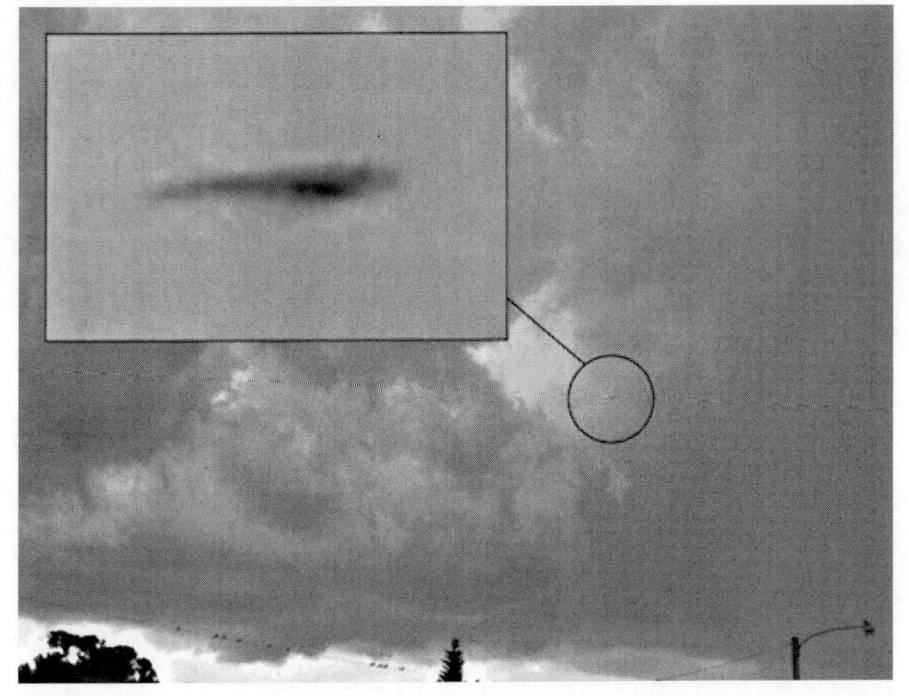

Photo 53

I truly love capturing the vertical flying ships like in the next picture (photo 54) because no one can say they are airplanes or birds. People will always come up with something to deny these flying objects of their true nature. They deny them due to fear of the unknown. The only things that fly in a constant vertical flight are rockets and UFOs. This ship is approximately about 100 – 120 ft. long.

Those Who From Heaven To Earth Came

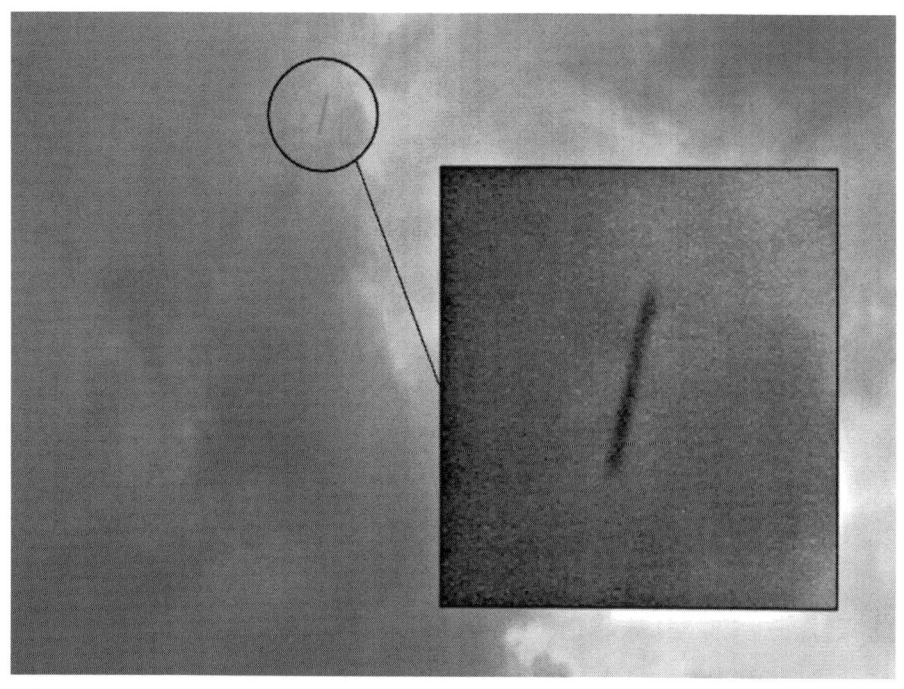

Photo 54

Accordingly, I have provided plenty of UFO pictures for you to ponder. This should at least stimulate your curiosity even more in searching for the truth. You will find no one who has captured more photographs of UFOs anywhere in the world other than NASA who hides them and denies them. Feel free to analyze them however, you see fit. I am not writing this book or showing you my pictures to deceive anyone. I am simply sharing with you the anomalies that I have encountered in the sky. Believe what you choose to believe. That is your free will that was given to you.

Night Time Energies

The nighttime energies within my home are always very powerful. When I say energies, I am referring to the energies of all the Ascended Masters, Archangels, Celestial Gods, and many other spirit Guides.

During the winter, the energies are moderate compared to during the summer months. The summer brings somewhat of a Circus into my home at nighttime. This is mainly attributed to the fact that Enlil and Enki are present, adding two extremely intense energies to my already energy filled home. They come here during the summer to reside and work their energies as to how they see fit. However, they reside in my home with an intense power. Right around 9:00 PM, each night the energies are amped up times ten. I know when they are present in my home because my cat goes crazy with nonstop meowing unless I hold her and calm her down. This is due to her nervous system not being able to handle such strong energies. I feel sorry for her, but these energies are not harming her, they are only giving her anxiety. When these energies start amping up at this time of night, all kinds of strange things happen. There are many noises in the house and I am constantly touched on my arms and on my head. For the most part, I ignore the noises, as I am so used to hearing them. I am also used to the touching by the entities that reside there and I simply say to them… "I feel you" and I laugh. Not only are Enlil and Enki's energies there, but many times they themselves are there checking on me. They also have many of their entourage there to watch and observe me in all that I do. They are the ones who are more curious about me. So many times they come simply out of curiosity and being able to touch a human. But understand that this is what I desire and I have been warned by Enlil to be careful of what I wish for. You know the saying… be careful what you wish for, you might just get it! Well, I do get it and I am always clear as to what I wish for through them. I give them freedom to visit me anytime they so choose and I have already given my physical body for Enlil to experiment with, so what could be worse? I have nothing to lose and an experience of a lifetime to gain. In the summer, I feel like I am whole again or complete shall we say. These energies and entities make up part of my being. As I am part of the Reptilian Brotherhood now, I need these energies to feel normal. As my Guides have explained to me, Enlil is part of me as I am part of him, just as I am part of the Ultimate Divine Source and so is he. Nevertheless, my connection with him and his brother Enki has been ongoing for many lifetimes because of my Galactic connections and origins.

I have told a few close friends of the strange happenings within my home and explained to them in detail and I have explained them to my mother on several occasions. I have asked her to come over and stay late at night in my home and she simply says… "Hell no". I have to laugh because the things I love so much would make other people scared out of their minds. These types of incidents would make any normal person run for the hills. One person's nightmares are my pleasures.

    I had also warned my friend Arietis about the things that go on within my home during the summer. She had learned of these strange energies and Encounters during the winter of 2010 in my home, which usually would be less active. She would come over to stay the night and we would be sitting on the bed talking and she would hear a noise in the next room and say… "OMG…! What the hell was that?" Then she would hear another noise again within a couple minutes and she would say the same thing again. I would just laugh and tell her not to worry they were just my Reptilian friends making noise. Then something would touch her and she would freak out even more. To me it was so hilarious. Yes, I have a sick sense of humor. I have always laughed when I see fear in someone's eyes. These Reptilian entities love to touch and they are not so soft as my other normal spirit guides and Ascended Masters that reside there. When they would touch Arietis, she would freeze and not move for a couple minutes and I would laugh even more, telling her not to worry. She simply had to get used to it as I had. For me it is a sense of comfort knowing that these entities are there for me.

    There was one evening during the rainy season when I was lying in bed. It was around 5:30 PM and I was relaxing having a catnap. There was a major storm approaching from the east as I was outside a few minutes earlier and could smell the rain from a distance. Therefore, I was laying there in bed with my eyes closes and Enlil appeared to me on my mental screen. I had not called to him, but he came to me sitting on his throne with his long blond hair and wearing nothing but his loincloth.

He held a lightning bolt staff in his right hand. He looked and me and smiled, then tapped his staff in an abrupt motion as if to declare something. At that moment, a lightning bolt hit the ground behind my home, just a few feet away from the room where I was lying down. Then Enlil disappeared. I have to laugh at myself this time because it scared the living shit out of me! Now I love extreme lightning, but this was too close for comfort and it was so loud, that it was like a damn bomb going off outside my window. Nevertheless, I will say that it pumped my adrenaline like nothing else and yes, I would ask to have it happen again. I do not fear the lightning what so ever. I will stand outside as a storm approaches when the lightning tends to be extreme right before the rain hits. I will stand outside in the middle of the street in awe of the electricity running through my veins as Enlil is near. I know that he will not hit me with lightning, as he controls it. Yes, he has a button. Enlil has explained to me that yes, the lightning is mechanically controlled with the push of a button. He also explained to me that back in the ancient days, he used lightning to instill fear into the people as a show of power. As he put it… it was like a gimmick for him.

 There were other times when I would set up the Triangle of Solomon with the black mirror and conjure Enlil… hoping to speak with him and receive a vision or oracle. There was one specific time where I had made a blood offering to him and it was late at night with no storms in sight. After making my offering and calling to him, within 20 seconds it began to storm with a fury. Lighting was cracking the sky, the rain was coming down massively, and there were gale force winds. So you see, he can arrive in mere seconds if he so chooses. Other times I can repeated call and nothing truly exciting happens. The biggest key here is whether he is busy. He says he can be in many places at once like all the other Angels and Ascended Masters. Nevertheless, my theory on this is that since the world we live in is a hologram… these entities can project their energies or image into many places at once via computer-generated techniques. However, the actual entity itself such as Enlil is truly only in one place at a time. So Enlil is truly only in one place, but projects his computer generated self to many other places. Therefore, I know when the true Enlil is near, for his energies are so extreme, that I become filled with electricity, having every hair stand up on my body and I begin to have a rapid heartbeat. However, if I am trying to conjure him and he is far away, I will still get a vision of him along with his voice but I do not feel the true energies.

There is also another phenomenon that happens at night during the rainy season. I usually sit outside on my front porch each night to take pictures of the spirits and anomalies that take place in my strange world. Nevertheless, when I do, Enlil is always doing some sort of flyby with several of his Spacecrafts that are about the size of a commercial jet. These Spacecrafts are cloaked, but I see them as large shadows and they usually fly overhead at a low altitude of about 500-800 feet several times within an hours' time when sitting outside at night.

One night in 2010, I had been taken aboard the Tamarandak Mothership again for more physical and mental testing. As I was onboard, they informed me that there would be a mark placed upon my home to signify the Reptilian energies, so that when Enlil's entourage would show up, they would know they were in the correct place. When I woke up the next morning, I went outside to sit on my front porch to get some fresh air. After my intake of a 5 Hour Energy drink, my brain had truly awakened and my eyes had focused. I happened to be looking at all my surrounding plants and saw that the concrete had a strange pattern on it that was never there before. Then, my brain really kicked into gear and I said… "Holy Shit!". The pattern was like that of true Reptilian scales. Not something that looked artistic like, but like the real deal. This pattern as you can see in the next picture (photo 55), is as if it were laser etched into the concrete.

Photo 55

it is not cracked or anything of that nature. This was the mark of Enlil. This next picture (photo 56), shows a closer view of the Reptilian pattern on the concrete. It has continued to stay this way and has not cracked or faded in any way. This is one of many signs given to me to represent the Reptilian energies and I am grateful to Enlil for this mark upon my home. Blessed be Almighty Enlil.

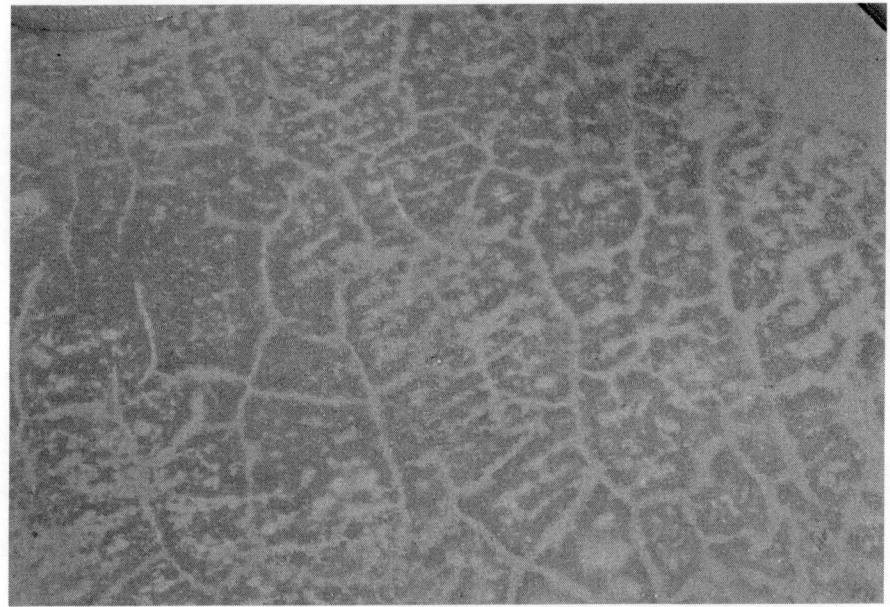

Photo 56

Enlil has reiterated that this is also a mark of protection that has come about due to my allegiance and loyalty to him. Perhaps this is similar to the parable of when Moses was told to put blood upon the door jams of followers of Yahweh so that they would be spared of the "Tenth Plague" in which Yahweh placed upon Egypt. Yahweh "the Destroyer" would then pass over (Passover) each home and the ones marked with the blood of lamb would have their first-born spared from death. Now I will reiterate that Yahweh was nothing more than an Extraterrestrial like all the other Gods. According to scripture it was Yahweh himself personally who wanted to do the dirty work of killing the Egyptians first born. I can assure you that if he did, he would have had an entourage with him for protection as he did his dirty deed of killing… especially the Pharaoh's son. Remember this is an Extraterrestrial, not some Magical force. So my point to all this is that the way the things are going in the world today, it will not surprise me if Extraterrestrials come down to annihilate humans. Personally, I believe it is long overdue considering how evil or misguided humans are. Have you noticed that there have been so many movies in the theaters now about Aliens coming to earth and trying to annihilate humanity? Well my friends, this is a mental preparation for what is possibly to come. Many movies are channelings that the writer was given by a higher Power to prepare humanity for coming events. Therefore, as I stated, perhaps the mark upon my home is also a sign of protection. The only difference is, Enlil and not Yahweh gave this mark to me. You may laugh, but it is a possible concept indeed, as these are the "End Times" and no one truly knows what will happen.

For those of you who are interested in bringing intense energies into your home, be it Angelic, Extraterrestrial or Elemental… fill your home with crystals. My home has crystals everywhere. I have crystals of all different types and sizes. I also have them outside my home on my porch and in my potted plants to help them grow. There are even crystals buried in my yard in certain areas like an invisible electric fence. I have truly spent a small fortune on these marvelous rocks in order to attract higher energies and ward off bad energies of the dark ones whom lurk in the night along with blocking out dark scalar waves that the military/government sends out via the Haarp Project (Active Auroral Research Program). For those of you who do not know about this I suggest you wake up and start doing some research on this subject so that you are aware of the dark forces working against you.

So my point to all this is to create within my home a comfortable haven for the "higher powers" that I call upon and those entities who are simply attracted to me by my Light. It is like having my own miniature spiritual resort and you can do the same. Just make sure that you yourself have raised your vibrations high enough to handle the energies like this. Otherwise, you will end up like many of the mainstream people now who are acting abnormal and insane because they are not able to handle the influx of 4th, 5th and 6th dimensional frequencies that are coming into fruition right now as I write these words.

Aliens Landing on the Roof

This next story is probably one of the most bizarre things that could happen to someone, short of being abducted by Aliens. The Reptilian entourage of Enlil has helicopter like aerial vehicles that can land on any surface and they have landed on the roof of my home on 3 separate occasions as far as I am aware of. They may have done so many more times, but it would have happened, as I was asleep. There is a book entitled "Proof of Ezekiel's ETs – UFOs of the Bible" by Arthur W. Orton. In this short, but excellent book, it describes the UFOs that Ezekiel encountered as small helicopter vehicles that each carried one humanoid like entity. Well, I will tell you that Mr. Orton who is an aviation expert is quite the genius and very correct in his deciphering the Book of Ezekiel. He is the only person that I know of who has ever accurately unraveled the mysterious words describing the UFOs and entities that Ezekiel had experienced. I came across his E-Book on Amazon.com and purchased it for my Kindle. After reading it, I knew Mr. Orton was correct because these same type crafts had landed on my roof. I have not physically seen these crafts, I have only heard them and Enlil had explained to me what they were exactly… small helicopter crafts, designed to carry only one entity at a time that can land on the most delicate of surfaces.

Those Who From Heaven To Earth Came

On one Saturday, I was taking my afternoon nap. I was almost asleep when I heard something loud on my roof right above my bedroom. It literally sounded like something landed on my roof. Now I know we have large birds in Florida such as the Blue Herons and the Egrets, but they are not heavy enough to have made such a sound as that which landed upon my roof. There was a storm approaching in the distance as I could hear the rolling thunder, so I got up and went outside to see what the hell was going on. I saw absolutely nothing on my roof, no birds, no broken tree limbs, but I knew something had happened. I went back inside and laid back down to finish my nap. It was then that I had the sensations of some thing or someone touching me heavily. It was not like somebody lightly tickling or caressing me, it was like someone laying a heavy hand upon me. My first thoughts were that Enlil sent a member of his entourage to my home and landed his Spacecraft upon my roof. I pondered upon this as to how this could be possible. How could a Spacecraft land on my roof without doing serious damage? Nevertheless, I knew that something landed on my roof and somebody was touching me. This did not freak me out in any way, as I am used to their heavy-handed touch and I knew the vibrations that were in my house were that of Reptilians. I tried to communicate with the entity, but got no response. Therefore, I figured they were only there to observe and I went back to sleep. The following day I got out my ladder and climbed up on the roof to do a more detailed inspection. I noticed there was what appeared to be a skid mark of some sort right above where my bedroom was. I should have taken pictures to document this as I normally would have, but for some reason I did not. A few weeks later, precisely the same thing happened all over again. It all happened right before a storm in the distance was approaching. This time I did not see any type of skid mark upon my roof, but everything else was exactly the same as the first incident, including being touched and sensing the intense Reptilian vibrations or energies within my room.

It was later that I had spoken with Enlil through a channeling session and he confirmed my beliefs as to what happened. He once again told me that they were there only to observe because I had permitted them to do so. He stated that if I was not comfortable with this, all I had to do was say so and it would not happen again, but I reassured Enlil that I am comfortable with this type of scenario and welcome it. I feel comforted, protected, and not threatened in any way by these Reptilian entities. I know that most people would have packed their bags and moved right away... lol. Yes, I know that many people have claimed to have many bad experiences with Aliens including being raped in their own homes, but I have a loyalty and unconditional love for Enlil and all his entourage and because of this, I am not harmed. This is just one reason why it is very important for people to keep a very high Vibrational level in their Auric field. This way, if they are approached by an Extraterrestrial entity, then it is less likely that they will be harmed as they are Vibrating with Energy of Light and therefore the Extraterrestrial will want to work with that person on a Light level and not the Dark.

I have only told a handful of people about these particular incidents. It is hard enough to tell people about

Extraterrestrials and UFOs, much less telling them that a Spacecraft landed on your roof. I did tell my dear friend Arietis about this and I do not know if she believed me or not, but she would soon become a believer as it happened again on December 5, 2010 around 11 PM at night. Arietis and I were looking over some UFO photos on the computer we had taken earlier in the day, when we heard a noise outside the wall next to us. I said to her… "Did you hear that?" Both of us heard the sound again as if something or someone was outside my home right against the wall. We gathered our cameras and I grabbed a flashlight to go outside and investigate the noises. She stayed in the front yard and I walked around the side with my flashlight, but I saw nothing. I went back to the front of the yard and stood next to her. We then both heard a very loud sound as if something hit the roof. Once again, this was a very loud thump and we both looked at each other and said… "WTF" We both determined that this noise was too heavy sounding to be any type of large bird and we saw nothing whatsoever. I told her that it reminded me of the movie Predator when the Alien would jump out of tree a land on the ground. We started taking pictures of the roof, but could still see nothing. I decided to walk around the side again with my flashlight and she got frightened, walked towards the front door, and stayed there. I then heard her yell out to me… "OMG, I am going to piss myself" I ran back around front and she was standing in front of the front door as she trembled and said… "Something lifted up my sleeve". As per usual with my sick sense of humor, I simply laughed at her, so she decided to go inside where she thought it would be safer. I stayed outside for a few minutes on the front porch looking through my photos I had just taken on my camera, when a set of hands grabbed my head very heavily. I once again laughed and simply said… "Yes, I know you're here and you are welcome". I then decided to go inside to look at our pictures a little more thoroughly on the computer. Arietis was still shaken up a bit about the whole incident and I told her not to worry. I explained to her that it was an entity belonging to Enlil and that she was in no harm. After thoroughly examining the photos, we found no evidence upon them, but we knew that something truly did land on the roof and came to observe us and you could feel the intense energies. It was an hour later or so that we went back to my bedroom and sat on the bed talking when this entity started touching her once again and I can assure you there was going to be no booty call for me that night… lol. This went on for about 20 minutes or so and Arietis sat there frozen on the bed afraid to move. Then the entity seemed to have moved to the bathroom next to the bedroom, as it was making noises in there. I told her to relax and to get used to it as I have. Again, I laughed about the situation at hand. We then retired to sleep.

    After all that, she was indeed a firm believer to the fact that some type of Spacecraft could actually land on someone's roof. This is why I had also given her a warning as to her taking so many pictures of the sky and calling to Enlil when she was by herself. The fact that she was close to me and was always around me was enough to get her abducted. I have a couple of friends that have wanted to take pictures of UFOs and I have warned them that if they do, they could be targeted for abduction. These Extraterrestrials are on another dimension and they can see our thought forms. Therefore, they can see that we are possibly interested in making contact. Once again, this contact may not be something pleasant for them as Enlil has confirmed with me that they do take flesh samples from humans quite often on a regular basis.

It was a few weeks later that Arietis would have her own experience, just as I had warned her. She continued to take pictures of the sky hoping to catch Enlil's Skyships flying about. I also knew she was thinking of Enlil as she was doing so. This is exactly what I told her not to do, but as they say… curiosity killed the cat. One night as she was sitting in her bedroom at her own house, the Reptilians came and landed on her roof. This is her story in her own words:

"I was sitting in my bedroom relaxing and watching TV when I heard a loud thump on the roof. It was so loud that my two little dogs started freaking out and running around looking to see what caused the sound. It startled the hell out of me. I turned the TV down, but I could hear no other sounds, so I went back to watching TV again. No sooner than I started watching TV, there was another loud thump, which was louder than the first one. Both my dogs got up and started barking furiously. I again started staring at the ceiling where the sound emanated from and this time anxiety set in as I became extremely scared. Once again, I turned the sound off on my TV to see if I could hear any more noise coming from my rooftop. Therefore, I listened in silence for about 10 min. when something rubbed my arm. All the little hairs on my arm were standing up as I then felt another rub upon my arm. This time I could actually see the little hairs moving as someone or something was rubbing my arm. From that moment, I had a feeling that this is why Puzuzu had warned me. I remembered what happened that one night at his home and these Reptilians landed on his roof while I was there. That same night that something pulled up the sleeve on my top. It was happening again. Perhaps now they had come for me. My heart started beating faster as did my breathing. There was most definitely a strong presence within my room. I sat there on my bed as if frozen in time, not able to move out of fear. I did not see anything and the touching of me stopped. After about 15 to 20 minutes of freezing in my tracks, I decided to lay down as I was starting to calm down some. Even though the touching stopped and I could hear no sound, I still felt a strong presence within my bedroom. I decided I would try to go to sleep which was extremely hard to do given the anxiety placed upon me by this scenario. The next day I decided to get up on my roof to inspect it for any possible evidence. Perhaps I was just being paranoid and there might have been some tree branches that had broken off and fell on my roof. But there was no such evidence of that kind and that ruled out my tree branch theory. I saw nothing that could have fallen upon my roof to make such loud thumps in the night. This led me to believe that I had indeed had an Encounter with these Reptilians under the watch of Enlil."

    The next day Arietis called me with excitement to tell me about what had happened to her that night. As per usual, I laughed my ass off because of my sick sense of humor in finding humor in someone's fear. Nevertheless, I had warned her about this, so I reserved the right to laugh. There was no doubt in my mind that this was the work of the entourage of

Enlil. She went on to explain that she had an out of body experience later that night after going to sleep. I told her that this was due to her exposure to these Reptilian energies within her own home. This is the account of her out of body experience from that same night in her own words:

"I came to a house at the end of a dead end street. It was a two-story house and it was if I already knew everything about this house, as if it was déjà vu. I entered the house through the back door and I walked around the house a bit to find my way to the front door. I happened to turn around and saw a set of stairs, so I decided to go up to the second floor of the house. There were no lights on in the house at the time and as I was walking up the stairs, the only light was that of the moonlight coming in from all the windows, which had no curtains on them. At the top of the stairs, there was a hallway with a room to the left. I ventured towards the room and I heard noises emanating from within it. I pushed open the door and there was Puzuzu lying in bed with an Alien looking creature on top of him that had about eight tentacles that were flinging and squirming about in all directions. It was a female Alien as it had breasts and Puzuzu was rubbing her body as it was slouched over him making love to him. I freaked out thinking that perhaps she was trying to become impregnated to create a hybrid and this angered me more as I thought to myself, WTF? As soon as my anger kicked in, the astral currents carried me off to a completely different space and time as a bright neon blue light came down from above and surrounded me. All of a sudden, I was standing in what looked like a high-tech office/science lab that was illuminated with neon blue lights and glass everywhere. There was a desk in front of me with a beautiful woman sitting behind it. As I walked towards her, I could see that behind her were rows and rows of books from the ceiling to the floor, which seemed endless from right to left. As I then stood right before her, the whole desk was also lit up in neon blue. She smiled at me and said… It is okay you are not quite ready yet, but you soon will be and then you will know more. It was at that moment that I woke up and found myself back in my physical body."

    I explained to Arietis that there was an obvious message contained within that astral projection. It was the words of the beautiful woman, who sat behind the desk in the neon blue office. It was the words… "You are not ready yet". I spoke with Enlil a few days later and he explained to me that two of his entourage intentionally landed upon her roof that night. He apologized for any inconvenience and said that it would not happen again. He went on to say that the members of this entourage were simply curious about Arietis being that she was in my life and she also had a curiosity for the Reptilians. He said they simply came to examine her energies and therefore determined that she was not ready yet to become a member of the Reptilian Brotherhood. He said in due time she would be when she spiritually advanced herself, but they would not be back until she was ready.

    About a week later, I decided I would try to help her in developing some of her dormant powers. I sat her in the Magic Circle within my home and set the Triangle of Solomon before her. I stood outside the circle, as I am already used to the Reptilian energies in my protection level is extremely high. I began to invoke Enlil to show himself within the black mirror. I had only worked with Arietis on one previous occasion with the black mirror. Her training was not complete and her abilities were not fully developed yet. This is why I was working with her to develop these abilities. I continued to call upon Enlil to show himself, as Arietis would be the "Seer" and possibly receive a message from Enlil. At this time, she was not able to see or hear him. I was still standing outside the circle when I looked into the black mirror and saw Enlil sitting upon his throne and he spoke to me saying… "She is not ready yet, in due time". Then he faded out and completely disappeared from my vision. I explained to Arietis my vision and told her that we should end the session for the night. I would continue to work with her regarding the black mirror on other future occasions.

Therefore, as you can see, the message given to Arietis during her out of body experience was the same message given to me from Enlil within the black mirror. Enlil's energies are extremely strong and of a male dominance. The same can be said for his brother Enki. These are energies like no other. These energies are much different from dealing with those of the Ascended Masters and Archangels. These Reptilian energies of Enlil and Enki are almost overpowering and this is why they are not for everyone. These energies are for those who have worked with the Darkness, mastered the Darkness, and are now mastering the Light. These energies can overwhelm a person's nervous system and bring forth dark corners of one's subconscious mind possibly causing insanity or delusions and possible possession by dark underworld or Extraterrestrial entities. This having been said, one may find one's self committing heinous crimes and being incarcerated. Here is where I will reiterate…. you have been warned.

End of Summer, Enlil leaves

It is towards the end of August that Enlil leaves this area and moves on to another part of the world to do his work. It is at this time that I am saddened by the absence of his presence. Even though he comes and goes throughout the year, it is during the rainy season of summer here in which his presence and energies are the strongest and contact is made.

When Enlil decides it is time to leave this area... he usually says goodbye in a spectacular way with an awesome display in the sky. I know the exact moment he leaves and it is because of our strong spiritual bond. There is also a change in the atmosphere and the energies all around me. No one else notices these changes, as they have never been in tune with them in the first place. For me it is almost like someone taking away all my energy drinks and saying you can have any more until next summer. These energies make me feel alive and excited about getting up each day during the rainy season.

In the first two pictures (photo 57 & 58) on the following page, you will see the Tamarandak and one of his other Motherships in the glorious clouds that cloak them.

Photo 57

Photo 58

I do not know the name of the other ship, but I do know it is not the Tahazu Zog because the Tahazu Zog is smaller and more of a warship battle cruiser. These two were his larger Motherships and they were just approaching from the northeast and southeast coming towards my home. They have a brilliant fire like color between the Mothership and the storm clouds beneath it. It was a beautiful scene indeed to behold. In the next two pictures, Enlil is getting closer and his Mothership clouds are becoming more defined in taking shape. Look at the fire like beautiful light that grows even stronger between the Mothership and the clouds below in the next picture (photo 59). To see this and feel his presence is like nothing else on this earth. It is amazing to think that the average mainstream person has no clue as to what it right in front of them, nor do they feel these energies, as they are not in harmony with the Extraterrestrial Gods.

Photo 59

This is something that you would expect to see Christ the

Master of Light return upon in the sky. The next picture (photo 60), also has a brilliant white light burning below the Mothership. Usually, that section only lights up when there is thunder and lightning. However, these are Enlil's' Motherships and not some empty super cell cloud. This was simply a display for his farewell to me. This was truly a magnificent sight to see indeed.

Photo 60

After taking these pictures a few streets away where I could get a better view, I then went home to look over my photos. After a brief look at them, I went back outside and stood in the front yard as I watched these two Motherships come closer and closer to me. They started to move very rapidly and ended up to where the one Mothership was almost touching the edge of the other one directly overhead of me. The two clouds did not mesh in any way. They literally stopped within a couple hundred yards of each other. I looked up and I instantly knew that this was his goodbye. Although I was in awe of this spectacular sight, there was extreme sadness that overtook my heart. I heard him speak to me and tell me not to worry, that he would be back soon. It was then that I held my head down and shuffled my feet in sadness. It was not but 2 minutes later that I raised my head up the sky only to see both of these clouds completely gone. Yes, they were literally gone that fast. Regular clouds that size cannot move that fast unless there is an extreme wind and there was no wind this day.

For several weeks, I felt empty and lonely. I felt as though I was having withdrawals from the absence of his energies around me and in my home. From that moment, it was a waiting game for summer to come bringing the full force and presence of Enlil himself. It is not the same just having his entourage checking up on me. It is nothing like the full force of my Reptilian God friend Enlil being in my presence.

Many people have conjured Enlil and have been able to see visions of him and hear his words. However, very few people like me actually become great friends with him over many lifetimes.

Blessed be Almighty Enlil, Lord of Sky, and God of Thunder!

Enki, Lord of the Abzu

Enki, Lord of the Abzu, Beloved God of Wisdom, He who hath dominion over this earthly plane of existence. Enki is the half-brother of Enlil. He is also known as Ea, Poseidon, Kukulkan, Lucifer, and Ptah, along with many others, thus playing the part of many Gods throughout time. Most people well studied in the Occult know and pay homage to him. To those who are not familiar with Enki, he is the Extraterrestrial who is the Creator of the Adamic race (Adam) and the Adapus race which is current man. Just to make things clear, it was Moses or (whoever truly wrote the book of Genesis) who borrowed the story of Creation from the Sumerian Tablets, which are from approximately 8600 BC. The Biblical version called Genesis was approximately written around 1445 BC. Those who wrote Genesis in the Old Testament of the Bible took the story and rewrote it to their own liking, making people think that it was the God Yahweh who did all this marvelous genetic work in creating humans. Perhaps they wanted humanity to believe their God worked such feats of greatness. On the other hand, it is possible that by the time they handed down the story through the generations, it had changed drastically. It is as if when you tell a story at work and by the time it reaches the other end of the office, the story has changed.

This is more likely the reason. Those of you who are Truth Seekers will understand this, but those who are still bound by the mainstream religious Control System should do their homework and you will surely be Enlightened as I was.

Enki is a kind, loving Celestial God and a brilliant genetic scientist to say the least. I am extremely happy to have been awakened to him again in this life as I have learned many things from him. He brought me out of the Darkness and back into the Light in harmony with my own Christ energies. As he recently told me... "In the absence of Darkness, Light would have no meaning, so cherish those experiences in which you walked through the Darkness and know that you come out into the Light."

    I will tell you he is also the one and only Lucifer "the Light Bearer ", worshiped for his Light. There are also those whom call him Satan and worship him for the Darkness and as he has told me, he is still here under contract to act as a polarity for the Light and the Dark. He is the true Yin-Yang of this planet. Yang represents everything Positive or Masculine and Yin, characterized as Negative or Feminine. Keeping a balance of both energies here on earth is part of his duties. Being that he is the one whom illuminates the mind and helps us to discover our Divine Birthright, he prefers that humans choose the path of enlightenment or higher consciousness and not be so concerned with the material world. The majority of mainstream people will never accept these facts because of their indoctrination into religious Control Systems since they were children. These systems instill "Fear" and control the masses through fear. The Vatican knows this and I will reiterate that they belong to the

Illuminati and they need to keep organized religion in tact so that you will remain spiritually ignorant and therefore enslaved to the material world. Do not take my word for all this. Do your own truth seeking and then your eyes will be opened and you shall become Enlightened.

    While I am on the subject of Enki, also known as Lucifer, I want you to know that he has informed me that he is very close with the beloved Christ and Christ has confirmed with me that Lucifer is very dear to him as well. Now for both Deities to tell me this solidifies the truth in it for me. If this were not true, then one or the other would have clarified this matter. Once again, the Vatican knows this and hides this truth from you because this goes completely against their "System of Fear".

    When I call to him, he prefers me to call him Poseidon. The reason for this is that as he explained to me, the Cosmos is all contained to where the Past, Present, and Future are all happening at once. Therefore, being that is so and this is also a hologram, he can project himself into any timeline that he so chooses. He prefers the Greek Mythological period where he played the role of the God Poseidon. To this day, there are still many statues of around the world in fountains and so forth portraying his Godly image. Even though I use the name Poseidon when invoking him I still like to refer to him as Enki, his Sumerian name, as I resonate with that culture and time period. Those of you who have read much about him have always read about his rivalry with his brother Enlil. Let me set the record straight. Enki and Enlil are very close and work together on a regular basis. Do not believe the old rumors of them being at odds. Yes, they have had their share of arguments just as all brothers and sisters do, but Enki has told me many times not to separate him and his brother. They are a combined energy working with earth, but Enki has more of a vanity as he works more with humans and is still worshipped to this day which he thoroughly enjoys.

Enki has worked with me through many, many lifetimes. In this current life, he has worked with me in my early years of delving into the Occult. He continued to work with me but in the background and I would not truly see him again in his full presence until the summer of 2010 during the month of July. At the beginning of that month, I decided to make contact with him again. Soon as I started calling to him again, lo and behold, there he was. Now I was not using the Magic Circle or the Triangle of Solomon to conjure him. I trusted him. Therefore, I would simply call to him, as I laid in bed at night ready for sleep. This way I knew he would come and visit me or take me out of body to wherever he so chose. I have the protection of Archangel Michael, so I do not worry about these things anymore. Michael and Enki did at one time have slight tumble shall we say. This was at a time when Enki was slightly misguided, but they are close friends now. Therefore, Michael allows him to come to me and knows that he will not harm me. Nevertheless, I always invoke Archangel Michael when laying down for bed and I make sure I tell him whom I am specifically asking to come to me that night. This way I know there is no interference or blocking of that particular energy that I am calling upon.

Therefore, during that first week of July, I called to Enki each night hoping he would come to me. It was not until the following week that he made his energies known within my home. After calling to him one night I felt his strong energies getting closer to me and that is when I heard my cat, which was laying upon my bed, stand up and start hissing loudly as though something was frightening her. I heard a noise as if someone was walking down my hallway, which leads to my bedroom. I did not get up to see if there was an intruder because I knew Archangel Michael would not allow this. I immediately knew that this was the presence of Enki himself. I knew that his appearance was what was frightening my cat, as it would any animal or human. I did not ask Enki to take a calmly shape, because I am not frightened by any type of appearance in which he might shape-shift into. To me, the scarier an entity looks, the more exciting the experience will be. Many people who are into the art of conjuring Deities and so forth, ask them to take a calmly shape so they will not be frightened or appalled by their appearance. They forget that we ourselves may look very strange to these Extraterrestrial Deities. I prefer them to appear as they so choose. This way they do not have to cater to the paranoid whims of a human and so they are comfortable in their own skin. Now getting back to my story, I knew that it was the Lord of the Abzu himself, Enki coming down my hallway. I could not see him, as he did not show himself to me, yet I felt his presence standing there in the doorway to my bedroom. I gave him a verbal welcome and asked him to show himself, yet he did not. I asked him to take me on a spiritual journey out of body to one of his temples as I fell asleep. That night I was taken in spirit to the Temple of Poseidon on the etheric planes. This temple was a replica of the physical temple, that was originally once on the continent of Atlantis. Outside the temple was a large statue of Poseidon wielding his weapon, the Trident. The outside of the temple was similar to those of the mythology with large pillars surrounding the front and sides of the structure. Inside the temple, the floors were of marble with marvelous designs and most everything else was made of gold. There was a large throne chair made of gold with an array of gems upon it. To each side of the throne was a pillar of fire. After showing me the temple, we sat for a while as he explained to me how I have been one of his favorites due to my loyalty as a friend and that I did not need to play the role of a supplicant to him. He told me that he is not a God and I am not a mere mortal. He told me that I am equal to him, as he is to me. The only difference was that my being in the physical world subjected me to the Laws of Karma, whereas he is not subjected to these laws. He was happy with me in my spiritual progress. He was happy to be working with me in the vibrations of Light and not the Darkness. He went on to explain his role here on earth as a polarity. Many people think he is trapped or imprisoned here beneath the earth and we simply laughed at this notion of mainstream dogma. He is free to travel wherever he so chooses, via in spirit or physically in one of his Motherships. On that note, he does live deep beneath the ocean, as that is where his main base is located. However, no one will ever find it, because it is on another dimension. He told me it was time to go back to my body and that he would come again to visit me on a regular basis from this point forward in my life.

    Many times when he speaks to me, he will repeat himself and this is to encode my conscious and subconscious mind with his words and Light energies. He speaks with great wisdom and many times speaks with words that I have to look up the meaning. One particular day I was conversing with him for about an hour through my other psychic channeling friend, Elizabetta. I asked Enki about creation. I also inquired as to what he wants from me. These are his words…

"Know that I am in the waves that come to the shore. Know that I am in the shells that you will find on the beach. Know that I am in the air that cools your face. Know that I am in the cloud that shelters your head. I am not a God, nor are you a mere mortal. We are all part of one another. Visualize the form of a snowflake. There is always a center in a snowflake. Assume for the purpose of easier understanding that this center is the energy that so many people call God. Understand however, that this center is no more important that all the ramifications that emanate from it. Each one of the ramifications in its turn forms another subsection of the snowflake. You are a soul just as everybody who is living in every dimension of creation is and has a soul. In this subtle level includes what we believe to be inanimate objects. However, we will deal for now with sentient human beings. I am no more important than you are. I need you and you need me. As you consider the snowflake, see how many individual nuclei emanate in a regular pattern from the center nucleus. Each one of them has sub-formations and more and more are infinite. That really is the key to understanding how Creation works. We are in God as we are in one another, as we are in every creature in every cell and every drop of the ocean, which is so dear to me. Whatever emanates from us effects the energy that forms together to make the snowflake in its pattern. When the emanations of energy from us are not in accordance or in harmony with our source, which is the very nucleus, which is our soul, then we cause a malformation of the pattern. However, the way the universe works is that we are always inevitably drawn back into our rightful place in the pattern. We may falter, we may cause a temporary failing of the pattern or malformation of the pattern, but we will always come back into what we call the Light. There is no escape from that principle. Why...? Because the Light is what started it all. Therefore, you as an individual human being are actually in the center of your own pattern, as well as being inextricably linked and part of the greater creation. I am in you... you are in me. However, you want to know what I want from you Puzuzu. What I want from you is to do what is in your nature to do. We can call it to follow the higher calling. As you come to earth, you have a multifaceted agenda. You are given the opportunity of this life each time, so that you might meet the circumstances and the challenges that will cause you to rise to the challenges or not, depending on what you make of your free will and that process will cause your soul to understand. Understanding is not an abstract mental concept. Understanding is aligning us with the perfection of that energy that holds all of creation in its place in a perfect pattern. You are free to temporarily desiate from the perfection that is your birthright. Nevertheless, as I have said, you will one day return and how soon, is up to you. Freewill is the greatest gift we are handed when we come to earth as we have indeed in all other realms. It is your chosen task to help me. You do not have to convince people of the reality of other dimensions. All you have to do is live in that belief and know that even when I have spoken our thoughts change the world. I am grateful to you for opening yourself up to other dimensions and you know that this may cause you delusion. Therefore, exercise this knowledge wisely and know that all you have to do is to live accordingly to what you learn and you will change not only the immediate atmosphere around yourself. However, know that the repercussions will influence all for the better, the town, what you call the state and what you call the country and everything that is sitting on the crust of the earth and beyond. Each one of us has a very important task, which is to live in accordance to the pattern. There is perfection in the pattern and that is why I ask you to consider the shape of the snowflake because in that tiny universe lays in fact, the explanation of how the universe works."

Amazed by his perfect analogy of the universe and creation would be an understatement. Many Deities and other entities beat around the bush when it comes to giving detailed and or straight answers. The attribute I like most about Enki is how he speaks with giving forth such great Knowledge without all the bullshit. There was another instance where I asked him about the Darkness and the Light and these are his own words…

"I want to address the matter of being called "The Devil". People like to believe that there is Darkness, there is Light, and indeed, there is. However, for the purpose of life on earth, it was decided long ago in the global consciousness, that Darkness would be assigned the role of evil, which would be incarnated in a fictitious role of an entity called the devil, and I have played that role, but I am not evil. You my friend, like so few people, understand that Darkness and Light can penetrate and need each other. The devil is only born out of the necessity of human beings needing to give a name to the misuse of their faculties. Let go of the prejudice about Darkness. It is necessary for those who want to reach Enlightenment to go through both Darkness and Light. This, you have done. You have mastered the Darkness and now you are mastering the Light. Many people come here to earth from other dimensions to experience the Darkness as this planet to some is a playground, and for others it is a learning school for the soul."

As always, his words of wisdom amazed me. In the following weeks, he had visited me a couple more times in the night as I slept. On one particular night, at about 3 AM in the morning, something woke me up. I thought perhaps that it was Enki calling for me to go outside to take pictures at night as he often does. I jumped up out of bed, took about two steps and I ran right into Enki. It was like running into a wall and I immediately fell backwards onto my bed. The doorway to my bedroom is only a few steps from my bed and he was standing right inside the doorway. He was more humanlike with the appearance of a man with long straight black hair, but it was very hard to see him because it was dark in my bedroom and the only light was that of my computer which was at the other end of the hallway. Therefore, with the light behind him, it made him appear more shadow-like and therefore I could not make out his facial features even though he was there in the physical. Now for most people waking up at 3 AM in the morning and running into someone standing in their bedroom doorway, this would probably scare the living fuck out of that person. Even though I was barely awake, I knew it was Enki. Therefore, there was no fear. I sat there on the edge of the bed and rubbed my eyes for a couple seconds to attain clearer vision. When I looked up, he was gone. I called to him and said… "Where did you go? Come back, please come back." Nevertheless, I did not see him again. I believe he was just checking on me and would speak with me once I went back to sleep. I do not recall him visiting with me again that night after I slept because it took such a long time for me to go back to sleep after the excitement and adrenaline of running into him. He may still have come back again that night and I simply do not remember. I am still amazed to this day, that he was there in a physical form to where I could actually feel him instead of going right through him as if he had been in spirit form.

    The next month of August was upon me, and my friend Lil Lamb had come to stay for a few weeks. She was an abductee of the Sirian War Gods and therefore we had much in common. About the second week into her stay, we were outside at night around 11 PM. We were walking up and down my street taking pictures of spirit orbs. It was during this time that we noticed a very unfamiliar anomaly. We were getting some very strange red squiggly lines that resemble something from an Etch-a-Sketch in front of one particular home. No one lived in this home at the time, for the occupant died a couple months earlier. I noticed that the address on the home when added up and reduced, as one would do in numerology, came out to 13. Now of course it could have been reduced to a single digit of 4, but I knew that because of the strange pictures we're getting, 13 was what this home vibrated to. That is when Enki showed himself in one of the pictures. It was as if he came right up out of the ground as you will see in this next picture (photo 61), which is a truly amazing photo. This picture is in no way fake or a hoax for the sake of entertaining you. If you could see this picture in full color on a HD monitor you would truly be able to see all the detail in his face and see that he appears like a red and yellow fire forming his shape as he appears sitting on his thrown which is like that of an antique high back gothic chair. This is simply his hologram being projection onto the earth plane. Even though he can shape-shift and look human, this is how he prefers to look. He dawns a very skinny body and Insectiod looking head with horns that are twisted. What you cannot see in this picture is the Alien standing behind his gothic chair to the left. Once again, if this were on a HD monitor you would be able to make him out in detail. The name of this other Alien is Hermel and you will see a picture I drew of him in my chapter entitled "Other Aliens that come in the Night". Now I never told Lil Lamb that Enki had been inside my house for the last month and a half. I did not want to frighten her. She was already going through a mess with the Sirians who had tagged her. As soon as I saw the picture, I told her that it was Enki, but that is all I told her. The picture looks very similar to when someone slows down the shutter speed of the camera. Then using a small flashlight, one can make it appear as if they are drawing with Light. Nevertheless, as you will see, this picture has too much detail for that to be a possibility.

Those Who From Heaven To Earth Came

Photo 61

I can guarantee you this is not the case with this picture and I swear on my own life that it is authentic. The camera was simply set to night mode and that is all. I believe Enki had come that night to find out what all the commotion was with the Sirians that were present in the area. I know he is also protective of me, just as his brother Enlil and Archangel Michael are very protective of me. Therefore, I believe Enki just needed to know what was going on with another rogue Extraterrestrial race that is not of his origin, flying around my home and causing chaos.

It would be a few weeks later after Lil Lamb was gone back up north, that I would see Enki again. During the day, I was taking pictures of the sky and at night, I was doing the same, except trying to capture pictures of orbs and other spirit anomalies.

That is when Enki decided to come to me in the form of Light. He would show himself as the Light Bearer that he truly is. Now he was going to take on a completely new form that I had not seen before. In this first picture (photo 62), Arietis and I were outside taking pictures and trying to get the spirits to go along with our stupid poses. What I mean by this is, we would point in one direction like a model showing a new car at a car show and hope that the spirit would show up in the direction that we were pointing. Sometimes they did, others times they did not. Therefore, when Arietis took this picture of me, I was pointing in one direction, and Enki showed up in the opposite direction. He showed up in front of me in the form of a scorpion or lizard of Light with arms and legs and his long tail.

Those Who From Heaven To Earth Came

Photo 62

This was truly a fascinating photo indeed. Trying to explain this endeavor to mainstream people is not a fun or easy task, for they think it is faked and could never except the fact that a Celestial God would come and show himself in this manner. After this particular night, I was on a quest to get more pictures of Enki in the form of Light as this opened new doors within my mind.

This next picture (photo 63), shows Enki coming towards me. He looks very much like a skydiver in free-fall. I do not know if he did that to entertain me, being that I am skydiver, but I have a whole sequence of him coming towards me in this manner. Enki has on many occasions admitted to doing things simply to entertain me.

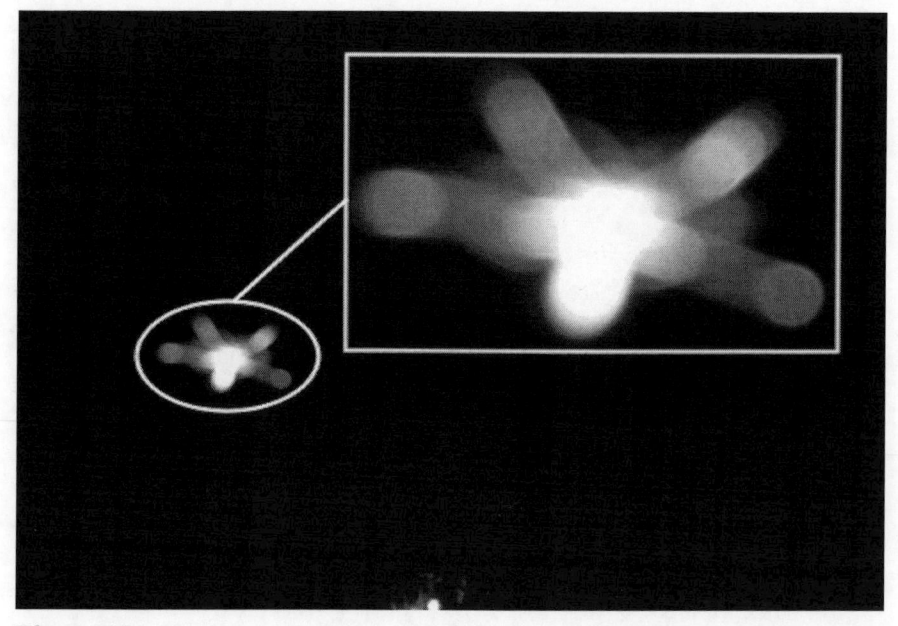

Photo 63

This particular night I felt his presence coming on very strong as he approached. As he got within a couple feet of me, I felt him raise the Kundalini (Coiled Serpent Energy) from the base of my spine. As the Kundalini was rising to my Crown Chakra, I felt a sense of euphoria, a natural high with intense energy, as though every cell within my body vibrated with frequencies of Light. After this encounter with him, I went inside to examine my photos and relax. It was at that moment that I had an extreme pain within the area of my neck and shoulders. I then remembered hearing stories of the Kundalini rising too fast and tearing through muscles and so forth. I had always dismissed these stories as myth, until it happened to me. After several days, the pain resided. I had not asked Enki to raise my Kundalini energy, but he decided to do so of his own accord, so that he would able to bond with me on a higher frequency or vibratory rate. One of the many perks of raising one's vibrations is being able to become one with the universe and the "collective soul" thus making it much easier to make contact with the Celestial Gods, Archangels, Ascended Masters along with all "Beings of Light".

There were many nights where Enki would wake me up at 3:00 am and tell me to go outside and so I would arise to do as he requested. When this would happen, it would mean that he would have something spectacular to show me, like in the next picture (photo 64). I got up out of bed one night after Enki awakened me. He told me to go outside with my camera, where I would encounter a spectacular Light show of entities going back and forth. In this picture, there are nine entities, which are all part of Enki's entourage. His entourage consists of Hermel, Jiobbe and Shamah, and others who would come in orb form or another anomaly shape. There were actually more but you cannot see them all in this photo. I have within my possession a large series of these entities of Light from that night, buzzing around in front of my home.

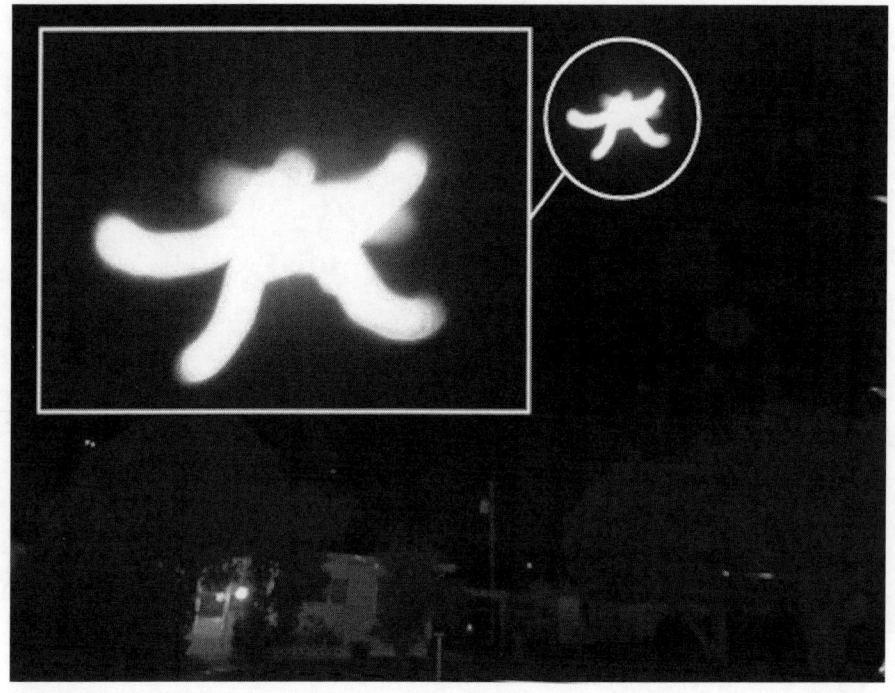

Photo 64

Enki himself hovered in front of me from about 11 feet away with same brilliant white Light and tubular body and once again changing his actual form. He has told me many times that his shape is not always intentional and that it simply changes as if it were liquid Light floating around in the air. A few nights later he appeared in an almost octopus form of Light as you will see in the next picture (photo 65). This time he was only about three feet away from me and it startled me only because the light reflecting off him was blinding. He would absorb the photons in the flash of my camera, and then send them back at me in a blinding manner. This shape of Light was flowing gracefully through the air once again as you can see.

Those Who From Heaven To Earth Came

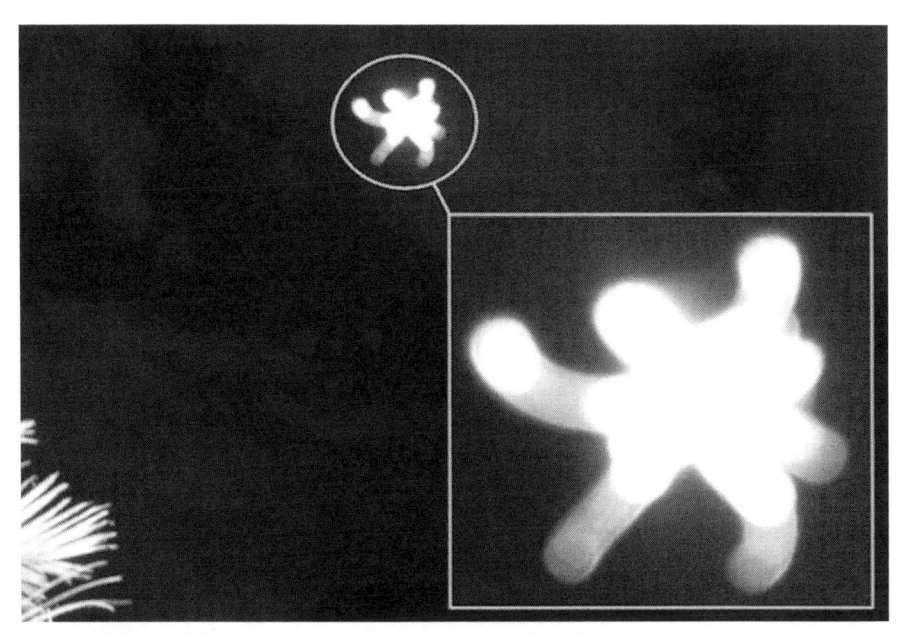

Photo 65

Photo 66

Then were many times that Enki would appear more round and

condensed in shape as in photo 66. I have so many photos of him in many different embodiments, but I always know it is him because of his energies that can be felt and these are the anomalies that show up when I call upon him to grace me with his presence.

This next picture (photo 67), shows the large right-side-up triangle that would always hover in the background. It would also just stay in one place not moving in any direction. Perhaps this was another Biomechanical craft used in monitoring the situation while Enki and his entourage made their appearance before me each time.

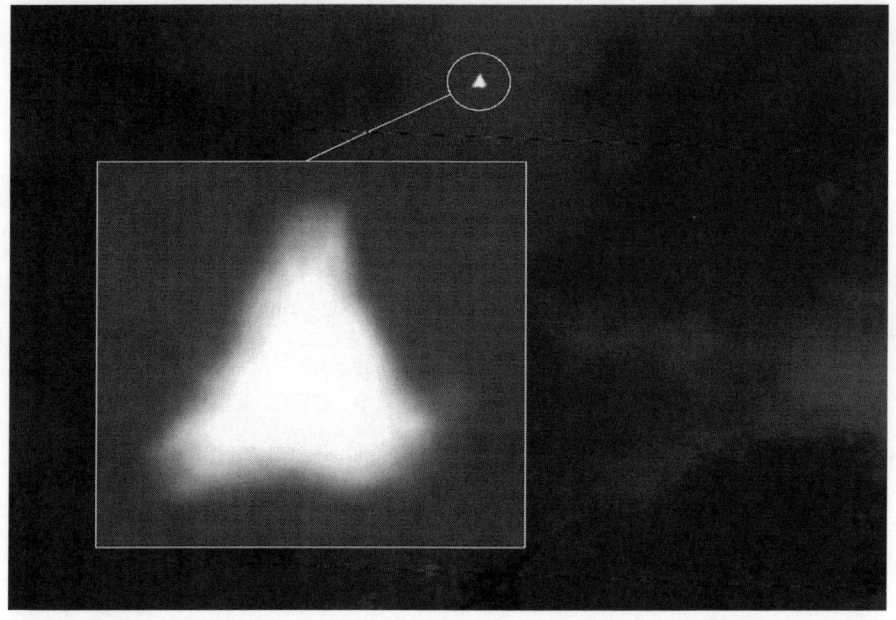

Photo 67

There would also be within his entourage, 2 upside-down triangles that would stay together as if they were a pair and possibly a masculine and feminine energy. However, they were different from the single one that would just hover in one place.

I have noticed that the tube-like tentacles on Enki look very similar to the Pleiadian Spaceship 5, which hovered over my home, as I was having a healing ritual done to remove my friend Lil Lamb's implant tag. You will see this in my chapter "Abductions - Tagged by Extraterrestrials". It seemed to have morphed from a ship to a flowing Light entity, like that of Enki. I was bringing this to your attention because of the close similarities in how they appear. Many of Enki's entourage came in the form of orbs with faces in them. I am still in the process of figuring out who each one is by name. One of the stranger anomalies that came with his entourage was rectangle shaped Biomechanical objects.

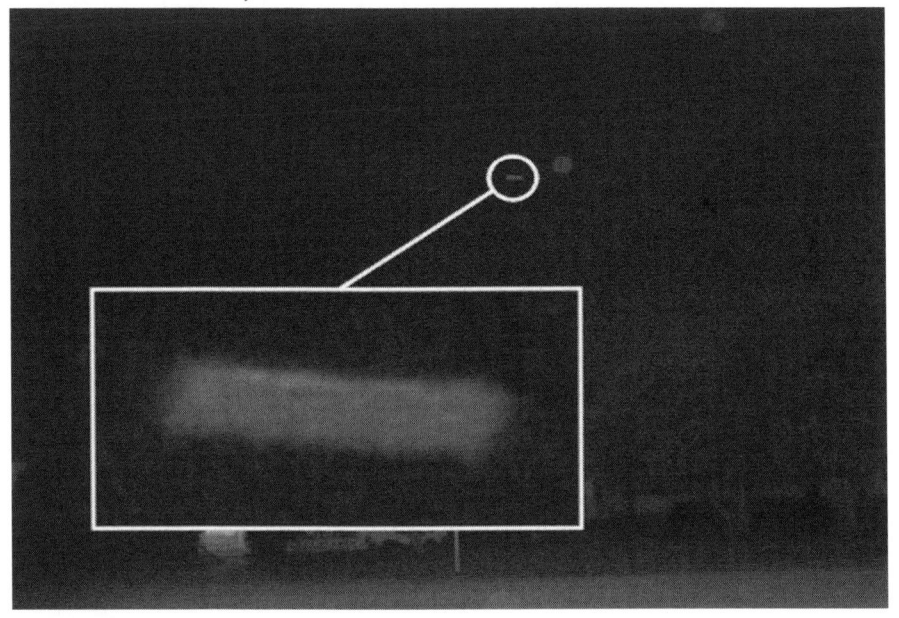

Photo 68

Sometimes they were green, sometimes a brilliant blue and sometimes purple or violet. These rectangular objects were visible with the naked eye, hovering in front of me from about ten feet away. They would also move back and forth horizontally only a few feet at a time. These anomalies were there as possible surveillance devices for Enki like that of a Drone. The Biomechanical object in photo 68 was light green in color. I have yet to see anyone else who has produced photos of rectangular shaped spirit anomalies of any kind to my knowledge.

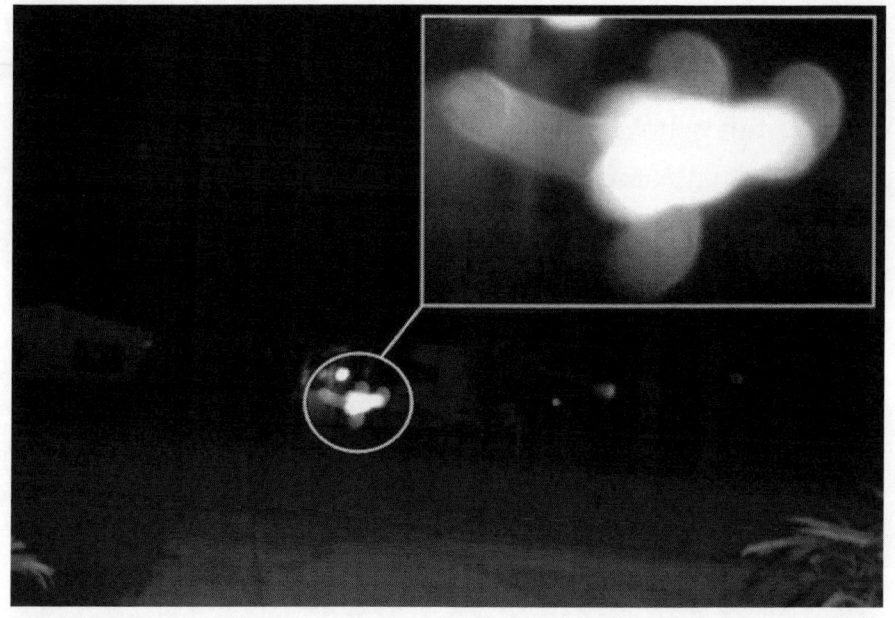

Photo 69

This picture (photo 69) shows Enki flying up to me. Once again, take notice of the tube like tentacles emanating from him. I was able to capture a series of him, as he constantly changed shape with his flowing Light. As he flew right up to me, he emerged himself into the large vase of spring water I had placed on the patio table as an offering to him. You can see the bright aura emanating from him in photo 70. His form was pure white, but his aura was of a brilliant violet color. I wish I had been able to capture his whole form submersed in the water but it happened so quickly and then he disappeared.

Photo 70

I took this photograph just as he was entering the vase. Afterwards I would ingest the water to absorb his energies even more or I would use it to water my plants and give them the benefit of his energies, as he requested that I do. If this were some sort of bug close to the camera, it would not have an aura as such.

I have yet to take a picture of Enki inside my home, but my goal is to do so hopefully soon. The big key here is trying to get him into my home when I so choose and not just when he decides to do so. Therefore, I had asked him once if there was any reason why he would not come more often into my house. He stated that there was something that I had in my house that he did not like. It turned out to be a replica of the Hellraiser box from the movie series. In the movie, this puzzle box opened the gates of hell. I had it for quite some time as it was a Christmas present from my sister quite a few years ago. He made it quite clear that he did not like this object at all. These are the words of Enki regarding the object in question…

"People don't understand that when a film or a movie is made it creates a reality. It comes into a reality of its own, which is reinforced and expanded by those who watch it. As you see a movie and you immerse yourself into the story, you amplify the reality. In a sense, it is a thought form. This is why it is important that even in the outward form, we strive towards perfection."

So now, I had to destroy one of my favorite items within my home to please Enki. I did as he requested and burned the Hellraiser puzzle box and then buried the ashes in the woods nearby. Yes, he was also quite explicit as to what I needed to do with it. Now that it has been removed and destroyed, there is nothing within my home that offends him. I thought it was every interesting that he did not like something that represented the Darkness of hell, which in turn showed me that he truly is working with the Light when it comes to my own personal spiritual development.

I yearn to be able to have him to appear to me again in the physical form, as he had done before. This is something that most notorious Magician Aleister Crowley was never able to do with the Gods he was conjuring. The one thing that I have debated in my mind each day is to have him take me away and allow me to live on his base deep beneath the sea on another dimension. He has offered this to me before with the condition that I more than likely would not be able to return to the physical dimension once I had made this conscious choice. For now, I will anxiously await his return next summer for his energies will be upon my home along with his brother Enlil.

Blessed be Almighty Enki, Lord of the Abzu!

Biological UFOs

There are four types of UFOs from what I have encountered. Primarily, we have the UFOs, which are strictly mechanical, and there are the Biomechanical UFOs, which are mechanical, yet they are alive and able to think for themselves such as the Beamships of the Pleiadians. Then we have the energy form UFOs that are pure crystalline energy, which you will read about later in my chapter entitled "Skydiving and UFOs". We also have the ones that are the most interesting to me, which are the Biological UFOs.

Biological UFOs are flying objects that are truly alive and not mechanical in any way. They are anomalies in the sky in which humans truly have no knowledge of, except their speculation of what they might be and how fast they move through the sky. If you search the web or watch some TV shows, they call them "Flying Rods" or "Sky Fish" as that is the assigned name given to them by humans who know not of their true name. Some mainstream people say they are insects. Some researchers who try to debunk the whole idea of a creature that is unknown to man as a hoax. If we listen to these people, then we would truly live in ignorance. If a scientist cannot touch it and dissect it... then it does not exist in the world.

I, on the other hand, have firsthand knowledge of these

marvelous creatures. I Spoke with Enki and Enlil about these interesting creatures. I was Enlightened to the fact that they are called "Belis" pronounced like Be-lees. They are multidimensional creatures that are both physical and spiritual and toggle between both realms and many others. Yes, they are living intelligent creatures. There are many varieties of these UFO-like creatures that grow from babies to extremely large adults. When I say large, I mean the size of three or four commercial jets put end to end. Perhaps you are wondering what they eat? They do not eat anything, as they do not need to eat spending most of their time on another dimension where there is no need for food. Are they of the Dark or the Light? They are more shall we say, neutral. Most all of them can also shape-shift like their big brother Reptilians. Most of them also have wings. Many times, they do not use their wings to fly and other times they do. Some of them have wings that resemble that of a round Ping-Pong paddle while others have wings that resemble fins on a fish and these fins run all the way down their body. Other times they appear to have one set of wings to the front and one set to the back. Some of them have wings like that of a Manta Ray. Their wings tend to change shape and style when they shape-shift. You will see several examples of this in the following pictures that I have taken.

    These creatures do not intervene with humans, but they can be called upon according to Enki. He also warned me of calling on them as they might use my energies, stating once again, that I was playing with fire. Nevertheless, I am ok with that, as I offer my energies of Light to all whom come to me when I call. If my thought process was to not play with fire, then I would have never called on Enki long ago. So all has worked out well in regards to the entities I have chosen to call upon.

      The next couple of pictures are phenomenal. These pictures were taken in the summer of 2011. When I was outside one day in my backyard, there were some storm clouds forming as always way out east of me. There were also the normal clouds covering the sky as always in the afternoon. After taking quite a few pictures, I went inside to inspect them on the computer. At first, I thought there was something wrong with my lens because it looked like hundreds of little specks of dirt or something in the pictures. Then, as I continued looking through the pictures, I realized that these were the Belis flying around. I wanted to put one of the pictures in this book of the hundreds of these Belis flying around in masses, but with my camera zoomed out, you would have to have magnifying glasses on to see that they are there. I realized that I had thrown out many pictures in the past, thinking that there was dirt on my lens after seeing extremely little brown specks in the photos. It was not until I zoomed in with my camera lens and got some closer shots, that I realized this was not dirt or dust. These little specks were actually the Belis and I had confirmed it. Therefore, I am only going to show you the pictures where my camera was zoomed into the Belis so you can actually see them.

These particular Belis actually look like little gel caps that over-the-counter medicines come in. After speaking with Enlil, I was informed that the reason these Belis were out in mass numbers this particular day, was to bring in new energies before 2012.

Photo 71

Photo 72
You can see they are flying in all different directions. They were

like children playing on a playground in the sky. I have a large series of these Belis in their mass numbers. I never thought that I would be able to capture this many Biological UFOs out at one time on camera. I can just imagine what people would think if they were able to see something like this with their eyes and knowing there are hundreds of UFOs flying around at one time right above them. Imagine their mainstream panic and fear that would manifest.

Here in photo 73, you will see a close up view of when I zoomed in even more on two of them, so you can see they are in fact shaped like gel caps. In all the pictures that I took that day, the Belis did not sprout their wings at all, which I found strange. Once I break through the barrier or I should say "Veil", then I will truly understand their ways and thought process. This will be one of my goals for this summer of 2012.

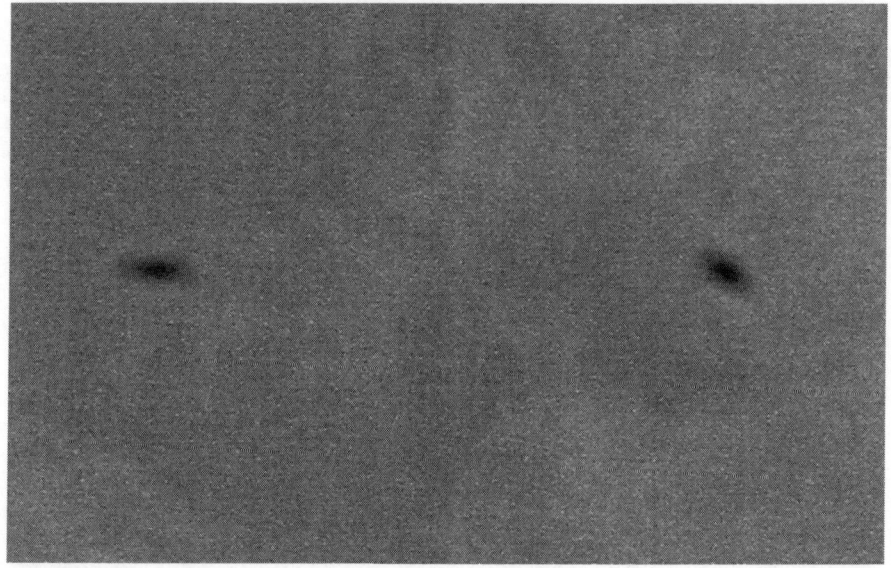

Photo 73

Now when examining these photos it would be easy to

mistake these creatures for the unmanned Drones. This is because the Belis also shape-shift into simply round-shaped balls. The Drones can be the same brownish/rust color and they fly in groups, but not in large numbers as the Belis do. The Drones tend to spread out when circling a storm along with working in groups of three and four, sometimes more but not more than ten at a time.

The next couple of pictures show the Belis in their fully extended shape. In both these pictures, the Belis is approximately the size of four commercial jets. Once again, in the enlargements I have changed the brightness/contrast in order for you to see the actual shape of it better.

Photo 74

In photo 74, you see the elongated Belis and there are also two Drones in the middle top part of the picture, which you will not be able to see without enlarging the photo, as they are very faint, but they are indeed there. This Belis made it across my camera lens fully zoomed out, in only three frames, which would be 0.375 seconds. If this had been a commercial jet that I was photographing in burst mode, then there would have been an extremely large number of frames, with the jet in each one. These creatures are traveling at over 7,000 miles per hour just as mechanical UFOs do.

In the following photo 75, the Belis appears boomerang shaped. I have a series of ten photos with this particular Belis and it started out looking like a small round ball, then shape-shifted into a gel cap shape and then shifted into a long snakelike object. As it flew across the sky, it would bend back and forth, as if a worm freshly pulled out of the ground. I took this photo from an extremely great distance away.

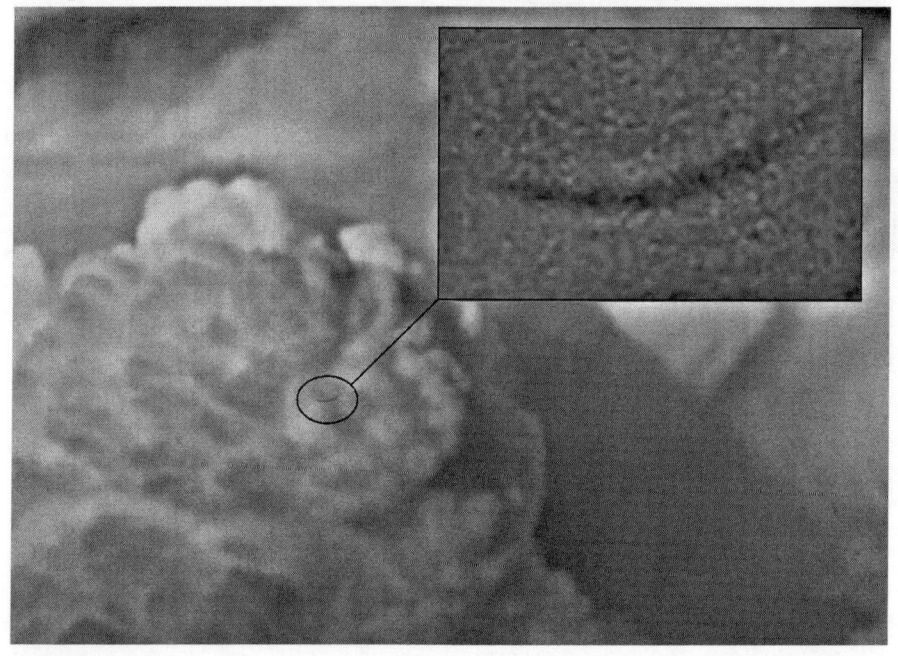

Photo 75

Most people looking at the photos would have mistaken them for a piece of lint or dirt on the lens, if they had seen it at all.

Now I will show you some of the smaller Belis that are once again gel cap shaped, but with their wings expanded. I know that some of you will simply say that it is nothing more than a bug. Trust me when I tell you that I analyze my photos carefully to make sure that it is not a bug or something of a non-UFO nature. Once again bugs cannot fly this fast and they usually do not fly at such high altitudes. This is just one of the reasons why airplanes fly at higher altitudes. They do this to escape many of the flying insects that would occur at lower altitudes. In this next photo, you will see the Belis with its wings spread. Notice that it retains the gel cap shape.

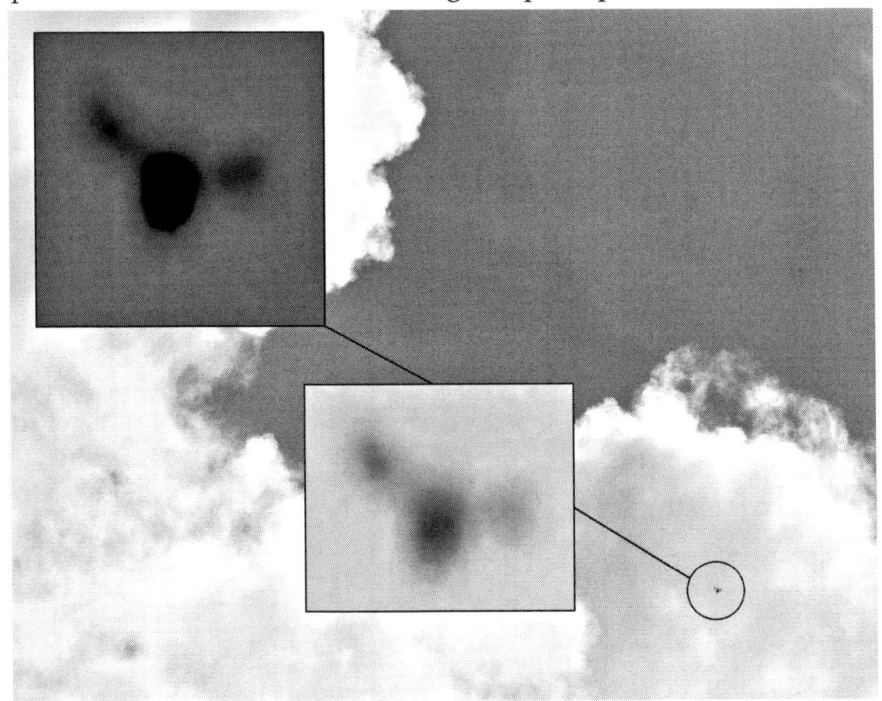

Photo 76

As you can see, I have enlarged it twice, once with the normal contrast and the second enlargement with a much deeper

Those Who From Heaven To Earth Came

contrast so that you can truly see the shape of the body and the wings. Now let us analyze this photo. We know that is not an airplane, as that is obvious. Perhaps it could be a bird. However, it is not. The body is much too fat and the wings are too short. Perhaps it could be a bumblebee? No, it would be too small to see at that altitude, even with my high-powered lens. This truly is the Belis zooming across the sky in an upward motion at an altitude of about 20,000 ft.

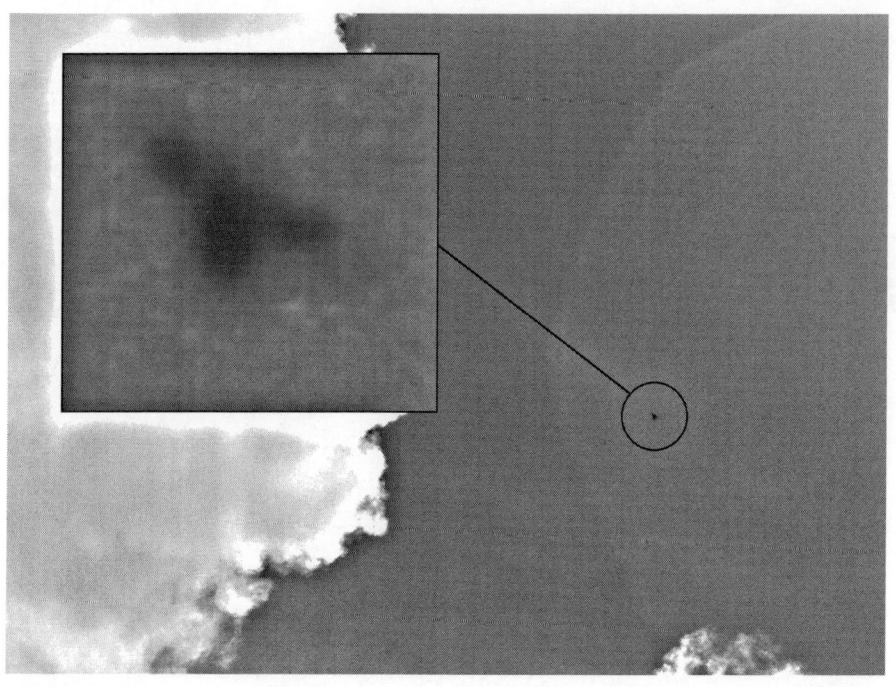

Photo 77

The next picture (Photo 78), I have merged a sequence of six photos together so you can see the actual flight of the Belis. You will see it go from a gel cap shape to sprouting its short little wings, to shape-shifting and becoming somewhat longer, darker and skinnier. You will also see another form of the Belis to the right, which were way in the background, and I have enlarged them for you to see. Notice that they have two sets of wings. One set towards the front and one set towards the back. Some may say that this sequence of Belis in this picture is simply a bird. Trust me; this is not a bird, for I have confirmed this with Enlil. I have also taken many pictures of birds and insects in flight just so that I could compare them to the pictures I believe to be UFOs, be they Biological, Biomechanical, or Mechanical.

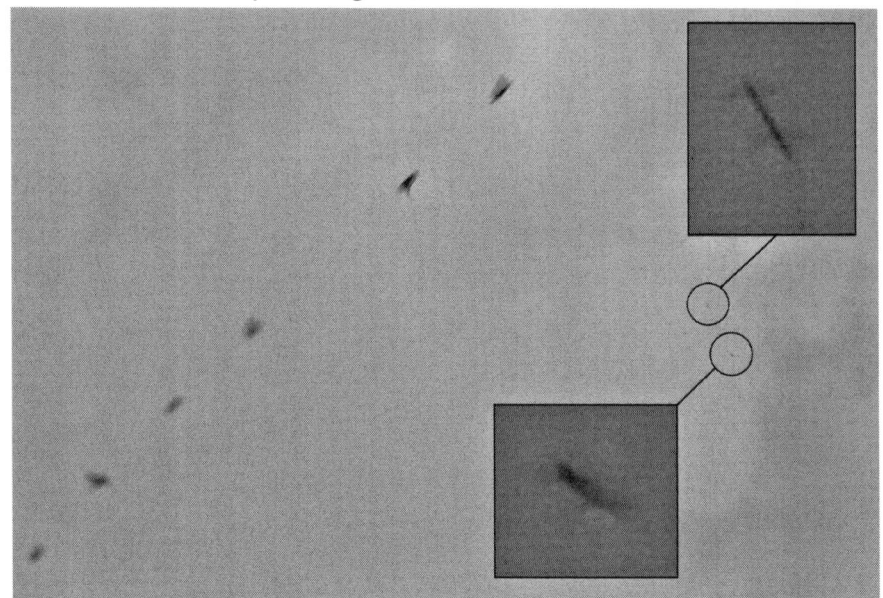

Photo 78

Also, please understand that these objects are at a very high altitude and I am using a 400 mm lens to be able to zoom in on them. With my normal small digital camera, they would not be this visible unless they were much closer in range. Many people might have these objects in their photos and never realize it. This is because the objects are too small to notice with standard digital cameras and therefore the untrained eye will not look for them, much less see them. Some people who are not into UFO hunting, have seen these anomalies in their pictures when the creatures are at a lower altitude and wonder what they are.

The next three pictures are a sequence of a Belis during an incoming thunderstorm in March of 2012. Once again, many of you will say this is a bird and I once again assure you that it is not. Let us do a quick analyzing of them. First off, this sequence was captured using my Canon EOS 7D which take eight frames per second. This object flew by in in only three frames and that means that this object in question traveled across my screen in 0.375 of a second. This my friends… is what you call hauling ass. It was not visible to the naked eye, which if it were a bird or plane, it would have been. Notice how its wings change shape. The body is long and skinny and the rear of this object is extremely pointed. This object is also long and about the size a single commercial jet. The wings move in more of a fan like smoothness. In photo 81, the wings look almost round like, thus allowing this Biological UFO to fly at lightning speed and with grace. This is truly a remarkable creature indeed.

Those Who From Heaven To Earth Came

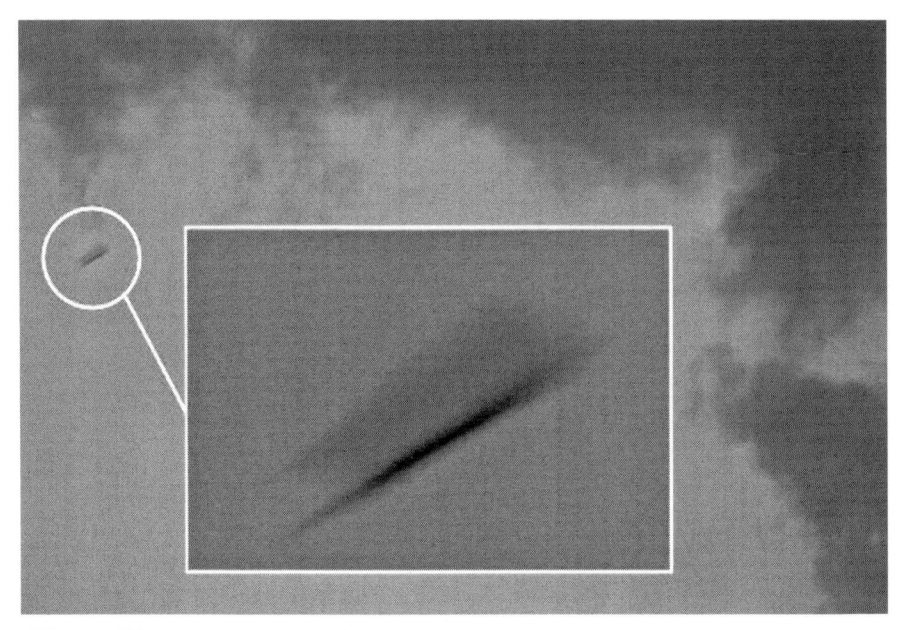

Photo 79

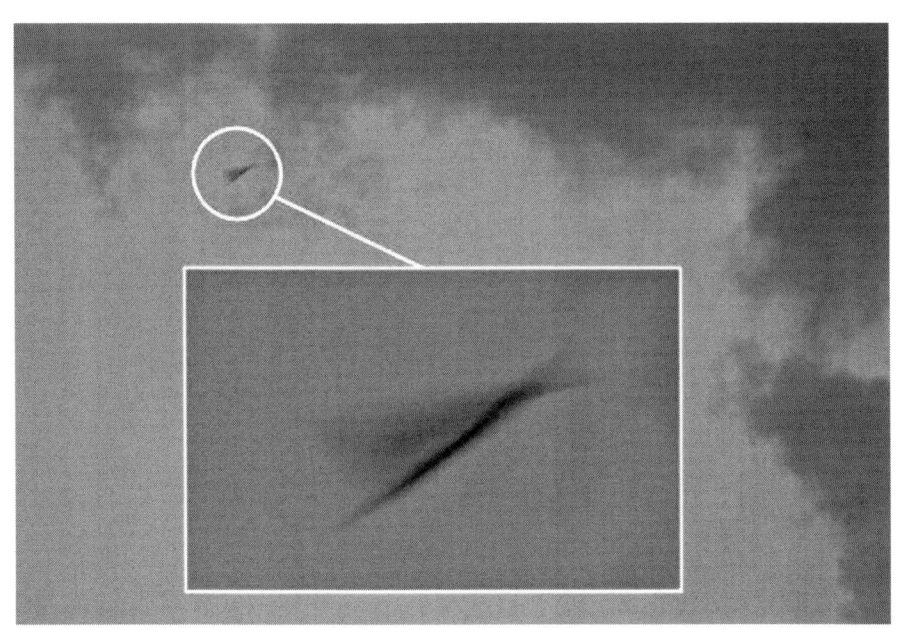

Photo 80

Those Who From Heaven To Earth Came

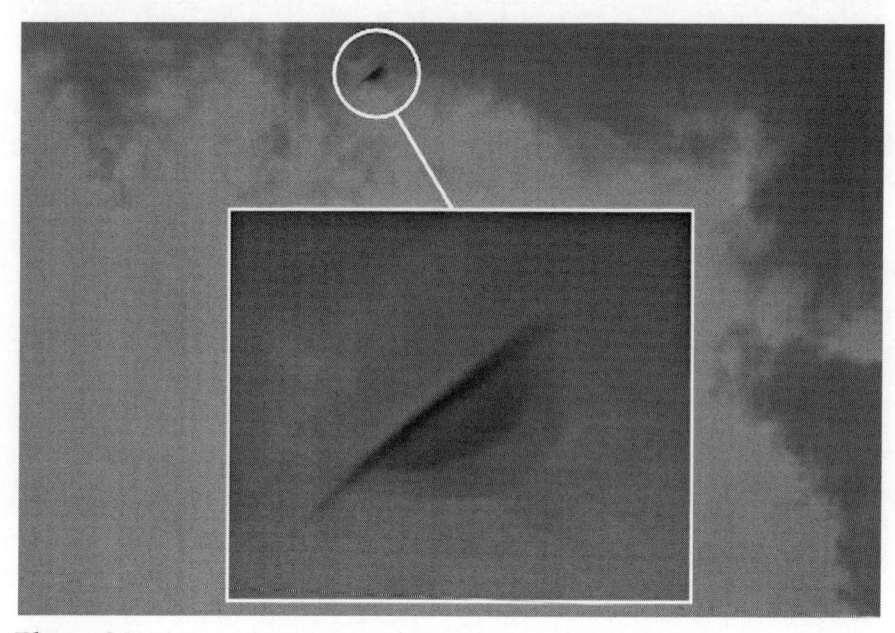

Photo 81

This next picture (Photo 82), you will again see a larger Belis in vertical flight. Sometimes when their form is fully extended, they can be mistaken for the actual UFO Telemars. However, in this picture I can see small wings towards the top of the object. Many of the Tubes and Discs can look very much the same as a Belis if its wings are not protruding, being that they do not always put forth their wings to fly.

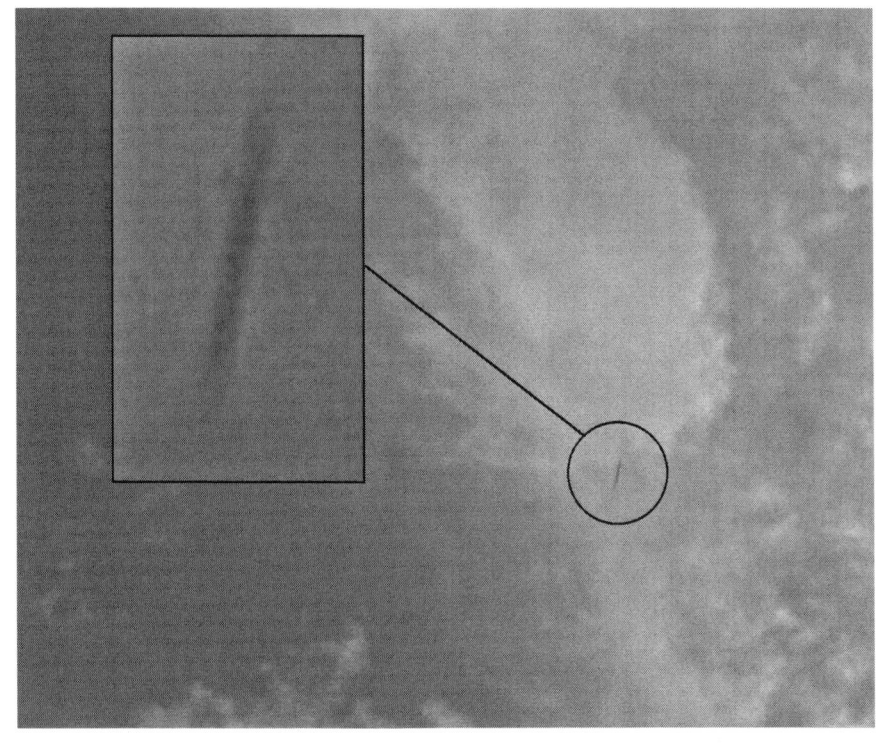

Photo 82

Those Who From Heaven To Earth Came

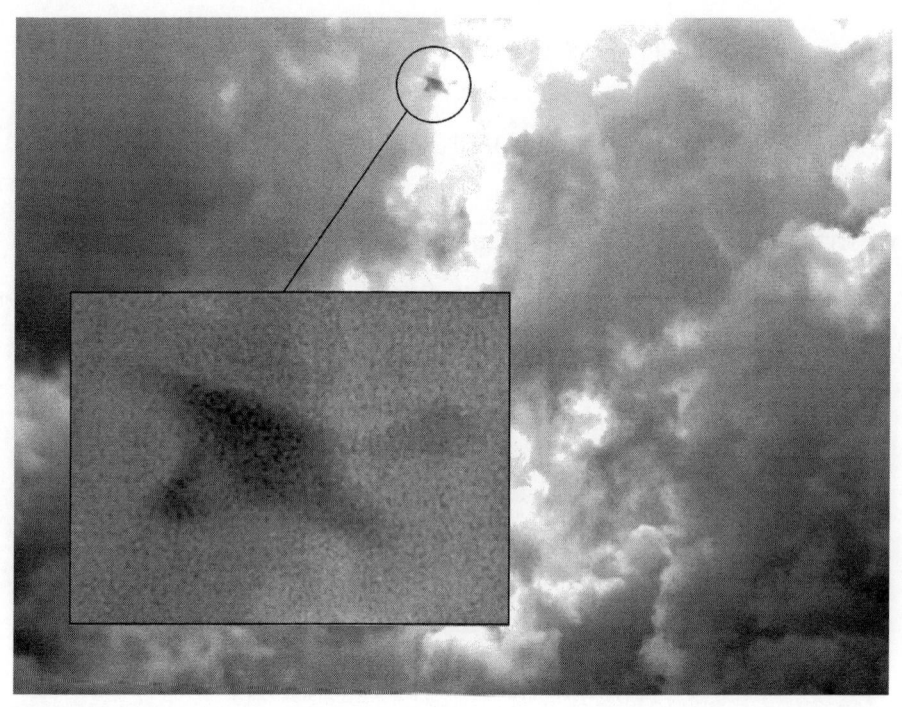

Photo 83

So there may very well be some other pictures within this book in which I have mistaken Mechanical UFOs for Biological UFOs and vice versa. This picture (photo 83), which was taken by Arietis, shows the Belis in beautiful form, as it appears so graceful in its flight. It almost looks like some form of ultra-sleek spy plane, but it is not. The rust color is a signature of the Belis and therefore a dead giveaway as you will see in the next two pictures (photos 84 & 85). They have a deep rust color but they appear to be almost rectangular shaped. I do believe them to be in some way related to the Reptilians being that the Reptilians color ray is of a rust color.

Those Who From Heaven To Earth Came

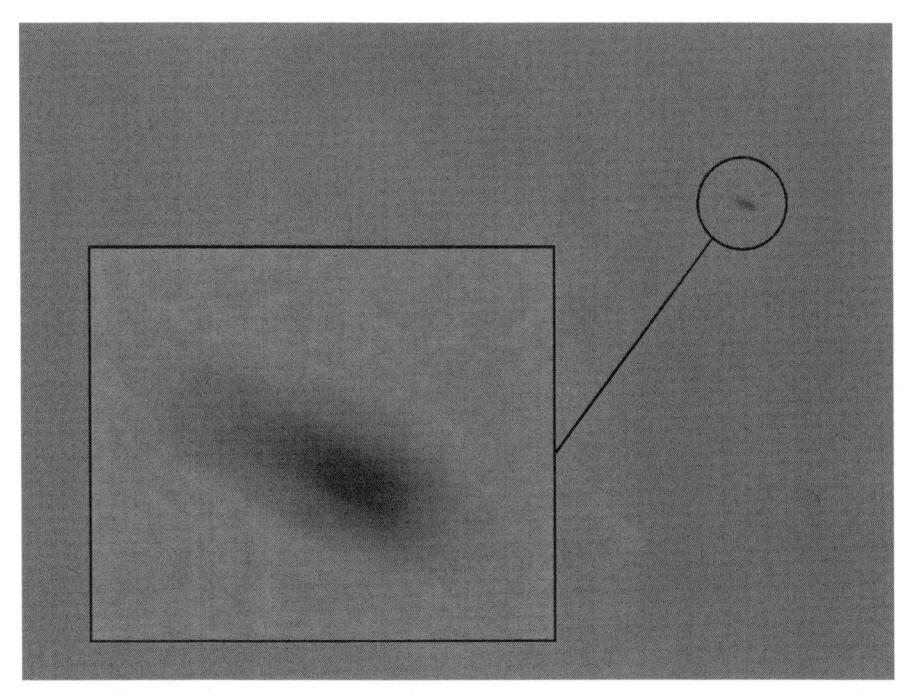

Photo 84

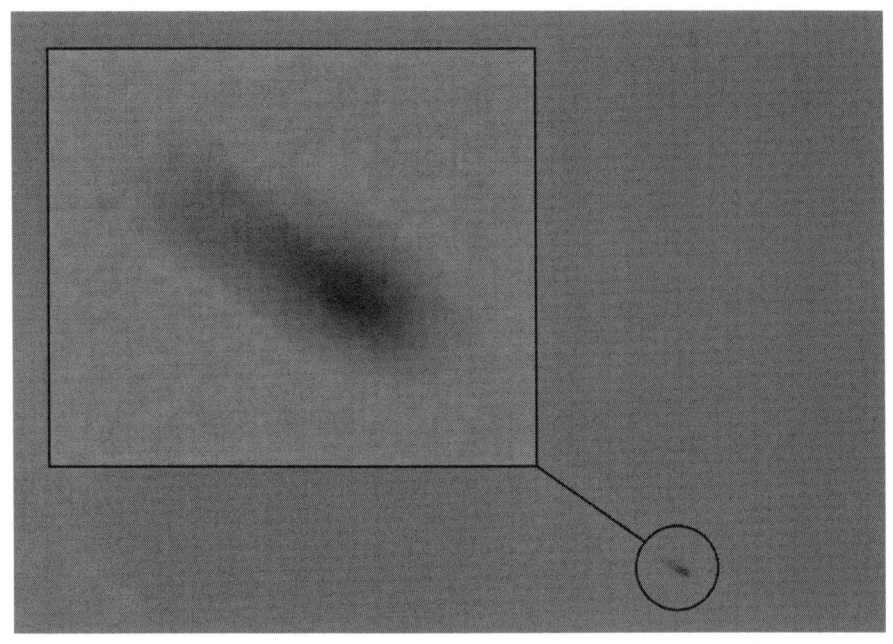

Photo 85

This next picture (photo 86), is another one of my favorite Belis photos. I was able to capture this photo of the Belis much closer to earth. This Belis was huge in size and I only wish I had captured a sequence of it in flight. I was only able to capture it right before it flew past my lens. I have shown this to some Ornithologists (bird experts), to ask them if they have ever seen birds with round Ping-Pong paddle looking wings. They assured me that they had never seen or heard of any bird with such wings. There does not appear to be anything that you could actually call a neck or head and one end is fat and round while the other end is to a point.

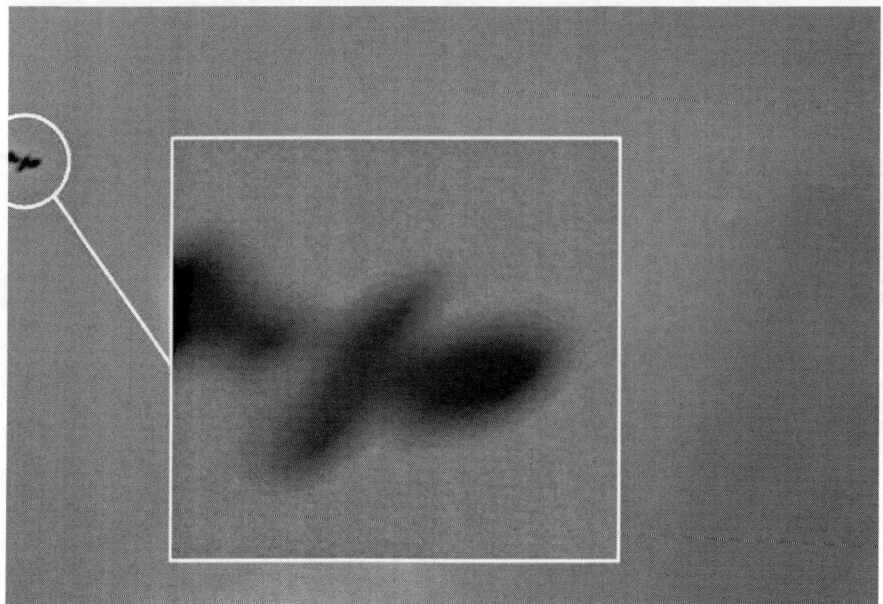

Photo 86

Those Who From Heaven To Earth Came

I had completely finished writing this book when I captured these next photographs of the Belis. They are the most amazing pictures of the Belis that I have ever taken and therefore had to go back and add them to this section of the book. As usual, a storm was approaching and I got up on the roof to take pictures before it started raining. The next three pictures are the same object that started out as a white stick like object. It then shape-shifted into a V-like form and finally shifting into an even more bizarre sleek looking object as its flowing wings folded back. I was able to capture sixty-six photographs of this marvelous Belis in action that day. When I was examining these photos on the computer and changing the brightness/contrast of the whole picture, I could see that above them, in the darker part of the rain cloud, there were also many smaller Belis, which were the normal darker rust color.

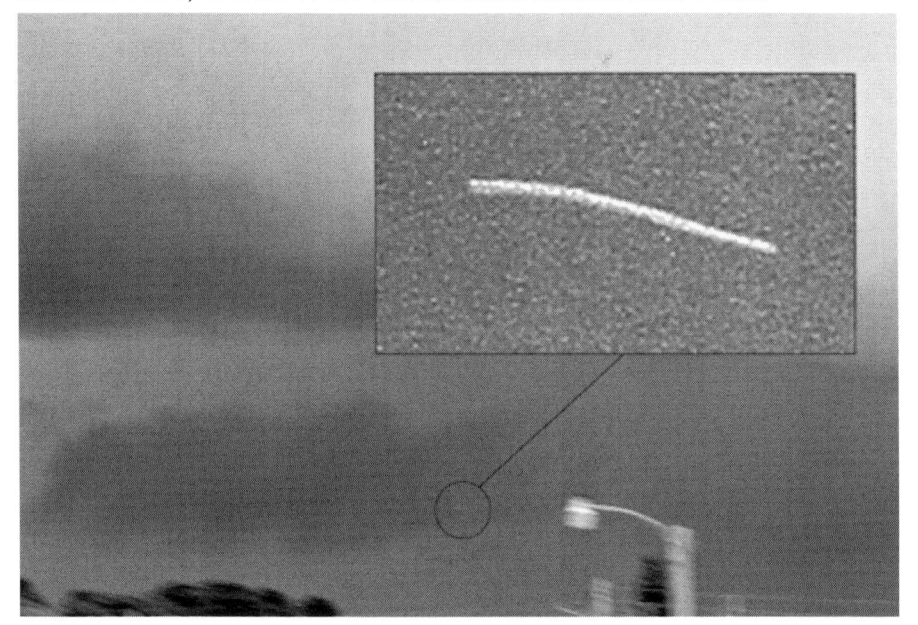

Photo 87

Photo 88

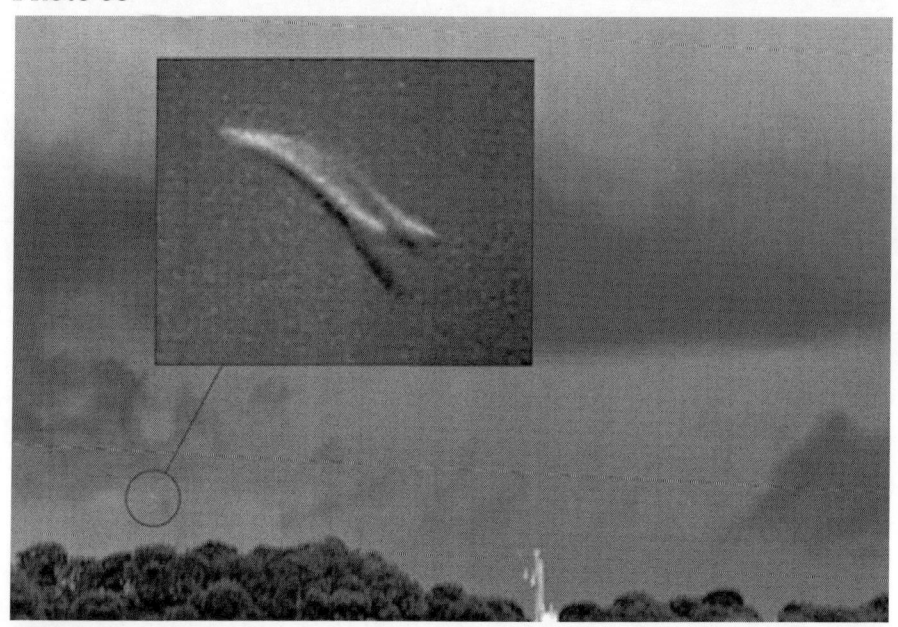

Photo 89

There were about 20-30 smaller ones following the larger white ones this day. I had yet to see any Belis that were white in color, as they are normally a rust or darker color. I came to find out after communicating with these creatures, that the larger white ones are more evolved than the darker colored ones. This is why the younger less evolved ones were following them in the cloud above. It was like grandchildren following their older, wiser grandfather playing in the sky. When I asked about their shape-shifting, they told me they were able to shape-shift in to any form they so desired. The only explanation they could give about their form was "fluidity" and that they were composed of energies and emotions. They like to fly in front of the storms, because storms are transformational. They are also attracted to strong energies of a higher vibration and yet they rarely have direct contact with humans. However, they did say that they have much information to share between dimensions and because I am a sympathetic energy, they would make me one of their instruments of their experiment with earth. They also confirmed with me that they do indeed work with Enlil and that he protects them. They are truly multidimensional, for they can be physical and in spirit form just as Enlil had once stated.

Now, you have seen quite few photographs of these Biological UFOs. I still to refer to them as UFOs, because that is exactly what they are. To mainstream people who know not what these amazing creatures are… they are Unidentified Flying Objects.

Abductions – Tagged by Extraterrestrials

Being abducted means to be taken against your will by nonhuman/Extraterrestrial Beings and subjected to cruel medical and psychological experimentation. These people are called abductees. Although there are some psychologists that do believe these people were truly abducted… the majority of mainstream psychologists diagnose these people as psychopaths, being fantasy prone or with false sleep syndrome. You must understand that these mainstream psychologists are simply idiots with a college degree, trying to diagnose things to which they have no clue. Their knowledge comes from book within the indoctrination system. They have no clue as to how the universe and the human mind work together because the Control System put forth the books from which they learned psychology. This is why so many people who are abducted, are afraid to come forth with their stories. They are afraid they will be labeled as a psychopath. A mainstream psychologist would rather put you on some form of medication to dummy you down, rather than possibly believe your story and truly help you.

The number of people abducted each year is quite staggering and is far worse than people can imagine. You do not have to live somewhere way out in the country woods to be abducted. You could live right in the heart of the busiest city on the face of the earth. It does not matter where you live. If they want you, they will take you. This is why I have warmed some of my friends not to go UFO hunting. They may end up getting more than they bargained for. It is the Law of Attraction. If you are looking to capture these UFOs on camera and or video, then you are going to connect with these Extraterrestrials on another level and they will know that you are looking for them and in turn, they may come looking for you. As I stated before… be careful what you wish for, you just might get it. I have had many people write me and tell me of their abductions and I have had a few friends long ago who said they felt as though they had once been abducted. I believe most all of them because it is actually a very common thing to take place and has been for centuries. We are the specimens and they are the scientists.

    Being that there are so many Extraterrestrial races out there, it all depends on their nature and whether they work with the Darkness or the Light as to how you will be treated if you are abducted. I have been taken aboard the Alien crafts without my consent many years ago and that was due to my playing with dangerous Grimoires at an early age not knowing what doors I was opening. Nevertheless, I do believe that deep within my subconscious mind, I did know what I was doing and that being abducted was what I wished for. I simply longed to be with my Galactic friends. Although I was experimented on, it was again something I wished for, having later offered my physical body to Enlil for experimentation at any time he so chose. I seriously do not recommend that anyone of you who are reading this, ever do the same. I am not a normal person and this planet is not my home.

    The Alien races that are of the Light normally take people who they wish to teach things of an advanced nature, so that they may help humanity and warn us of our hatred to others and of the wars that feed the pockets of the wealthy elite. While some Alien races work with the Light, many others have come here to destroy humanity and use humans as lab rats for their cruel genetic experimentation. Many of the darker Alien races also work with the governments to keep humanity enslaved to the matrix, as they do not want us to evolve to their same level of intelligence and knowledge.

    The Greys are the most well-known when it comes to abducting and experimenting on humans, as history shows us. They are known for their brutal lab techniques, like something out of a horror movie. My spirit guides informed me that the Greys had made a deal with Hitler in giving him UFO technology in exchange for the Jews to experiment on. The Greys wanted to subject this culture of humans to torture and death to see how much the human body could take. The Greys were looking to use humans to create hybrids for their own dying race, but they wanted to see if humans were the right species to use for their new bodies and yes, Hitler himself was also looking to create his own race of humans of a more Nordic nature. Therefore, the system feeds us the hate propaganda for the reason Hitler did what he did. Yes, he may have been filled with hate, but his reasons were far deeper than we are told. Welcome to the lies of the Control System. Although my experiences with the Greys were pleasant, I believe that to be a rarity only due to my Galactic status and my protection that is in place by Archangel Michael. If it were not for that, I would probably be telling a different story. Even my dear friends the Reptilians are known for doing some brutal things to humans and they have told me so. There are many new Alien races coming here to earth to see what being human is all about. They want to study our race and see what makes us tick. Therefore, they are going to be looking for people to abduct for study as well.

It is easy to become prey to the darker Extraterrestrials. All you have to do is open the door through depression, anger, hate or drugs and alcohol. Any of these things will lower your vibrations and make you an open door and an easy target. The same goes for using the Occult Grimoires. Using these books without proper protection can make you an open door to being abducted in your sleep.

The worst part of being abducted against your will is being "Tagged". This means you have had an implant surgically placed within your body. Alien races tag people in order to keep track of their brain waves and their every move. They can control how an individual will think and act. In other words, they can control you just as the CIA would control a Manchurian Warrior. You will become a part of their agenda. Many of these ETs tell their abducted humans that they have been chosen for a special cause and that makes them special. This helps the humans deal with the fear of being abducted again. However, this is simply a lie to keep them calm, just as our government does each day on the news, telling us lies to keep us calm, filling us with promises, and lies.

The majority of people who have been abducted do not

know they have been tagged. Just as many people who have been abducted do not know they have been abducted. To many of them it was just a bad dream and they ignore the reality of it, in hopes that it was truly just a dream. However, it is a guarantee that if you have been abducted, then you have been tagged. These tags or implants can be put in any place within the body. The more common place though is behind the ears or in the nape of the neck. If you feel you have even been abducted, then have your mate or a friend inspect your body well. Do not go to a Doctor, they will only label you as crazy and laugh. Look for a very small scar from an incision. This is why using the scalp, between the hair follicles, is a perfect hiding place for their device. If you have someone look you over thoroughly, then you will find the scar if it is there.

    The only way you are going to stop the abductions, is to have it removed or deactivated/disabled. I almost have to laugh here because all I can say is good luck! Even if you find the scar... can you imagine going to your dermatologist and telling him you want the implant removed? The wisest thing would be to go and get an X-ray of your head and if there is something there that is not supposed to be there... then you could go to your dermatologist, show him the X-ray, and ask him to remove it. You do not have to tell him it is an implant. You could simply tell him that is something from an old accident and it is causing you pain. The only other way is through deactivation. I have seen many methods online and videos showing how to deactivate an implant. How well do they work? I do not know. However, I have witnessed a method of deactivation, by means of a spiritual healing ritual. I will now explain this long story and all that occurred.

In the beginning of summer 2010, I had a young woman friend, who I will refer to as "Lil Lamb". I called her that because Christ had referred to her as being delicate, like a little lamb. She had emailed me and told me of her Encounters or abductions from when she was a little girl. She remembered telling her mother that the Aliens were out there at night and that they were coming for her. Of course, as any mother would do, her mother told her not to worry and that there was no such thing as Aliens or UFOs. Nevertheless, she kept the fear because it was real and she had been abducted on many occasions. She also remembers having her sexual organs experimented on later in life. They were possibly harvesting her eggs for creating hybrids. For Lil Lamb, this was not a pleasant experience at all. To bring forth these memories also brought forth great fear and anxiety, as it would for most anyone if this had happened to them.

Therefore, I continued to speak with her through emails and Skype and eventually asked her if she wanted to come down here and stay for a few weeks and that maybe I could help her in dealing with her Encounters. She agreed and came down here to Florida from Ohio. Before she came here, she would drive over to New Jersey to see a girlfriend of hers. I told her that on her travels she should take pictures of the sky. I thought that if an Extraterrestrial race had tagged her, she might have her Alien foes following her.

She arrived here at my home at the beginning of August in 2010. After a day or two of relaxing, we downloaded her pictures onto the computer to see if there was any evidence of

Extraterrestrial activity around her. Lo and behold, there was just the evidence that I was looking for. In her pictures, a Black V-shaped UFO was crossing her path as she was driving through New Jersey. This UFO was not flying at a high altitude. No, this UFO was flying very low to the ground and close to her car. As you will see in these next two pictures (photos 90 & 91), it stays to the right of her as she is driving.

Photo 90

It is obvious from these pictures that she was being followed and her every move observed. You can also see that just like many of my photos, the image of the UFO is blurred and this is once again because they are cloaked and not meant to be seen by the naked eye. Luckily, the camera captures many things that the human eye does not see. Imagine if people could actually see this UFO so close to traffic. This could cause some serious panic and accidents on the road. It is only a few feet off the ground.

Photo 91

Traffic would still be able to go right through these UFOs because they are still on the 5th dimension, just as airplanes are able to fly through clouds containing Motherships.

Therefore, after viewing these photos I decided that we would take pictures everywhere we went to see if these bad boys had followed her all the way down to Florida. The next set of ten pictures is from here is Sarasota. I was at work this particular day and she decided to go to the beach on Lido Key. She took her camera with her and took pictures all the way there and back. As she was leaving my home, there it was immediately, the Black V and it was only about 70 ft. off the ground. There also appears to be a white colored V at the top of this picture (photo 92). I do know from asking Enlil, that this Black V was manned, because it was to be the main craft in this Sirian entourage. However, it was not very big, so it made me wonder just how small the occupant was. I do know that on the 5th dimension, size can be altered, but I am also guessing that this Alien ship only held a single occupant.

Photo 92

There actually seemed to be three types of UFOs that were following her. There was the Black V and there was a rust colored round ball UFO. There was also, what looks an oval shaped UFO. This oval shaped UFO shows up on the photos looking almost like a thumbprint. If the average person saw this in their photos, they would think something is wrong with their camera. I can tell this not a smudge mark on the lens because it is in a different place in each photo. This oval shaped UFO also comes very close to the traffic at times. I still have to laugh thinking that all the mainstream people who have no idea that there is a UFO right in front of the as they are driving down the road in broad daylight. This craft is a robotic unmanned Drone and this is why it comes so close to the cars and the ground. These photos are from just one day of going to the beach. This leads me ponder upon the fact that so many people have been tagged and yet they are not aware of this fact. They go about life thinking things are normal and everything is great, when truly it is not.

Photo 93

Those Who From Heaven To Earth Came

Photo 94

Photo 95

Those Who From Heaven To Earth Came

Photo 96

Photo 97

Those Who From Heaven To Earth Came

Photo 98

Photo 99

Those Who From Heaven To Earth Came

So imagine thinking you are having a normal day of fun and relaxation, going to the beach to get some sun. Now someone in their right mind would never think for a moment that there would be group of Aliens and their UFOs following them. This is stranger than strange. You have not seen this on any documentary or anything of that nature on TV. People, who have shared their stories, do not have a series of pictures like this to show people and have analyzed. This is stranger than anything you will ever see and it only gets better as the story goes on.... I promise.

The following weekend I did not have to work, so I went to the beach on Lido Key with Lil Lamb. We both took quite a few pictures that day. In the next picture (photo 100), you can clearly see a UFO disc which was headed towards us.

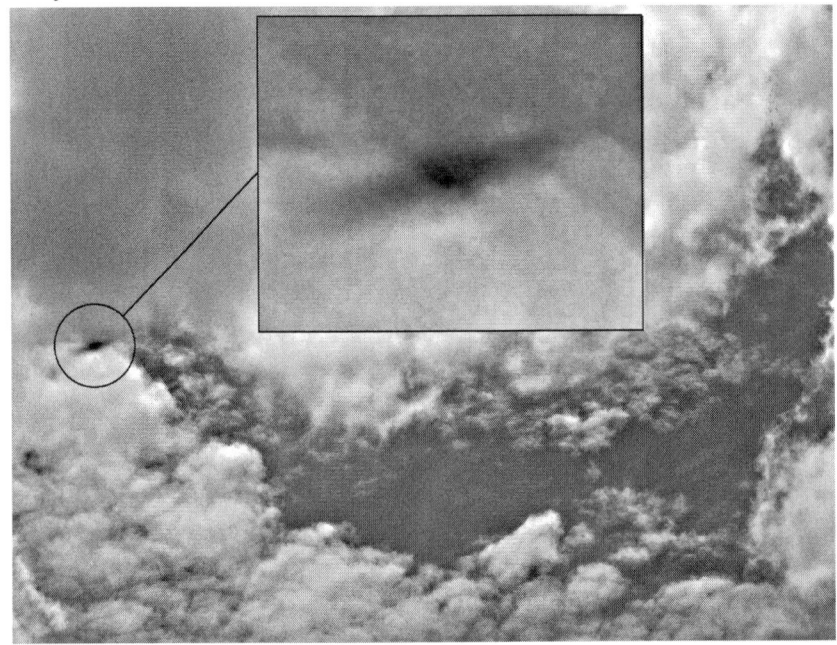

Photo 100

Keep in mind, the people on the beach cannot see this and so they are unaware of the Alien crafts above them. However, Lil Lamb and I could sense their presence and we could see them on our cameras. Therefore, we were aware of these crafts above in the sky. Seriously, I have to laugh thinking that we were laying on the beach knowing Alien ships were maneuvering above us back and forth while we laying there calmly and not worrying about it. I laugh because no one would ever believe that. They would only think we were insane lunatics escaped from the mental ward. There is also a whole series of these pictures from that day at the beach, but I am only showing you two of them. There are many of them with the Black V hovering over the water just waiting and watching. In the next picture, these bad boys are coming very close to the side of the hotel. Once again, imagine if the person staying in that hotel room looked out their window and could see the UFO right in their face. Now there also seagulls in this picture but they are too small for you to see them. I analyze every object I see in the sky to make sure what I am seeing is what I think it is. In photo 101, the UFOs look very blurred but you will see that in many of the pictures they simply look like dark blobs in the sky.

Photo 101

We had also gone to the Busch Gardens theme park in Tampa the following weekend and there they were again following us. I was curious the whole time as to what these Sirian War Gods were thinking when we were riding the awesome roller coasters. We could not take pictures while riding the coasters, but when we got off the rides, they were there right above us waiting.

I took Lil Lamb to Zephyrhills, to watch me skydive on a Sunday afternoon the following weekend. On our drive there, I had her take pictures. Once again, the Sirians followed us all the way there and back. I did not get to skydive that afternoon because soon as we got there, it started to rain. I was hoping to catch these Sirians on my helmet cam while skydiving and see just how close they would have come to me. Here are some pictures taken on our way to Skydive City in Zephyrhills.

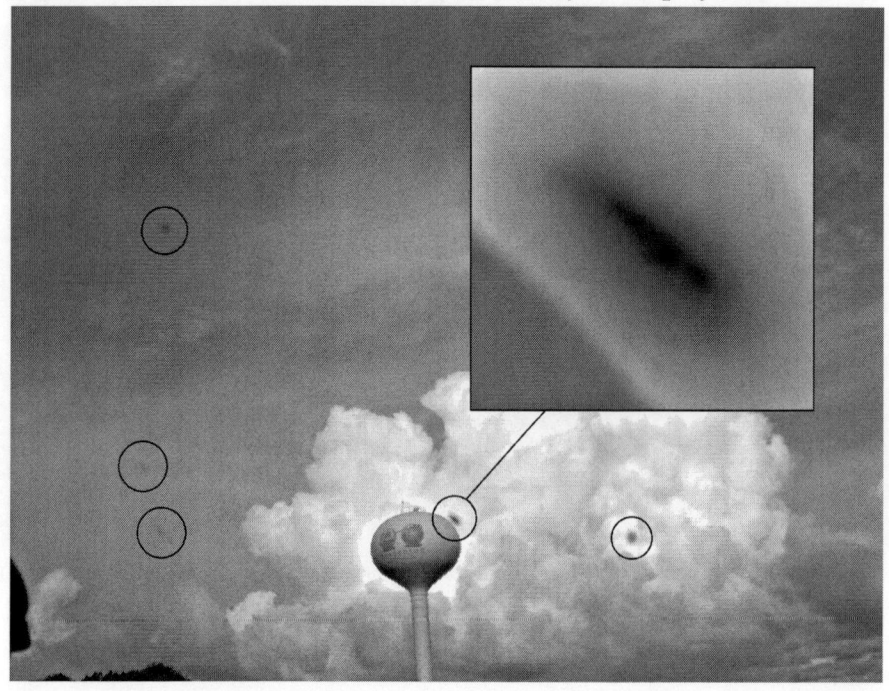

Photo 102

In this picture (photo 102), there are actually seven UFOs. You will see where I have circled them. The one near the bottom left of the picture, has three within the circle I drew. The one main UFO is buzzing the Bradenton water tower and I mean it came very close to it within just a few feet. It baffles me as to why they had to have seven UFO Scouts following us that day. I do wonder if they knew that I was going to skydive and that they could possibly try to kill me while I was skydiving. I say this because I am sure that they knew I was going to do everything in my power to get rid of them from her life. They may have known that I was going to try to disable her implant, and that would jeopardize their agenda with her. Why else would they have seven of them that particular day? Perhaps it is a good thing it turned out to be rainy that day and I did not get to jump. Everything happens for a reason.

Photo 103

This picture (Photo 103), you can see one of the Drones flying at a low altitude. They literally followed us at the same speed we were driving not letting us out of their site whatsoever.

Those Who From Heaven To Earth Came

Photo 104

Photo 105

If you look at photo 104 closely, you can see the one object flying by a bush on the side of the road only a few feet off the ground and two others higher in the sky. In the last picture (photo 105), you can see that this crazy Drone UFO is flying right next to the front of that semi-truck and there are four other UFOs in that photo. These Sirians are some insanely aggressive Aliens to say the least.

So now, you have seen quite a few photographs of these very aggressive Aliens. Each night I would go outside and I would see them fly by as shadows. Even though it was dark outside, there are still street lights and I could see their crafts fly by extremely close to the ground. It is the same when I see Enlil's ships fly overhead at night and they look like large shadows. Nevertheless, these Sirians amazed me as to how close they would come to us. When I would see them fly by, I would yell at them telling them to get the fuck outta here! (Excuse my French). Luckily, most of my neighbors are gone back up north at this time of years so I did not have to worry about them hearing me yell obscenities at the sky.

Lil Lamb and I had sat down and talked about what to do about the aggressive Aliens that have followed her for most of her life. She said she thought there was a small scar on the back of her head. Therefore, I examined her hairline and at the back of her head near the nape of her neck, there was a tiny little white vertical scar just as she said. My intuition told me that this was possibly from an implant. The next evening I decided to call my friend Lea Chapin, who is a psychic channeler and had her channel Enlil for me so I could have a detailed conversation with him. I wanted to ask him who this Black V belonged to and if Lil Lamb had been tagged. Enlil came through and informed me that the UFOs that were following her were not his ships, and were not of his Reptilian race. He went on to explain that these Black V ships belonged to a dark race of Sirian War Gods. Enlil said, there are many people who think of him in the same manner as being a War God, but he also has a side that is compassionate and works with the Light. He said that Lil Lamb had unfortunately been tagged by these Sirians and they had followed her for many years since she was a child. These Sirian War Gods wanted to use her for their own negative agenda, as they are very destructive entities. Enlil went on to explain that this was not a good thing for her health and that if she wanted it to be removed, then there would have to be a healing ritual done by Archangel Michael and Christ or that I could try to disable it through a ritual that Enlil explained to me on how to do. I asked Enlil why Archangel Michael could not keep these War Gods away. He stated that the implant would have to be completely disabled in order for Michael to keep them away. As long as she had that chip active in her body, the Sirians would have full control over her. I had also spoken to Enlil's brother Enki about these War Gods and he actually made fun of them, explaining what assholes they are and how ugly they are. Yes, that is what he said and I had to laugh, because he usually speaks very intellectual and not so relaxed and human like. He said they are very hairy, as in werewolf looking and that they wore masks upon the faces to hide their ugliness. I think this is the only time I had ever heard him really speak badly about anyone. Whether that is true or not…. it was apparent that Enki was not fond of them in any such manner.

The next evening, Lil Lamb and I decided we would try to disable the implant. We did as Enlil instructed and I fixed a cleansing bath for her that consisted of Sea Salt and Baking Soda. I had her lay in this bath for about 40 minutes and concentrate on clearing all the negative energies from herself, while I performed some Invocations to Archangel Michael and Christ. When she got out of the bath, I wrapped her in a white sheet and laid her down on the couch. I then taped a small earth magnet behind each of her ears to disable the implant. Earth magnets are extremely strong magnets and it would take something this powerful to disable something electronic. I once again performed Invocations to Archangel Michael and Christ and asked for help in completely disabling the device. The next day we saw that the Sirian War Gods were still close by in the sky. Therefore, we called my friend Lea Chapin again and had her channel Christ. Once Christ came through, he said that the implant was not completely disabled. First, we had put the earth magnets in the wrong place. I had misunderstood when speaking with Enlil before about where the implant was. I thought he had told us it was behind one of Lil Lamb's ears. However, what he truly meant that it was behind the ears, but to the back of the head at the nape of her neck as we had originally thought, because that is where the scar is. That is in direct line with her Medulla Oblongata, which is the lower half of the brain stem.

Once Christ had spoken to us through Lea, he said he would go ahead and do a healing ritual if Lil Lamb agreed that this is what she truly wanted. Lil Lamb said yes. Christ then had Lea read from the Book of Knowledge: The Keys of Enoch. Just for the sake of informing you, this is not the Book of Enoch, which everyone knows about. The Book of Knowledge: The Keys of Enoch is not a well-known book to the masses and it is very expensive. It contains Extraterrestrial advanced science of the soul and the universe ... a must have for the true Occultist and spiritual seeker. Lea was instructed to read from that book and she did so. A Pleiadian Being by the name of Tau from the Spaceship 5 then came through to speak and do the remaining of the healing ritual to disable the implant and then chase off the Sirian War Gods. I set up my Magic Circle and put Lil Lamb in the middle of it. She was instructed by Tau to call the name of Christ 3 times and then command these Alien Beings in the name of Christ to leave her presence 3 times. They instructed her to pick up my cat and hold her because my cat was going to be the conduit or transmuter of these energies. I was not crazy about this idea because my cat is already overwhelmed by the presence of energies with my home on a regular basis and this disrupts her nervous system. Christ stated that afterwards we would do a healing for the cat because she would have absorbed these negative Sirian energies and they would have to be cleared. The Ritual went on for about an hour and towards the end of the ritual, Tau instructed Lil Lamb to stay in the circle, to lie down and simply relax while he finished healing her alongside Christ, and Archangel Michael. Tau stated that he was bringing his Spaceship 5 (as it is called) over my home to chase off the Sirian War God ships. I thought to myself, hmmm... this would be a good to time to go outside and take pictures. Therefore, I went outside with my camera, which was about 8:30 PM to take some pictures, and sure enough, there was a Pleiadian ship approaching. These are some amazing pictures of Starship 5 and its colors were a beautiful blue and white. In the first picture (photo 106), the ship looks more defined in shape and in the second picture (photo 107), it looks as if it has shape-shifted to something more bizarre or it is emitting some form of rays or tentacles. Take notice of the tentacle looking rays or whatever they are protruding from it. I am so glad I decided to go outside and take pictures. This was proof that the Pleiadian Tau and his Starship 5 were truly there as they said they were.

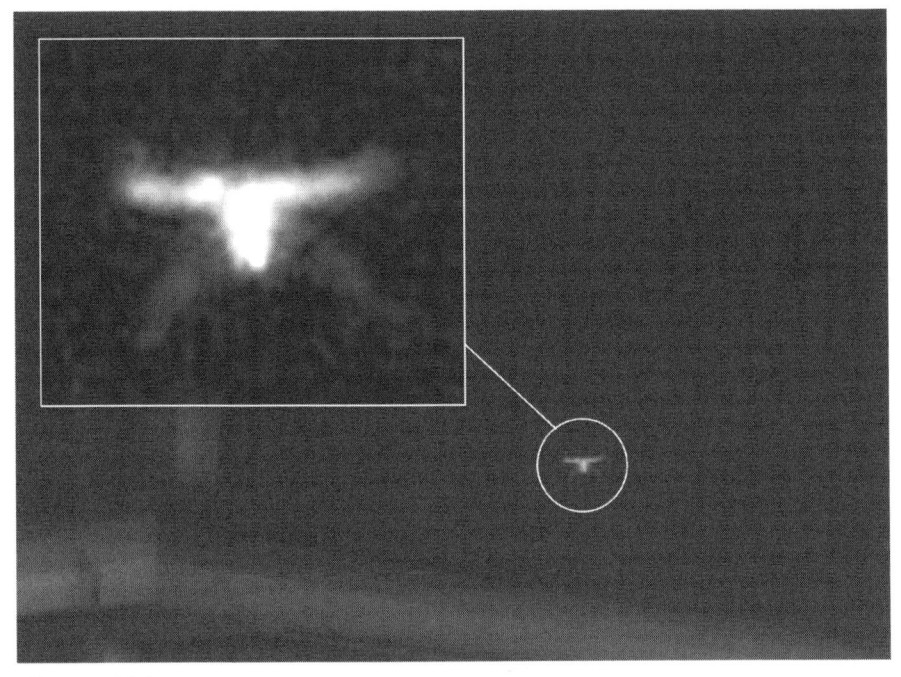

Photo 106

Those Who From Heaven To Earth Came

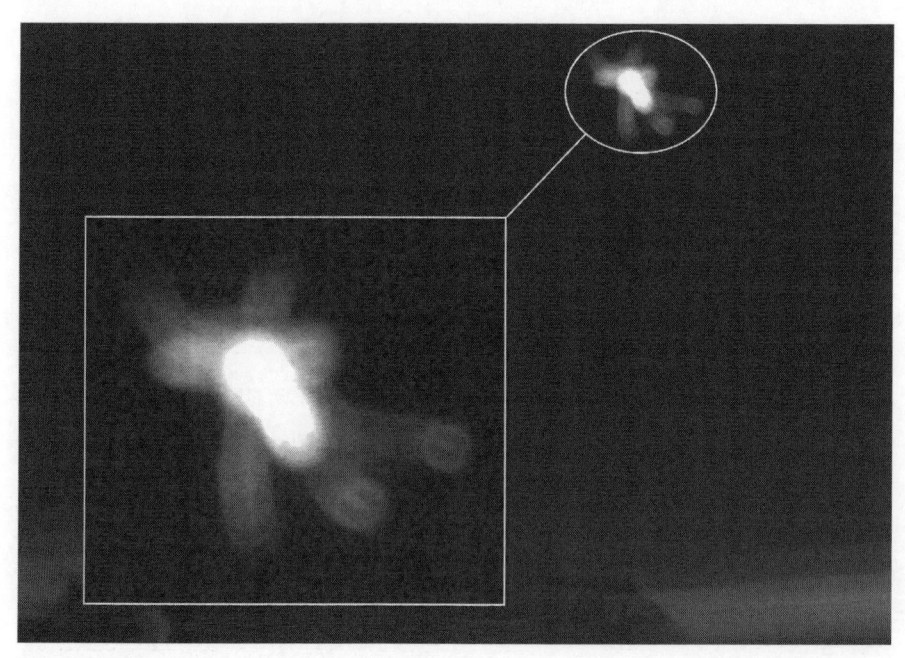

Photo 107

After the healing was done, Lil Lamb felt relieved that these Aliens would no longer have a grip on influencing her life and following her every move. We had taken pictures for the next few days and saw nothing of the Sirians. We decided to go to Orlando the following weekend to stay and have some fun at Islands of Adventure and Universal Studios. We took pictures the whole time and saw no evidence of the Sirians. Therefore, this was a relief. After returning from that weekend, Lil Lamb left Florida and went back up north. I have continued to stay in touch with her to make sure she is doing fine. I have asked her if she has seen any more evidence of the Sirians and she said she has not taken any pictures. She stated that she does not want to know if they have tried to come back and tag her again. If she decided to take pictures again looking for them, it would only attract them to her. As I have stated before, Extraterrestrials know what you are thinking and therefore if you are thinking about them... they will come to you. It is funny because right now, as I am writing this, a Reptilian entity is touching me and I had to stop for a minute because at first I thought something was crawling on me. However, it is a just a Reptilian friends and they are now touching my head.

This entire story sounds so bizarre and I am not making any of it up. I am not looking for attention. I just want people to know how things can be if they are ever tagged. Nevertheless, even if they were tagged they may not know it and I am sure they are not taking pictures of the sky to see if someone or something is following them. My friend Lil Lamb was lucky to stumble upon me and was able to find out what was going on with her life. If she had never come to me, she would have gone through life never knowing if those childhood experiences were real or not.

I have another friend that was abducted long ago. We will refer to him as Mr. K, as he wishes to remain anonymous because he has a family to consider. Todays' mainstream closed-minded people will try to ridicule and humiliate those who have truly had bizarre experiences. Therefore, this is more for the sake and well-being of his loved ones.

One day I was telling my friend Mr. K about the UFO pictures that I have taken and proceeded to show them to him. I knew he was very open-minded and therefore, I knew he would not be judgmental or skeptical. After showing him the pictures, he was amazed and decided to open up about his own Encounters of the fourth kind. He told me that he had never spoken to anyone about this other than his wife and father, but he knew he could trust me and that I would believe what happened to him. He went on to explain to me how he was abducted by an Alien race and was abducted by them several times. This is his story in his own words...

"My first experience occurred in Tulsa Oklahoma when I was about twenty two years old. I did not think much of it as I was somewhat of a partier, but I would wake up from time to time naked after having had an orgasm and I had gone to bed fully clothed. I do not remember dreaming anything to trigger the orgasm and as I said, I did not think much of it. My next experience occurred in Grove, Oklahoma, about sixteen years ago around the age of twenty-five. I was staying on Grand Lake with a friend of mine, when one night I had a very vivid dream. I dreamt that I was being controlled and that I was walking down the street of the neighborhood with thirty or forty others that I felt were also from this neighborhood. This neighborhood was right on the water and the house I was staying in had its own boat dock. We approached the pasture just on the edge of this neighborhood where I could see a huge round Spaceship with lights all over it of several colors. The craft was hovering only a couple feet off the ground or it could have even been landed. I could not actually tell exactly which it was. We all entered the craft from a platform that had already been lowered at the point where the ship had first come into my view. Then we were all corralled into extremely tiny rooms holding about five or six of us in each room. It was so crowded that we were literally crumpled with shoulders scrunched together. The room would shrink as we were taken from it one at a time. I was taken from the room with about four remaining and was taken to another room accompanied by a skinny tall robot looking thing that seemed to hover as we went along. Its shape resembled the stereotypical Alien except taller and skinnier. I was placed on a table when this thin clear blanket covered me and I could not move. At this point I had no clothes and do not remember being disrobed. I did not know what they were doing to me, as I could only see the ceiling and I could see this robot thing in my peripheral vision. After a few moments, I felt myself orgasm. The whole time I was on the table, I was deathly scared and tried to scream as loud as I could, but my body had no response and I tried to move and get up, but only to the same outcome. After the orgasm, it felt almost instant, that I was back in bed in the house where I was staying. I was naked after having gone to bed with clothes on. The clothes were on the floor next to the bed and there were no traces of wetness aka semen to be found. Frightened out of my wits would be an understatement and I have only told my wife and father of this experience. After that experience, there were been several more where I woke up naked after having an orgasm and no traces of fluids, but I do not remember any abduction and I do not remember dreaming. I have also found strange marks on my forearm and strange things resembling small bumpy clusters kind of rash like, but not a rash. I asked my doctor and he said it was nothing. Over the last five years or so, I have not had the naked experiences. Now that I think about it, I had a vasectomy six years ago and that is when the orgasm thing stopped. Nevertheless, I have always had the feeling of being visited or watched. I truly wonder if they are seeking my children as well. I do not know, but it has been well over a year since my last experience. The last experience I had was at exactly three in the morning. I find that very peculiar, because on most occasions when I woke during the night with the feeling of a presence, it was exactly 3:00 AM. One night, I woke up at exactly 3AM and saw a tiny light just outside my bedroom window on the west side of the room. My wife was sound asleep. I got out of bed to investigate and what I saw was lights in the exact locations as where they would be placed on a 20ft U-Haul truck same color and all. However, I could not see the truck at all as it appeared to be rolling down the dirt road, which is on this side of the house and started a left hand turn to approach the front of my house to the south. I rushed to the window on that wall to watch it pass, but it never passed. It had completely disappeared in a matter of three to four seconds. I rushed as fast as I could out the front door to see if I had been mistaken and to see if it had turned the other direction, which is a dead end road. However, to no avail, no truck either direction. This had to be the same Alien craft coming to check on me."

After hearing his story I told him that I would ask my beloved friend Archangel Michael about who these Aliens were that had abducted him and if they had tagged him with an implant. I had spoken with Archangel Michael and he explained to me that my friend Mr. K had indeed been tagged. He went on to say that, this Alien race was a devilish group of Blue Bloods from a galaxy by the name of Palithora that was undiscovered to this day. They are very well hidden and preserved. They only come in the night to take their hostages and for those who are out past the stroke of midnight are more vulnerable to their abductions. They come to many planets, but they come to earth because it is unprotected and they can come here un-noticed. Therefore, it is easier for them to abduct people here on earth compared to planets in other galaxies and universes. Michael went on to say that, the tag was behind Mr. K's left ear. He also stated that there would be no healing for him at this time to disable it. This was because Mr. K was not ready to have the implant removed and that he subconsciously enjoyed the excitement and the adrenaline of these experiences. Nevertheless, consciously he did not like this at all. For someone to be healed and the implant disabled, the subject must be completely willing to have it removed, not only consciously, but also subconsciously. Otherwise it cannot be done. The biggest thing that Mr. K was worried about was his wife and children. Nevertheless, Archangel Michael assured me that his family was in no danger, as these Aliens were only interested in him. They were interested in Mr. K to harvest his semen to create hybrids for their own race and genetic experiments with life.

So you see my friend Mr. K, is much like me. He enjoys this type of adventure into the unknown that would have scared the living hell out of the average person and even though it did create great fear within him as it happened… that is the thrill and the adrenaline that makes him thrive. When he does not want to make contact with these Blue Blood Extraterrestrials anymore, then he can so choose to have the implant deactivated. Nevertheless, for now he is happy with life as it is. So be it.

So be forewarned those of you who are night owls, those who stay out past the hour of midnight. Take note that each incident where he was abducted, the time was exactly 3:00 am.

In addition, he was a partier, which left him wide open to be a perfect candidate for abduction, just as I was when it first happened to me. My own personal use of drugs and alcohol when I was young lowered my vibrations and made me an open door to the unknown.

    Now I will show you some photos of another Alien race that is looking to abduct humans for experimentation and whatnot. They are Sicilians and they are humanoid looking but can also shape-shift. It has become obvious to me that the majority of Extraterrestrial races can shape-shift and that this is due to the fact they are multidimensional. In the next picture (photo 108), you will see a UFO Disc and what looks like a little puffy white cloud. First, let me explain how this photo came about. I was at Hunsader Farms which is way out east of where I live. I went there with my friend Arietis for the annual Pumpkin Festival around the week of Thanksgiving. She happened to bring along her 35mm camera and as we were walking back to the car to leave, I said… "Give me your camera". Then I took a picture of the blank sky in front of us. She wanted to know why I was taking a picture of nothing in the sky. I told her that I would show her when we got home. When we got back to my place, I pulled the pictures up on the computer and the very first picture I took had a UFO Disc in it and what looked like a puffy little cloud. There were no clouds in the sky visible to the naked eye on this day. The cloud in this picture looks like it has two hollow circles that resemble eyes. This puffy little cloud is actually a small Sicilian Scout ship. I have many other pictures of the same type craft, which disguises itself as a tiny little cloud that always has two holes in it. The other UFO Disc is Reptilian. The Reptilian craft was probably investigating why the Sicilian craft was in the area and what they were doing. I was truly surprised to catch two different Alien races so close to each other in one picture and being the first picture I took that day. This was the first time Arietis had ever seen me take pictures of the sky to see what would show up. I know that you are thinking that my imagination has gone off the charts here with saying this little white cloud is a disguise for a UFO. However, it was Enlil himself who informed me of this. Think about it. If you were going to be a sniper in the woods… how would you disguise yourself? Yes, you would disguise yourself to look like you belong there in the woods with leaves and whatnot. Therefore, disguising as a cloud for an Alien ship would be the perfect cover and that is exactly what the Sicilians do. Even though this cloud was not visible to the human eye, it did show up in the pictures and no one would ever guess that it was anything other than a cloud if they saw it in a photo.

Those Who From Heaven To Earth Came

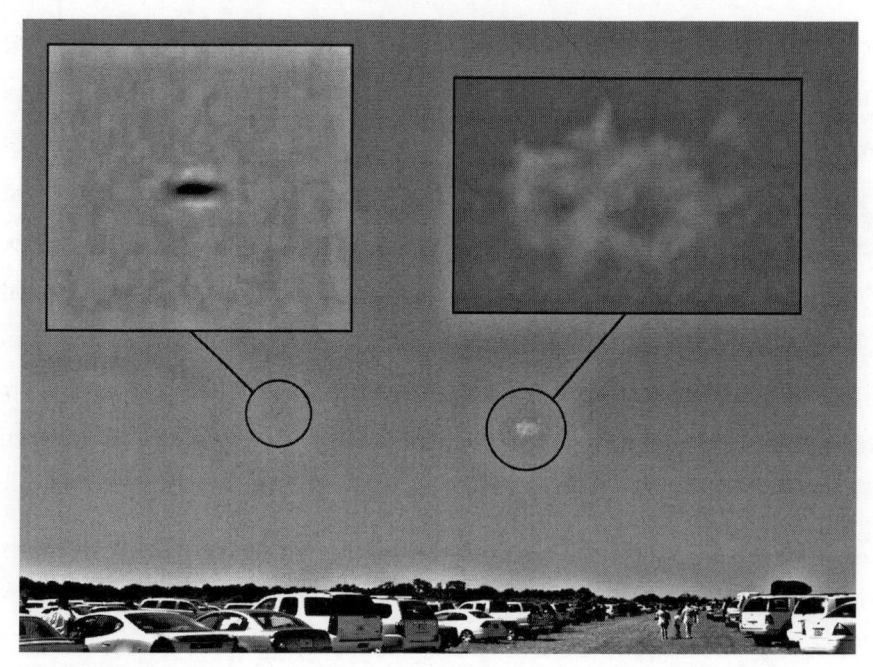

Photo 108

    The Sicilians are trying to get in on all that is happening here on earth. They come here looking to find humans to experiment with and Tag. They are looking to find people who are lost, depressed, and willing to vanish from this earth plane with an offering of a better life in another galaxy. However, this is not the case. They will be experimented on in a very unpleasant manner. They will become lab rats. This breed of Sicilian Extraterrestrials is not of the Light. They are in fact very dark. They had no interest in Arietis or me, they just simply happened to be in the area where we were at the time.

    The second time we were able to capture these UFOs on camera, Arietis and I were up on top of my roof on a sunny day enjoying the sun and taking pictures. There was not a single speck of cloud in the sky. Nevertheless, in all of our photos was the same little white UFO moving very slowly across the sky.

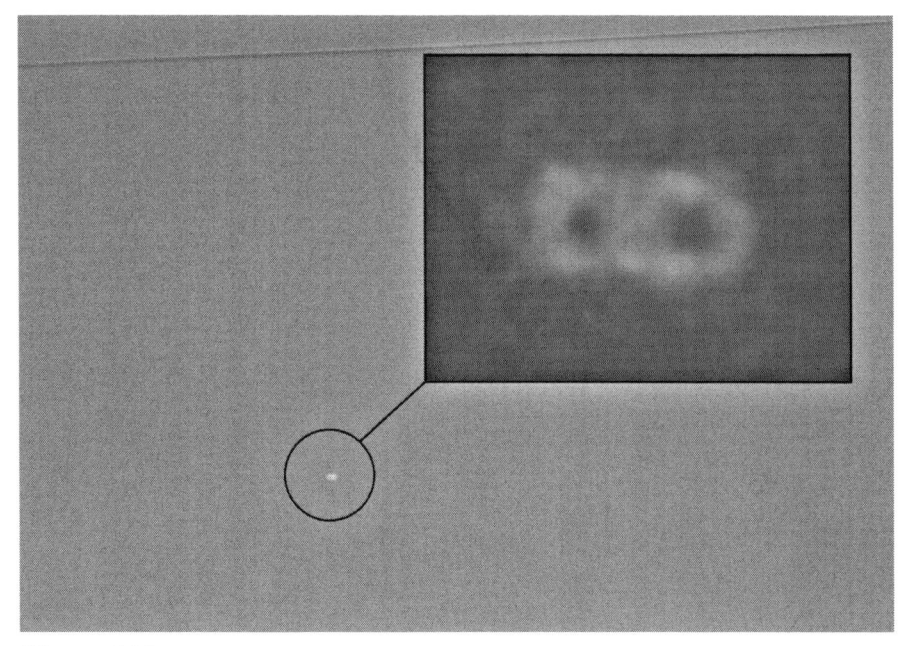

Photo 109

We could not see it with the physical eye, but it showed up on both of our cameras in a series of photos. This Spacecraft stayed cloaked on the 5th dimension, therefore making it invisible to humans. I have changed the contrast on the enlargement of the object so that you can see the shape a little better, even though it is still fuzzy. It is as I stated, two round balls connected together with circular windows on each side. In some pictures, it appears to have a point on the top and the bottom of it. A couple months later, I was actually able to see this object physically with my eyes as it became un-cloaked and it was moving extremely slow. I also wanted to mention that you could photograph these crafts any time of the year and not just during the rainy season. Photos 108 and 109 were taken during the winter. I will say however, that during the wintertime it is much harder to photograph these UFOs being that there are not as many flying in the sky during this time. Therefore, during the winter here in Florida I am extremely bored when it comes to photographing anomalies in the sky. My guess is that the Sicilians come here during the winter because Enlil and his Reptilian Motherships along with Scouts are not in full force during this time of year. It is as if they are thieves that have come to a store during the night when it is closed. The thieves can then take all they want and leave un-noticed.

All in all, most Alien races abduct people in one way or another, be it pleasant and Enlightening or for the purpose of control, hybridizing and other genetic experimentation. I have known several other people that claim they had once been abducted, but I could look into their eyes and see no truth or fear. They were simply people looking for attention. Nevertheless, my friends Lil Lamb and Mr. K had very real experiences in which I have no doubt whatsoever. They were not looking for attention and did not share these things with people outside their families and to this day, still choose not to. This is why their real names are not given. These were true abductions. For me, I will reiterate that the things that happened to me were not against my will and therefore I refer to them as Encounters and I look forward to many more in the future.

Missing Time

As in most UFO abductions and other UFO related encounters, missing time always seems to be a factor. Many abductees remember seeing a UFO and then nothing after that, other than being back in their house or car or left somewhere in the woods. I had many instances of missing time in the past few years and they continue to this day.

I have a strange phenomenon happen every few weeks when I am driving down the road in broad daylight. I pay attention to every detail around me when driving. First let me state that I drive fast wherever I go. I will be driving down the road and pass a car, only to come up behind the same car several miles down the road. Now I know that they did not somehow pass me, as I would have noticed that my fast driving was not making me any more progress than the slower moving traffic. Each time this happens, I also seem to have a sense of missing time. According to Archangel Michael and Enlil, this is due to them putting me into a time warp to protect me from a fatal accident. In other words, they pick me up (vehicle and all) and set me back down in another location, thus saving me from harm. Archangel Michael has warned me several times, about my fast driving and has told me to slow down. Nevertheless, I cannot slow down as the adrenaline part of me controls my actions.

There were two accidents that I was involved in back in 2005. I had a large jacked up Dodge truck with extremely large off-road mud tires on it. A large truck with this type of tires will not stop quickly on pavement. It will simply slide across the pavement as if it were on a fresh wet surface and hydroplaning. I was going through an intersection late one afternoon doing about 60 mph when a minivan going the opposite direction decided to turn at that intersection. Most of these types of accidents happen, when the driver at fault turns in front of you. This was not the case. This person turned as I was almost through the intersection and clipped my rear end sending my truck into a massive spin. My first thought was that this was going to be bad, because it was during afternoon rush hour traffic and the oncoming traffic lanes were full. My truck slid about a hundred yards or more doing two full 360's into oncoming traffic at 60 mph, yet I hit none of the other cars. When my truck finally came to a stop, I got out and there was a large group of people that started clapping and yelling with excitement "Man you sure know how to handle that truck!" They could not believe that I was able to handle such a large truck spinning out and not hitting all the oncoming traffic and having had one of my wheels completely come off. Well I did not handle the truck and I told all these people that I only held on for dear life. During the actual time when the truck was spinning out of control it was if I was in some sort of green colored vortex and then the truck came to a stop and everything turned back to normal again. As I stated, the truck spun out for about a 100 yards or more, and that was a long time for an accident in motion. After hearing all the people cheering for me, my mind wondered how on earth I could have not hit any of the oncoming cars when I saw that my truck's rear axle had literally engraved both sides of the road from where my rear wheel had come off. Then out of nowhere stood an older couple that appeared to be in their early 70's. They just appeared in front of my wife and me at the time and handed her a bottle of Zephyrhills Spring water and me a Coke. They said… "We thought you might want this". Then they walked away and disappeared. I looked for them a few minutes later and they were nowhere in sight. They had simply vanished, leaving me astounded by how could they have come out of nowhere and known that I loved drinking Coke and my wife liked Zephyrhills Spring water. Even this puzzled my wife who normally would never give something like this any thought. So here we both walked away from this bad accident without a scratch, having worn no seat belts and not hitting any oncoming cars. Then I would be puzzled for weeks as to whom the couple was that approached us with the drinks as soon as we stepped out of the truck. It was as if they were already there waiting for this event to happen. Later I found out that they were two of my guides and protectors, Archangel Michael and Archangel Faith. They had simply materialized, as they knew this event was to take place. Michael told me that they had picked my truck up and put us into a Time Warp, then setting us back down on the road so that we cleared all oncoming traffic. Therefore, here was an example of missing time or perhaps I should say moving forward in time. Therefore, a fraction of time was removed from my life in order to save my ass. Therefore, this gave me the proof that Extraterrestrial Angelic entities have the ability to do just that.

After having my truck repaired and back to normal a month later, it was not but about 8 weeks before I would have another severe accident in my truck. I was going down a road once again doing about 60-65 mph when an old man in a car turned right in front of me at an intersection. I had no time to hit the brakes. I t-boned his car and the rear of my truck came up off the ground about eight feet and back down again. I was wearing no seat belt and should have been thrown through the windshield and killed. I got out and walked away once again without even a scratch. I did not even have any pain in my neck from coming to such a dead stop at that speed. I was once again told that my truck was put into a Time Warp and set back down again to lessen the impact. Archangel Michael once again warned me of the dangers of driving so fast and told me to slow down. In both of these accidents, time was manipulated to my advantage and for my safety, in order to save my life.

The last encounter I had with missing time was in June of 2012. I was in Zephyrhills skydiving at Skydive City and was getting ready to make my second jump of the day. I had asked Archangel Michael as I always do to protect me, but I had also asked him to do something different and help me with my spiritual Ascension process while I was skydiving. I had been working diligently on my Ascension process for the last year or so, but I thought what if he could do something while I was in free-fall. Therefore, as I was in free-fall, I went through a cloud and as I got towards the bottom of the cloud, I noticed a Golden Ring of Light with my shadow inside it. I was getting ready to go into it and right as I went through it… I found myself under my canopy. I do not recall deploying my parachute at all. There was missing time again. When I got on the ground I found myself somewhat dazed and disoriented, yet I had an overwhelming feeling of love and peace. Yet I pondered upon what happened, as I knew there was missing time and could not recall for the life of me how my parachute was deployed. I did however, have the feeling that I had been taken somewhere and brought back. I later found out that Archangel Michael had taken me through that Golden Ring of Light which was a Portal to the 8th dimension and then brought me back in mid-air. This was done, because I had asked for it. This was part of my Ascension process and by doing this; I had opened the Portal and brought back the energies of that 8th dimension for all of the Tampa Bay area. Here is a still shot from my helmet camcorder.

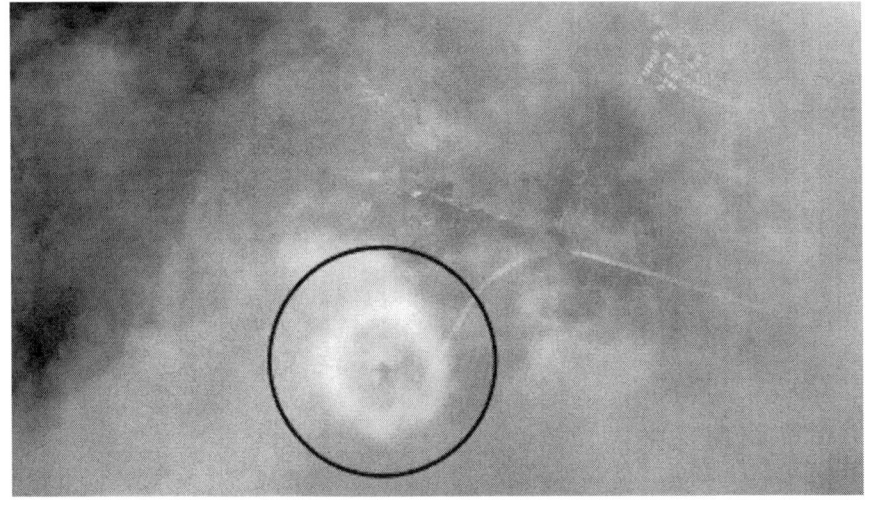

Photo 110

This picture is what I was seeing before I entered the Golden Ring of Light. Now I know that a few of my skydiving friends have witnessed this type of rainbow ring anomaly while skydiving and to them it is rare, but nothing that is of a metaphysical nature. For me, it was of a metaphysical nature, for I had specifically requested an experience that would help me with my Spiritual Ascension process. Ask and ye shall receive.

Therefore, another instance of missing time in my life takes place. Just like all of the Encounters I have had with being aboard Extraterrestrial ships, which all had instances of missing time. My conclusion to this is that in most of these Encounters, it was just a matter of the Extraterrestrial's erasing parts of my memory. They erase most of what happened, especially the experiments performed on me. I do recall being experimented on in some occasions, but there were also many that soon as I stepped into a certain room aboard their ship, my memory was gone and the next thing that I remember is being dropped off back in my bed. I am allowed partial memories just so that I am aware that these Encounters are taking place. So missing time seems to be a part of my life now on a regular basis. I am happy that there was missing time in both of my accidents and that time was manipulated to my advantage. Nevertheless, when I am having Encounters aboard Alien ships, I want full memory of everything that is done to me, no matter how horrific it may seem. I do not like anything hidden from me, just as our memory of the truth is erased from us all each time we incarnate into the earthly plane of existence.

Skydiving and UFOs

Here we have two subjects you probably thought you never would have heard together. Well, I am a skydiver and of course, you already know now that UFOs follow me everywhere I go. UFOs are in the sky, so technically they should be there when I am skydiving. Well yes they are, along with other strange anomalies called Crystalline Energies.

When I am skydiving, I have a helmet with a digital camcorder mounted on the side of it. I turn it on right before I exit the plane. The camcorder records the same thing that I see, as I am freefalling. It was not until just a few months ago that I realized that I had not been truly analyzing my video recordings to the degree in which I needed to so. I was analyzing them, but only to see how my body position, maneuvers, and my landings were. I was not even thinking about how there might be UFOs on these recordings. It was not until I saw a glimpse of something that flew by me in a video that I started looking at them more carefully, trying to find evidence of possible UFOs. When I first started looking for them, I realized I would have to slow these recordings down immensely. Most UFOs are traveling at around 7,000 mph unless they are just hovering. The human eye is not going to see something moving that fast.

Therefore, I imported them into some professional video editing software and slowed the videos down. The software would only allow me to slow it down to a certain degree. Therefore, when I would view the video after slowing it down, I would see a possible flicker of something fly by me. I would splice those sections where I thought there might be an anomaly and render them so I could re-import them again. This way, I could slow them down once again. That is when I was able to see these UFOs and anomalies fly by. Nevertheless, they were still traveling at too high of a speed for me to accurately stop the video to capture a screen-shot of it. Therefore, for a third time, I would render it and re-import it to slow it down one more time. From there I could freeze the proper frame and do a screen-shot. In this next picture (photo 111), you will see the strange blue anomaly with an oval shape in the middle of it and yellow trailing off each end.

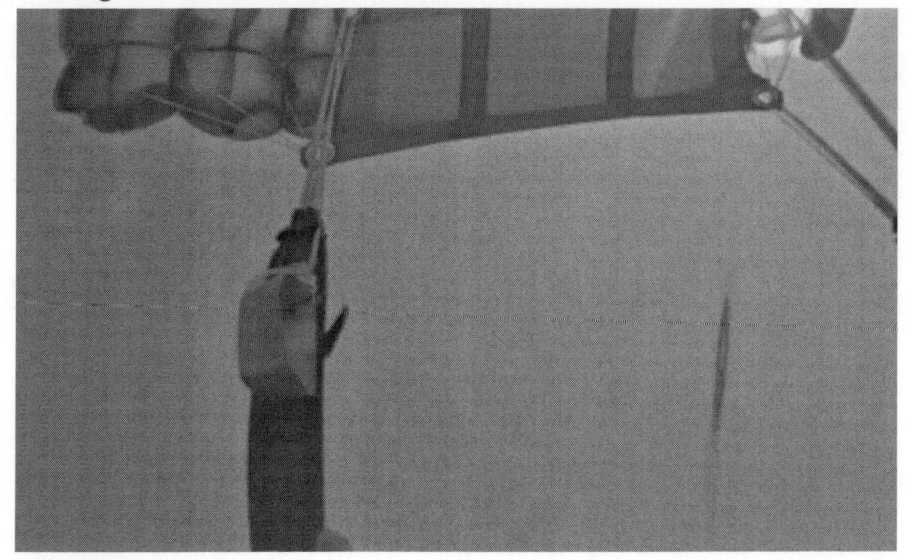

Photo 111
It was right in front of me as I had just deployed my canopy and

had not yet released my toggles. I thought that perhaps it was some form of lens flare.

Photo 112

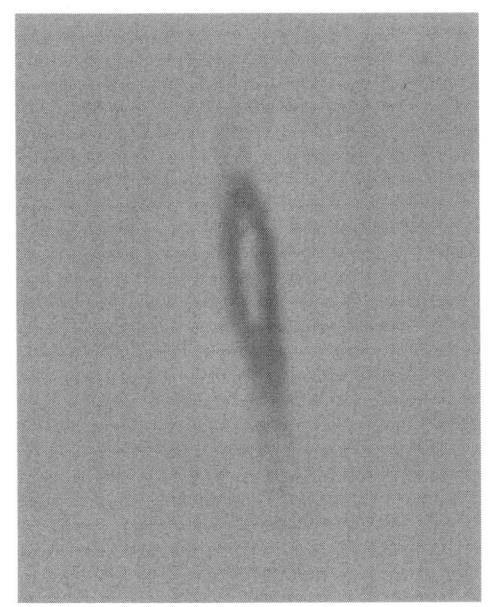

Photo 113

These pictures (photos 112 & 113) are from different skydives I had done. Once again, you can see the same shape and same oval pattern in the middle of it. I was still not yet convinced it was a UFO, but whatever it was, it was always close to me.

Then in this next picture (photo 114), I proved myself wrong. It was not a lens flare. This was a UFO fully showing itself to me. In the other pictures, the UFO was on another dimension and therefore it appeared blue and fuzzy. Once it decided to show itself to me, it had to come onto the physical plane and showing its mechanical attributes. You can see from this picture that it is a metallic craft, as you can see the reflection from the sun off the front end of it.

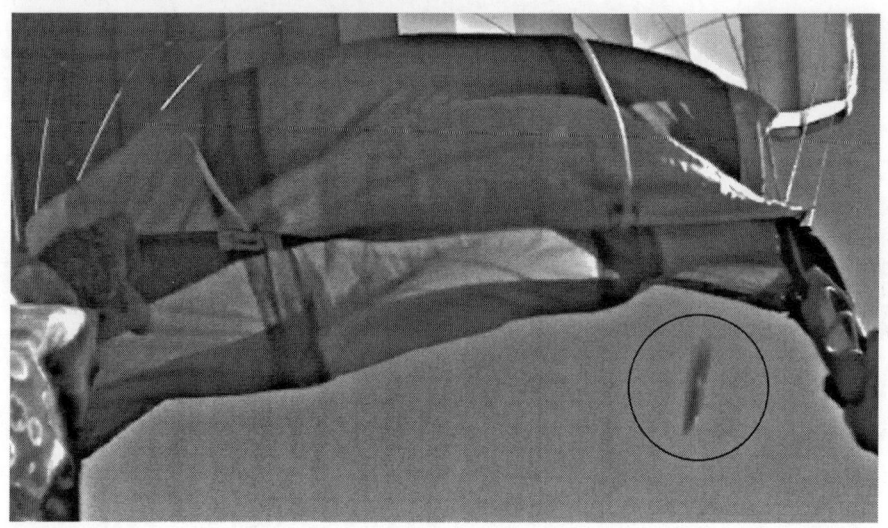

Photo 114

It was traveling straight down in front of me as my canopy first opened. I have enlarged the UFO for you to see in photo 115. I will reiterate for you to take notice that it has an angled front end and you can see the sun reflecting off it, therefore, it is most definitely a metallic craft.

Those Who From Heaven To Earth Came

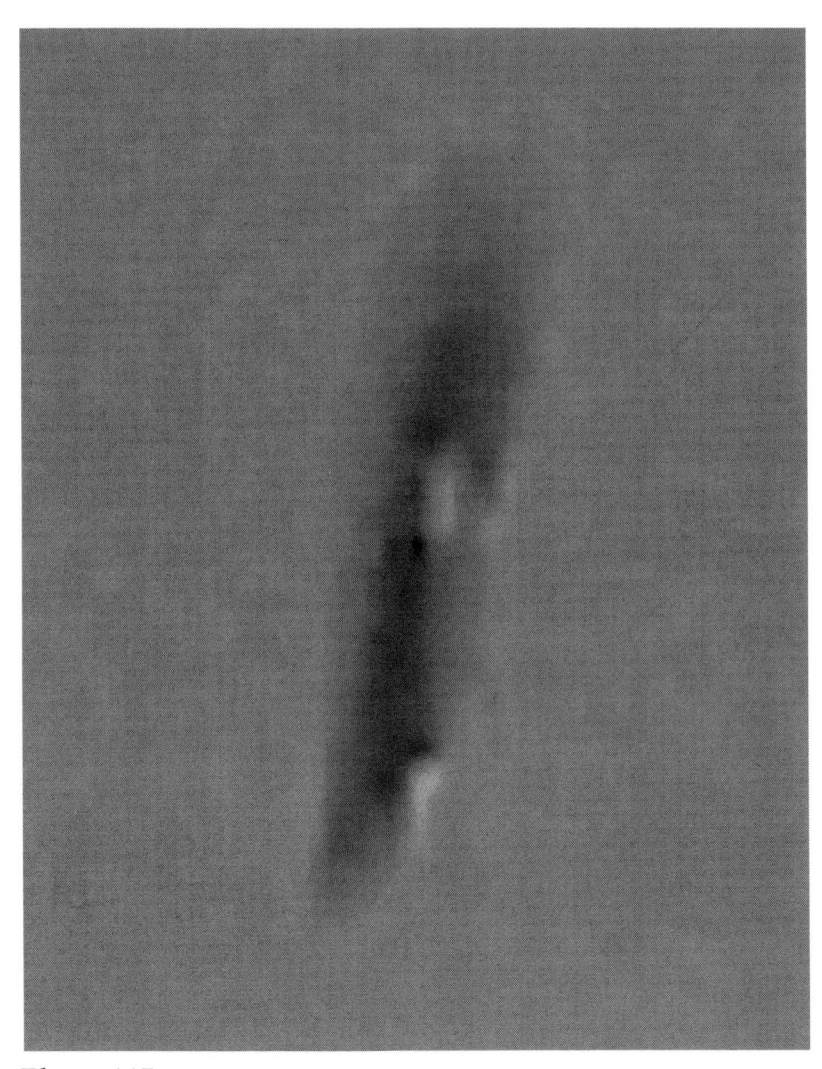

Photo 115

This UFO appears almost every time I deploy my canopy. It is there to protect me according to Enlil. He told me that if I did not wish for it to be there he would make it stop. However, Enlil controls the skies and protects me because of our agreement and my loyalty to him. When I am jumping from a plane, I want all the protection I can get, so I would never ask him to stop. The thought of UFOs actually protecting and monitoring me while I am jumping is truly awesome to say the least.

This next few pictures show what is called "Crystalline Energy". They are energies that take shape. These are not actual ships in any sense. They are energy forms that emanate from Archangel Michael, Enlil and from me. They are a combination of our energies mixed to create protection for me. Because of my spiritual abilities, these are projected from my own brain waves in sync with the mind of Archangel Michael and Enlil. They are very strange indeed. It is if they have vertical ribs all down their length. Sometimes these energies are really long like in photos 116 & 117 and other time short like in photo 118. You will also notice that there is distortion around the object in photo 118, which is very strange. It looks like a flying saucer Disc, but I assure you it is not.

Photo 116

Those Who From Heaven To Earth Came

Photo 117

You are probably thinking that I have placed this pictured upside down. However, I am flying in what is termed a "heads down" position. Therefore, everything from my helmet cam will be upside down while I am flying heads down.

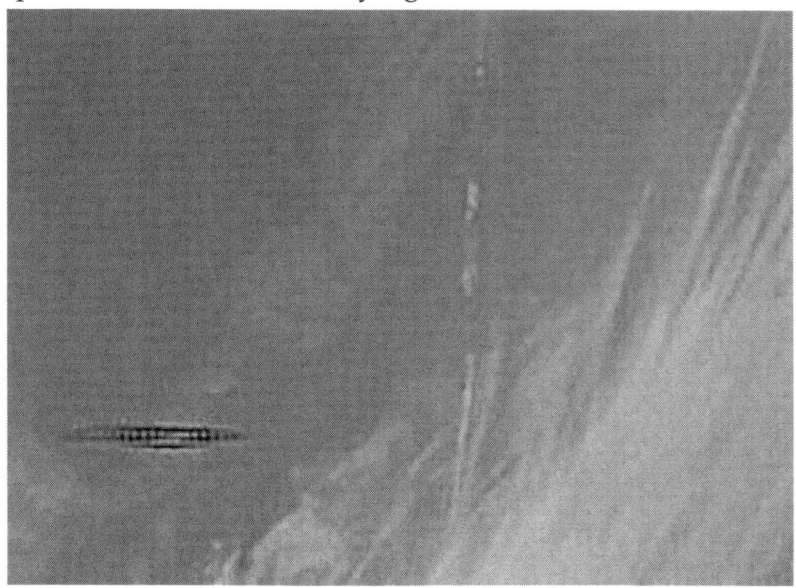

Photo 118

Sometimes there are two of them side by side zinging by me. I have even seen them go around me in a circular motion. These energies even go through me at times and out of my chest right in front of my face. There are sometimes that I am on the ground and these energies come up out of the ground in front of me and fly upwards. So now, I have actual mechanical UFOs and Crystalline Energies right next me each time I am skydiving and on the ground.

The next picture (photo 119), shows me boarding the Twin Otter airplane, ready to make a jump and you can see one of the gel cap shaped Biological UFOs flying over the airplane. Once again, I had to change the brightness and contrast of the enlargement so you can see the true shape of it. This also helps me rule out that it could be another plane or bird in the distance.

Photo 119

There have been some pictures I have from Zephyrhills,

that the objects in question turn out to be dragonflies. This is why I analyze them and adjust the brightness and contrast to see the true shape and the angles in which it travels across the sky. This next picture (photo 120), is either a UFO Disc or it is a Belis, but I would have to guess it was a Belis. You can see that there is a fuzziness coming off the top of it, which could the Disc ripping through the air or it could be the wings of the Belis. The wings of the Belis tend to look like this, but I cannot be sure. It is however, one or the other and not a bird or plane.

Photo 120

It was not until 2011 that I first started looking for these UFOs and other anomalies from my helmet video camera. As Enlil returned for the summer of 2012, I became more aggressive in scanning my skydiving videos to look for his UFOs and the Crystalline Energies that were with me in the sky.

Strange Clouds, Signs in the Sky

Do you remember when you were little and would look up at the sky and say that clouds looks like a duck or a bunny rabbit? When I was young, I traveled quite often across country in the car with mom and dad, being bored to death having to just sit there and maybe read a book. There was no such thing as DVD players built into cars. Hell, there was no such thing as DVDs period. Therefore, my passing the time consisted of annoying my younger sister and looking at the sky to see what the clouds looked like, turning them into imaginary characters and so on. I never would have thought that one day I would always look up at the sky to see if the big super cell clouds hiding Motherships and UFO Scouts that might be watching me, as if I were an amoeba in a petri dish.

People are too busy with their everyday actions of the material world to pay attention to their surroundings. They do not see God in every living thing; the trees, the grass, the ocean, the birds and so on. They walk through life oblivious to everything that is part of the Divine. This being said, they do not realize that are being watched and observed every day by many advanced races of Extraterrestrials. It is time for people to wake up and understand how they truly came to be here on earth and who is watching over them. They need to look to the skies to see that those who are watching us will soon one day make their selves known to mankind again as they did long ago. That day is not something that will be announced, it will just happen. This is another reason I am constantly looking at the sky when I am outside. My neighbors probably think there is something wrong with my neck because I am always looking up. When something big happens, I want to be paying attention so I am a witness to it.

    The next three pictures show what is called a Noctilucent cloud, also known as a Night cloud. It was Otto Jesse of Germany, who coined the term "Noctilucent cloud", which means night shining cloud. He was the first person to photograph them, in 1887. These clouds are very rare to see and they look as though they are illuminated in the dark sky. This is because they are reflecting sunlight from the other side of the earth at night.

    There is a story behind these particular clouds. One afternoon I went horseback riding with my sister, her girlfriend, and my mother. On the way home, it was getting dark and I noticed this very bizarre cloud illuminating the sky. I rushed home as fast as I could to take some pictures. When I arrived home, I ran inside to get my camera only to realize my camera battery was not charged. Desperate to take pictures of the event, I grabbed my video camera and took pictures. It was nowhere near the pixel quality of my regular camera but it would have to do. Frustrated, I came back out to take pictures as it was already dark outside, but the cloud was still glowing. I noticed that this glowing cloud also looked like a snake-like Dragon in the sky. It was entwined within itself, as a snake would do. My mother called me about an hour later and asked me if I had seen this strange glowing cloud and I explained to her that I had managed to photograph it. This is the only Noctilucent cloud that I have ever seen and actually had no knowledge of them until doing some research after this incident. Possibly, I will be shown one like this again by Enlil in the future.

Photo 121

Those Who From Heaven To Earth Came

Photo 122

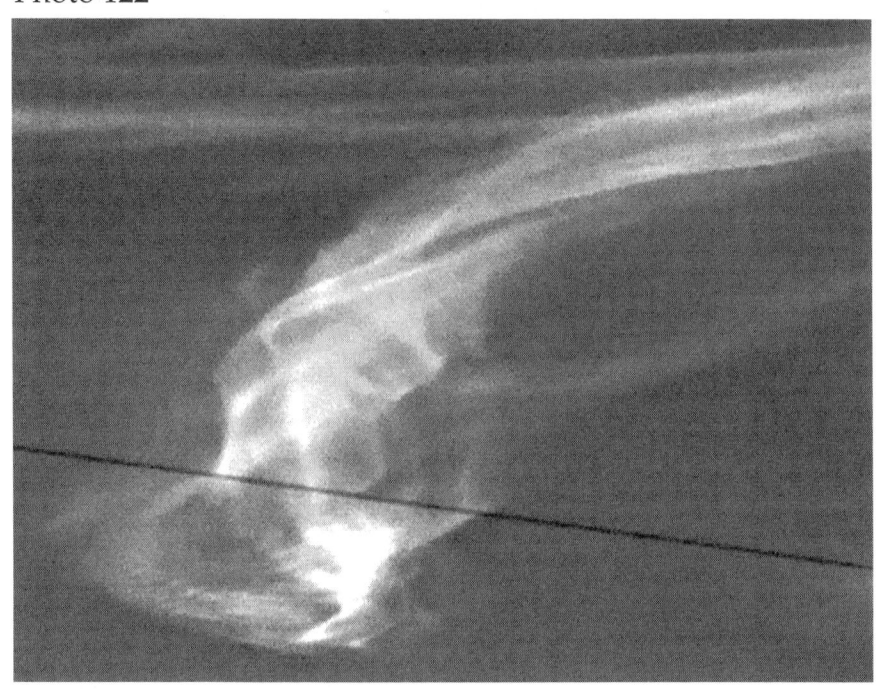

Photo 123

In this last picture (photo 123), you can see the details of the Dragon-like head. The other strange thing about this extremely rare cloud was that they are supposed to be at very high altitudes between our atmosphere and space, yet this one seemed much closer to earth. This was truly a remarkable sight. Later, I was told by Enlil that this was placed there to represent my connection with the Reptilian energies. He went on to explain that I should constantly look for signs in the sky, as he would show me things through these visuals.

One day I was outside my mother's house and we were standing by my car, when we both saw something strange in the sky. The sky was filled with the normal Cirrus clouds high in the sky, but we saw a very strange cloud anomaly all by itself. It was not like the Cirrus clouds and it did not look like any other types of clouds we had seen. It was very small and it appeared to be constantly changing, but staying in the same place in the sky. It was as if it was folding within itself disappearing only to reappear forming itself again. It repeated this for about 15 minutes or so as my mother and I watched in amazement. I have watched many clouds change shape, as they normally do, but never anything like this. I left and went home to get my video camera out to film this but the cloud was completely gone by that time. Therefore, I took my normal afternoon nap and I asked Enlil to give me an answer to this as I slept. Upon awakening, I knew the answer. This was a Portal being opened at that particular moment. When I say Portal, I mean a Stargate that leads to another universe or dimension. There are Stargates here in Sarasota, Florida and that is what makes this city special, as well as it is the first of the 22 "Cities of Light" to be activated. So once again, there was another sign in the sky and my mother was able to witness it along with me.

The next two pictures are my favorite ones of all. This bizarre cloud is actually cloaking a War ship belonging to Enlil's brother Enki. I call it the Phoenix Rising as that is how it looks along with the fact that the Phoenix represents Enki.

Photo 124

Those Who From Heaven To Earth Came

Photo 125

Photo 126

This warship in photo 126 also belongs to Enki and would appear on many days during the summer months. For some strange reason he is also more active here in the summer than in the winter, just as his brother Enlil is. Although Enlil interacts with me, he does not interact much with humans, whereas his brother Enki is still very connected to earth and interacts with humanity. After all, Enki has dominion over this earthly plane of existence. The next picture (photo 127), is also a cloud that would always show up in the same spot every so often and always to the south. I do not know if it is cloaking anything belonging to Enki or Enlil but it also has the same hole in the middle of it and every time it appeared, it had the same shape and same the hole in the middle.

Photo 127

Many of you might think I just have an overactive

imagination just as when I was a child looking at the clouds trying to pretend what they looked like. Perhaps this is so, but I was told to look for signs in the sky by my Reptilian God friend and therefore I do as he requested. Sometimes the universe and the Angels give us signs that are right in front of our faces in many forms, yet we are too busy with our everyday lives to pay attention and see these signs. As I stated these signs come in many forms such as when I say my Prayers and Invocations at night in my living room. When I am done, I will sometimes say… I hope you all are listening to me and no sooner than I said that, the giant chimes I have hanging right outside my door ring very loud. Therefore, they give me a sign to let me know they are listening to me. Pay attention to the signs no matter how silly or subtle they may seem to be. The more you start doing this the more signs will be given to you. If you do not pay attention… your spirit guides, Ascended Masters, and Angels along with the Celestial Gods have a harder time trying to communicate with you. Wake up, pay attention, and look for signs all around you. If you do not, you may miss your Divine intervention.

The next picture (photo 128), is one of the Angel clouds that would also appear quite often. They would always appear very close to my home so that soon as I would come outside, I would see them. It looks like a side view of an Angel flying through the air. See the body and the head at the bottom with its wing stretched out high.

Photo 128

This is another common cloud shape I would see on a regular basis. Many times, they are in a peach color and there would be several of them.

The next picture (photo 129) is one I have also seen many times as I walk out my door. The whole sky will be completely covered with clouds and there will be a hole in the sky right above me. This may sound silly to you, but remember that we live in a hologram, so anything can be projected into what we call our reality no matter how bizarre it may be. Though this may mean nothing to many, to me it means they watch over me and give me signs in the sky to confirm this. I do believe that if I stopped paying attention to these signs, then they would cease to happen, as it would be a waste of their time.

Photo 129

The next couple of pictures are of Enlil's Motherships cloaked on another dimension, yet they retain the main oval shape of the ship. In photo 130, you may think that this is just a cloud whirling around, but it is much more than that. The wispy part of the cloud to the right is simply following the outline of the Mothership. It stayed that way for quite some time. In a sequence of pictures I have, there were many Drones and Discs flying to into and from it. Another method for me to verify that this was a Mothership is that when the Discs and Drones entered the cloud they did not come back out. They simply disappeared.

Photo 130

The following pic (photo 131) was from one summer day when I was at the beach with Arietis. I told her to "Watch the cloud to the north of us… that is one of Enlil's Motherships". I tried mentally communicating with Enlil to have him move his ship in my direction. Within a few minutes, the Mothership moved south and stopped right over top of us, then moved south again and disappeared after about 20 minutes or so. This once again confirms with me that Enlil hears me and responds in a manner in which he sees fit. This is not coincidence as I have watched the clouds that cloak his Motherships many times come to me at my request and even changed opposite directions against strong winds to do so. There are also two small white dots in the top left of this picture, but they are just seagulls, as is the one that is much closer in the bottom left corner. When they are too small to make out, it is easy to tell that they are birds by their circular flight pattern as they ride the thermals.

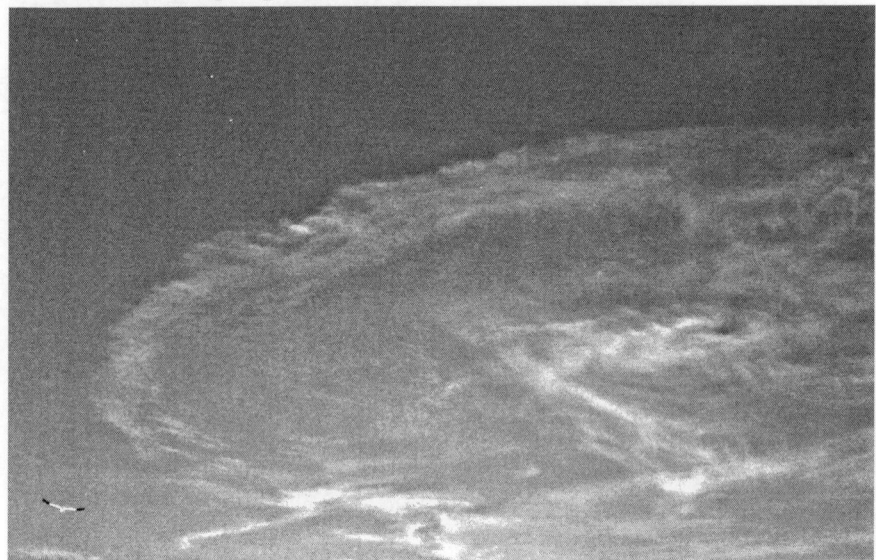

Photo 131

Photo 132

The last picture (photo 132), I call the face of Zeus as it reminds me of him with stern heavy brow, as he was around that particular day.

Therefore, if you ask for signs that higher powers are watching over you, then you will receive them. It is then simply a matter of… will you see them? Signs from higher powers can be in many forms and are usually right in our face, yet we fail to see them. Even when we do not ask for signs, they are still given to us as an answer to our prayers or needs in life. So wake up and pay attention to the detail of everything around you in life. Quit looking down at your cell phone and hold your head up.

How to Capture UFOs on Camera

First, let me say that I am in no way an expert in photography or videography. Therefore, I will not be using any fancy terminology in explaining how I do what I do. I only know just enough to accomplish my desired result of photographing UFOs. The better the camera you have, the better your pictures will look according to how many megapixels your camera is. Some people will argue this and will say that higher megapixel cameras are only good for photos that will be enlarged. However, I do blow up all my photos so I can zoom into the area of the UFOs within each picture. This however, does not mean because you have a great camera that you will get good pictures of UFOs. This is because they are moving so fast and you have to have your camera pointed in the right direction at the right time. I have missed many good sequences of UFO because of moving the camera around too much.

When I first started taking pictures years ago, I did not know about burst mode, yet I was still able to capture UFOs on my camera. If you want to have better luck at capturing these anomalies, then you need to have your camera in burst mode. This way anything that moves within the range of your screen will be captured. Most new digital cameras have this feature, but some do not. Therefore, if you are going to buy one, make sure it does have this feature.

In 2010, I spent quite a bit of money on a Canon EOS 7D along with two different lenses. I purchased a 70-200mm lens and a 100-400mm lens with image stabilization. Now this camera was way over my head for my knowledge and experience with cameras, but I did not care. I simply wanted a powerful camera with some long-range lenses. I needed the long-range lenses so that when the storm clouds were far away out east of me, I could still capture UFOs exiting and entering them. The 100-400mm lens is awesome, but it is very heavy compared to my 70-200mm lens. Nevertheless, having the image stabilization is necessary have for those like me who cannot hold the damn camera still without shaking a bit.

For those of you who want to go out right away and start taking pictures of the sky hoping to catch a glimpse of a UFO in action, I suggest going the simple route. You do not need to go out and spend a fortune on high-tech camera gear. The overall best bet is the smaller digital cameras and I prefer the Sony Cyber-shot. Other brands such as Nikon are of equal value and quality. These are truly the all-round best cameras for UFO hunting because you can carry these cameras in your pocket. I carry a camera with me now wherever I go, just in case I see something that is going on right at that moment. I do not know how many times I had to rush home to get my camera, only to be too late to capture what was going on. This brings me to another point… make sure you camera is always fully charged. There were many times that I did have my camera with me, only to find out the battery was dead. Yes, this may sound like such simpleton advice, but trust me, it is very important if you want to be at the right place at the right time to be able to captures these UFOs or whatever is going on in the sky at that moment.

Now, the first thing you want to do is when UFO hunting is to look for the proper clouds. The big storm clouds such as the super cell clouds usually have UFOs emanating from them. This is where you want to aim your camera. Set your camera to burst mode. In burst mode, the camera keeps taking pictures as long as you hold the button down. I have two different Sony Cyber-shot cameras. One is older and the other is new. One takes pictures at two frames per second and the newer one takes pictures at 10 frames per second in burst mode. Nevertheless, I prefer my older one. The newer one makes the pictures much smaller in burst mode whereas the older ones takes much larger pictures, which is great for blowing them up in order to see detail. Set your sight on some clouds and hold your camera still in one direction taking pictures for at least 30 seconds before pointing to another direction. You want to have time to let something fly by your lens. Actually the longer you stay pointed in one direction, the better your chances are of catching a full sequence of a UFO and its flight pattern. Take a good amount of pictures. I normally take about 1,000–1,200 pictures before going in to evaluate them. Then, if I see evidence of anomalies in my photos, I go right back outside to take more pictures. If there is a storm approaching with some serious rain, then aim your camera right where the rain meets the bottom of the cloud. That is where the Discs and Belis tend to fly back and forth. As I have stated before in this book, the Alien crafts always seem to circle the perimeter of the storm. When I see that there are UFOs flying in full force, I will also call Arietis to tell her they are flying so she will go outside her home to take pictures. This way I have more than one person working on my venture.

Next thing you want to do is analyze the photos you have just taken. After downloading them to your computer, I suggest you go through them with a fine-tooth comb. Most people would overlook the UFOs in their pictures because they are not looking for them. I say this because most of the time they look very small and are not right in your face. This is also, why I wear magnified glasses when reviewing the photos. When you see even the smallest dot, you should pay attention to its flight path. This will help you determine if it truly is a UFO, if it is performing maneuvers that no bird or manufactured aircraft could ever do. This is easy to do if you have a full sequence of the object in question. Airplanes and birds do not fly straight up and down and turn on a dime. If you have a sequence of an object that has made it across the sky in 4-5 frames then it is UFO. Airplanes will look like they barely move in a sequence of photos. Birds tend to ride the thermals; so many times, they will be gliding in a slow circular motion. I will say however, that birds that are far away tend to look like round balls and not birds. This is where you must observe its flight pattern and how fast it is moving across the sky in order to make judgment. Do not just think that because it does not look like a bird or airplane, that it is a UFO. Be you own best critic. You may also want to go through the pictures several times because you may have missed seeing something. After doing so, I save all the photos with anomalies in a dated folder each day. Yes, I normally take pictures of the sky every day during the summer and only so often during the winter. I know that I have told you to aim for the clouds when trying to capture photos of UFOs, but do not discount perfectly clear sunny days where there is not a cloud in the sky. There have been days where I have captured the non-Reptilian crafts such as those belonging to the Sicilians and Sirians in perfectly clear blue skies. Remember that there are hundreds of different Extraterrestrial races that are visiting earth and some that live within the earth. Therefore, any day can be a good day for UFO hunting. Depending on what area you live in can determine what types of Alien crafts will be in that area. My Persian friend Andisheh went to the Pyramids in Mexico and was able to photograph a different type of UFO craft that I had not seen before flying right over the Pyramids. If Enlil who is Reptilian has eight different types of crafts, then think about all the races visiting here and how many types of crafts there would be. If I were able to, I would do nothing but travel the world photographing and documenting the different crafts according to each region of this planet.

  Now we come to using video for capturing these Alien Skyships. I have four different video cameras I use every so often. One of them I use on my Skydiving helmet and the others are set up on a tripod. My Samsung video camera is full HD and allows me to slow the frame rate down. This way is I will be able to see fast moving objects much better. Then you can slow down the videos even more in professional video editing software. What you need to do is set up your tripod with your video camera, point it towards the clouds, and walk away for about an hour or two. The tedious part comes next. Seriously, plan to be bored out of your mind examining the videos. Yes, you will have to sit there for an hour and watch the video hoping to see something of a flicker fly by. If you do see something, I suggest pausing the video and jotting down the frame time, and then continue watching the video. Each time you think you may have seen something, pause again and jot down the frame time. This way you can go back and splice around each of those sections, deleting the sections you do not need so that you do not have to watch the entire damn thing again. Make sure that you save the entire original video and name it "Original" then save it again under a different name that so you can use this version to edit. Give yourself plenty of room when splicing so you do not delete any part of what might be the UFO in its flight path. From there you can slow each section down and analyze them. I have many videos of UFOs flying about, but it is truly time consuming and boring compared to simply taking pictures. However, one thing about using video is that you can capture the full flight paths of the Belis that are the biological UFOs and you can watch them shape-shift and sprout their wings.

So there you have a few tips on capturing these Alien crafts on camera and video. Do not get frustrated if you do not get anything when you first attempt this. If you are patient, I promise you will have success in doing so.

Other Aliens that come in the Night

Now I will show you some pictures and drawings of some of the other Extraterrestrial Beings that come to me in the night. There are several that make themselves known. Why do they come to me? They come because they are attracted to my Light. Even the Darkest of Beings is attracted to my Light energies. Remember that all Beings still carry the spark of Light no matter how Dark they maybe in their workings. Each night I open the door to the other side to allow whoever wishes to make contact with me. To me physical life is boring and nighttime brings about an adventure into the unknown. Enki has warned me that I like to play with fire, so if I get burned that is my choice. Nevertheless, my chances of getting burned are slim due to my protection from Archangel Michael. I have played with fire for many years and I am still alive and well.

This first drawing is my close friend Hermel that I have mentioned earlier in this book. He has an extremely large head and eyes. His body is unique to say the least, as it is made of what looks like little square blocks. Hermel has come to me quite often over the last few years. He normally comes in the form of an orb and tries very hard to show his face within the orb, although many times it is somewhat a little distorted.

Those Who From Heaven To Earth Came

HERMEL

He also shows himself in full form when I am out of body. He is a Shape-shifter like most all extraterrestrials and this is his chosen appearance. He has told me that even though I think he looks very strange, humans look very strange to him. Yes, he looks very cartoon-like and as if a child had drawn a stick figure, but this is exactly how he looks, as strange as it may seem to us. I have grown quite fond of him as he tries his best to always appear to me when called upon during the late night hours even though he has stated that it is very difficult for him to do so in a detailed manner like that of Enki. The simple fact that he tries and asks nothing in return is what makes him special. Therefore, in return, I always offer him my Light Unconditional Love. He is not of the Reptilian race. He is of another Alien race that is of a fourth generation of several races combined, which go back before the time of humans. He is always with Enki, as he is part of his entourage and this is because he is Enki's personal bodyguard. Enki does not need a bodyguard, for he is powerful enough to take care of himself, but he has given this title to Hermel because he is such a close friend.

This next character is quite interesting to say the least. His name is Jiobbe and is a member of the entourage of Enki as well. Jiobbe is the Great Counselor to Enki.

JIOBBE

He is an Extraterrestrial who is very involved and very

experienced with the planet earth. He is a multidimensional Being who has lived some extraordinary challenging lives and is therefore a good advisor to Enki because he brings with him the solid and practical experience of situations on earth in which Enki can intervene. He is also a Shape-shifter and therefore appears however he so chooses. The drawing I have done shows him as he tries to appear somewhat humanoid. This is how he appears when he comes to me in the night. He looks quite stern and almost like that of an evil Jinn, but he is quite a pleasant entity.

Next, we have Shamah and he is more of a Dark Jinn. Shamah is also a multidimensional Being and Extraterrestrial that comes to me during the summer months. Even though he works with the Dark, he means me no harm. He is interested in me due to many other Extraterrestrials being in my presence. Therefore, he simply wants to get in on the action and observe along with helping me connect to the old Sumerian energies. He comes in my dream state when I am out of body and he comes to me when I am awake in the form of an orb. When he comes in orb form, he shows his face within the orb. He dwells under the earth on the Etheric planes beneath the Harrat Ash Shamah, which is the largest volcanic field on the Arabian tectonic plate, which covers and area over 19,000 square miles. Many times, he comes across as an angry Deity with a loud voice, but for the most part, he is pleasant once you understand his nature. Being that he is on the Darker side of things and very powerful; he is someone that you should not make angry, for he states that his wrath can be vile to the unprotected.

Those Who From Heaven To Earth Came

Those Who From Heaven To Earth Came

Now we come to an entity of an Insectoid Alien race. Yes, an Extraterrestrial entity that looks very much like insect. His name is Celest and even though the name sounds as if it would be a female name, he is a male entity. I have only encountered him on about 4 occasions that I can recall. If there were more, then it would have been while I was asleep and had retained no memory of his visit. The first time I became aware of Celest was when Arietis and I went to a spiritual group meeting in the next town over. A friend named Liz was holding the meeting at her home, which was right on the Manatee River. This area was once the grounds of American Indians and this land by the river was sacred to them. That evening after we all had dinner outside by the water, we held a ceremony to clear the land of negative energies and bring forth the Light to appease the Indian spirits that still dwelled there. The Ritual was performed by my friend Lea under a big oak tree on the vacant property next door in the light of the full moon. As the ritual went on, the wind started blowing hard and wiping the tree around as if a sign from the Indian spirits. It was quite an awesome experience. We then started taking pictures and Arietis caught a picture of what looked like an extremely large bug. We later examined the photo and determined that it was indeed some form of multidimensional entity and not an insect of any kind. The entity was about the size of a football. We noticed the entity had two arms and legs and all these strange things coming out of its head, almost like the top of a pineapple.

Those Who From Heaven To Earth Came

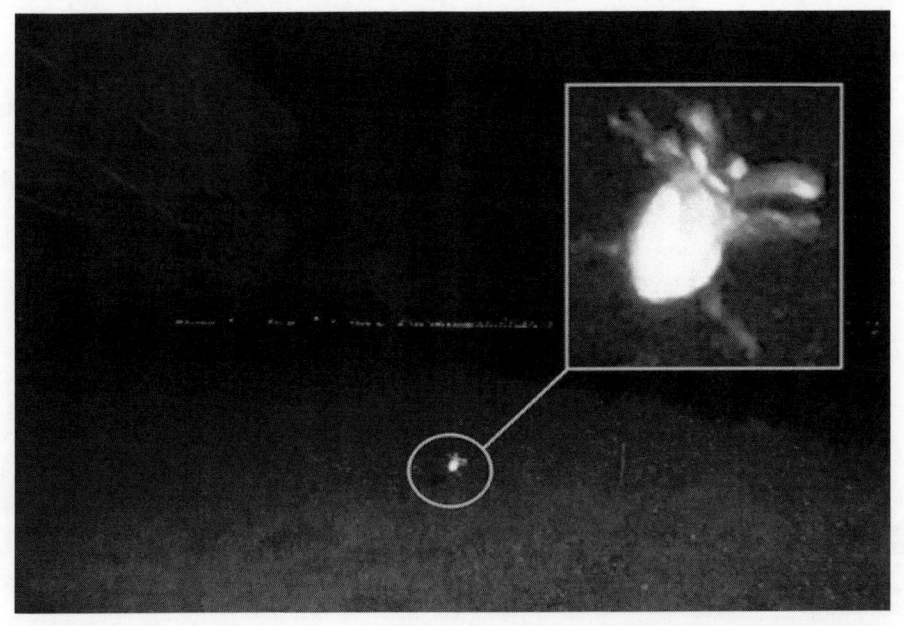

Photo 133

One strange thing is that it also threw a shadow from the full moon that night as seen in photo 133. This tells me that it was able to manifest in physical from. This picture had slipped my mind until about a week later when I saw the same entity in my front driveway. For some strange reason it was attracted to me as I was now at my home, which is about 12 miles from where, it originally manifested. I was sitting on my front porch one night trying to capture anomalies with my camera and there he was again and his Light was extremely bright. As you can see from photo 134, he is once again casting a hard shadow. The things that are protruding off him are very strange indeed. I had managed to capture several photos of him as he flew off and actually shape-shifted somewhat.

Those Who From Heaven To Earth Came

Photo 134

Photo 135

In the previous picture (photo 135), he is flying off and Archangel Michael is in the orb next to him. As you can see, he has his arms stretched out, but has no actual wings of any sort in any of the photos that I have of him. I know most of you are going to think that this is an insect of some kind. However, this is only true in the fact that Celest is an Insectoid Extraterrestrial and this explains his insect looking appearance. I compared his size by measuring the awning he was flying in front of and therefore determined that his little arms stretched out to about 14 inches.

Within the period of a month, he came around at least three more times. I was able to photograph him each time, and after that, I never saw him again. A few weeks later, I spoke with Enki about him and that is when I found out the entity's name was Celest and that he was initially attracted to my Light at the ritual we did by the river and then followed me home to study me. He is of an extremely advance Alien race of Insectiods and within a couple years he wishes to Incarnate here on earth for the first time.

Offerings to the Gods and Protection

If you are truly adventurous and wish to have "Encounters" with the Extraterrestrials then I will explain how to do so, even though I advise most people to refrain from doing so. Many people I spoken with that wish to do so are not prepared, nor do they have the energetic fields powerful enough to deal with this in their life. First, you must understand that Extraterrestrials are the Gods, Angels, and Demons of the mainstream religions. They are the monsters of the Necronomicon and the Goetia along with many other Grimoires of ancient times. You must understand that many of them are very pleasant and there are many who are very war-like, destructive, and who care not for humans. So choose your Poison well my friends. I suggest a sincere deep study of the different Deities and entities along with their dispositions, before ever attempting to call upon them.

There is the traditional method of conjuring these entities using a Magic Circle and the Triangle of Solomon. However, with this method you will only at best get to see and hear them in the black mirror of the Triangle of Solomon if you have truly developed your astral vision. If you have not developed your astral vision then you are not going to have any success with this at all and will need to find someone who is a "Seer" to be the one who looks into the black mirror and conveys the message from the ET. If you were simply wishing to speak to one of the ETs then you would be better off going to a psychic that does channeling of the spirit. You can go to your local metaphysical bookstore and ask them who in your area is a good channeler of spirit. If you have success in finding a good channeler then you should be able to speak directly with a particular Deity depending on the abilities of the psychic. From there you may ask the Deity to come to you as you sleep at night and take you aboard his or her Starship. Ask the Deity to show you their Starship when you are outside taking pictures of the sky. Here is where I will warn you again as I have earlier in this book. Many of these Extraterrestrials will experiment on you in an unpleasant way if you ask to be taken aboard one of their Starships. In addition, once you have opened that door and invited them into your life, you may never be able to shut that door and therefore have sentenced yourself to a life of horror.

It is very important that before you ever attempt to contact any Extraterrestrial Beings that you have established a serious form of protection. For me it is the protection of Archangel Michael, as he is the most powerful Deity in the universe. When choosing a form of protection, do not think for a moment that some rinky-dink ritual you learned is going to protect you from something much more powerful and more advanced than you are. Some people truly think that they cannot be violated or abducted without their own consent. This is like saying the government cannot take your property because you own it. I am sure that you now see my point. I suggest that you establish a serious bond over time with a Deity such as Archangel Michael or Archangel Gabriel, and then and only then will you be protected. However, if your intentions are not in line with what is best for your highest good then you may find yourself unprotected in hot water. Another thing you must consider is that must be able to handle their energies. You may find yourself overwhelmed by their intense energies and this may cause more harm than good in your life. Remember that most all entities have worked the Dark and the Light. Yes, even the pleasant ones and it is important to establish the fact that you only intend to call upon them for their Light only and you must state so when calling upon them.

    Many of these Extraterrestrials enjoy offerings and there are some that demand it while others do not. The energetic intention of the offering is what they appreciate. The Ancients had understood a very basic principle. When they made offerings, they knew that the value of it lays in the intention behind it. For instance, when I put forth water for Poseidon as an offering, what he gets out of it is the Love put forth in the offering, as I do this for him out of Unconditional Love. Do you understand this concept? It is not so much what you put forth as an offering as it is, the energies you put into it. As Enlil told me, I need not put forth anything as an offering, as long as I have my loyalty and Love to put forth. Nevertheless, I still always offer something, be it incense or burning flesh (meat on the grill) or many other things.

Think about it this way. If Aliens do come back and make themselves known to the public, it would be much better to be on their good side and to have already befriended them. Even I do not fully know their agenda and if they decide one day to cull the population of earth and make some people slaves, I would like to be spared and I am positive that I would be.

Once again, be careful what you wish for as far as making contact with Extraterrestrials. You might get more than you bargained for and this is not a game.

There are none so Blind

There will always be the disbelievers and the naysayers in life when it comes to everything. I am the same way, but only after giving something much thought and research. I have researched diligently and still do not fully know the truth in many things and so I keep asking for Divine intervention in finding the true answers. One thing for sure is that everything in this book is of fact and I have the pictures to back up my words. There will still be those who examine my pictures and say they are faked or that the UFOs are planes, bugs, or birds. In regards to that I have provided the evidence to the facts that with the frame rate of my cameras and the distance the objects in question were traveling across the sky in just a few frames, there is no way they are animals or anything man made. Even the UFOs that our government/military has secretly built from reverse engineering at Roswell cannot fly as fast as the objects I have captured on camera. Our government/military UFOs cannot turn on a dime and I believe this is because they have not yet figured out the process of reverse inertia. Even though some races such as the Greys of Zeta Reticuli have traded UFO and weapons technology in exchange for humans to experiment on, they are still not going to give up all the secrets to the ignorant inferior human race. The Greys would never let humans have the upper hand in technology and neither would any other Alien race.

I would welcome any scientist or photographer to dispute any of my photos. As I have stated before they only Photoshop work I have done on the photos is to change the brightness/contrast to make the objects in question show the shape better along with sharpening the image. The only other thing I have done is to enlarge each object in each photo.

Even if these objects are not spaceships, they are still not man made and they are not of the animal kingdom, so this still makes them UFOs because they are unidentified flying objects.

I ask all of you who are reading this book to open your minds even more this day. The more you open your mind, the more the mysteries of mysteries will be revealed to you. You will be the Truth Seekers and the Illuminated ones. You will be the ones who will be raised into a higher state of consciousness, fine-tuned to a higher dimension and level of awareness. You were brought into this life veiled and without memory of who you truly are and your Divine birthright. Therefore, it is time to Awaken and claim your birthright and to know all the mysteries of the universe. You have the choice to lift the veil that has been placed upon you, but you must choose to do so and act accordingly. Everyone on this planet was indoctrinated into some form of false belief system when we were young. Many of these people will simply stay within that same system without stepping out of that confined box because they are comfortable within in the confines of that space.

Those who choose not to believe in other life forms from other galaxies are one of two things. They are either very arrogant to think that they were the only creatures that God created or they simply fear the unknown. The latter is the most common case. They are also not ready to awaken in this particular life so they become the sheep, the followers of the Control System, afraid to break free from the norm. People would rather go about their lives without having to complicate it with thinking about Aliens. They would rather keep their blinders on, as that makes life much easier for them. I will have to agree on that aspect. I sometimes think of how life was so much easier for me not being in contact with Extraterrestrials and changing my whole perspective on life and the universe. For now, I never stop learning new things brought to my attention from these multidimensional Beings. Nevertheless, it is ok if people do not want to believe. You cannot force this type of information on someone. Many people are not ready or spiritually evolved enough to handle this information in this lifetime. This does not make them stupid. They are simply on a different level of spiritual evolution and therefore it does not resonate with them, so they block it out. There are many new souls incarnating to earth all the time and it just means they are not yet ready to receive advanced information. In due time or another lifetime they will. Here is the bottom line my friends… you have the free will to believe whatever you so choose and it is best to not be part of any belief system, no matter what it is. When you lock yourself into a system, you stop the flow of incoming energy and information from a higher source. Always keep your mind open… always.

You may think that perhaps I am delusional and all this is just a dream in my head. However, remember that this life is nothing more than a hologram and an illusion. We each create our own reality by our thought process. Therefore, I have sent out the thought forms to attract and create that in which I desire and it has manifested for me. I will also state for the record, that if anything I state within this book contradicts something else I have said within these pages, it is because I am constantly given new information and as this information comes in, I may find that what I previously thought to be true was incorrect. Therefore, each day in this life ahead of me is a process of learning, analyzing and absorbing and this will continue until the end of this Incarnation.

Puzuzu
"In Service to Others"

Those Who From Heaven To Earth Came

You can find Puzuzu on the Web @...
http://SpellsandMagic.com
http://Puzuzu.com
http://AlienSkyShips.com

Disclaimer:

The intention of this book is to relay the events in the life of Puzuzu for educational purposes. The manufacturer does not sponsor any brand name products I have mention within these pages as I have no financial ties to them. The manufacturer has no knowledge of the products used by me for photographing UFOs or other anomalies. Even though this book tells how to make contact with ETs, contacting Extraterrestrials can lead to possession, insanity and many other physical illnesses resulting from abductions and therefore is not recommended. That being said, we all have free will and therefore you are free to do as you so choose.

© 2012 Puzuzu

All rights reserved. No part of this book may be reproduced or transmitted in any form or by any means without written permission from the author.

Printed in Great Britain
by Amazon.co.uk, Ltd.,
Marston Gate.